MULTISPECIES

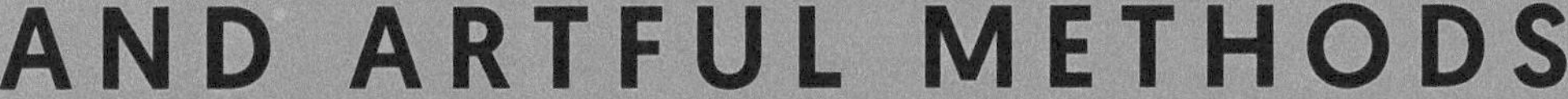

AND ARTFUL METHODS

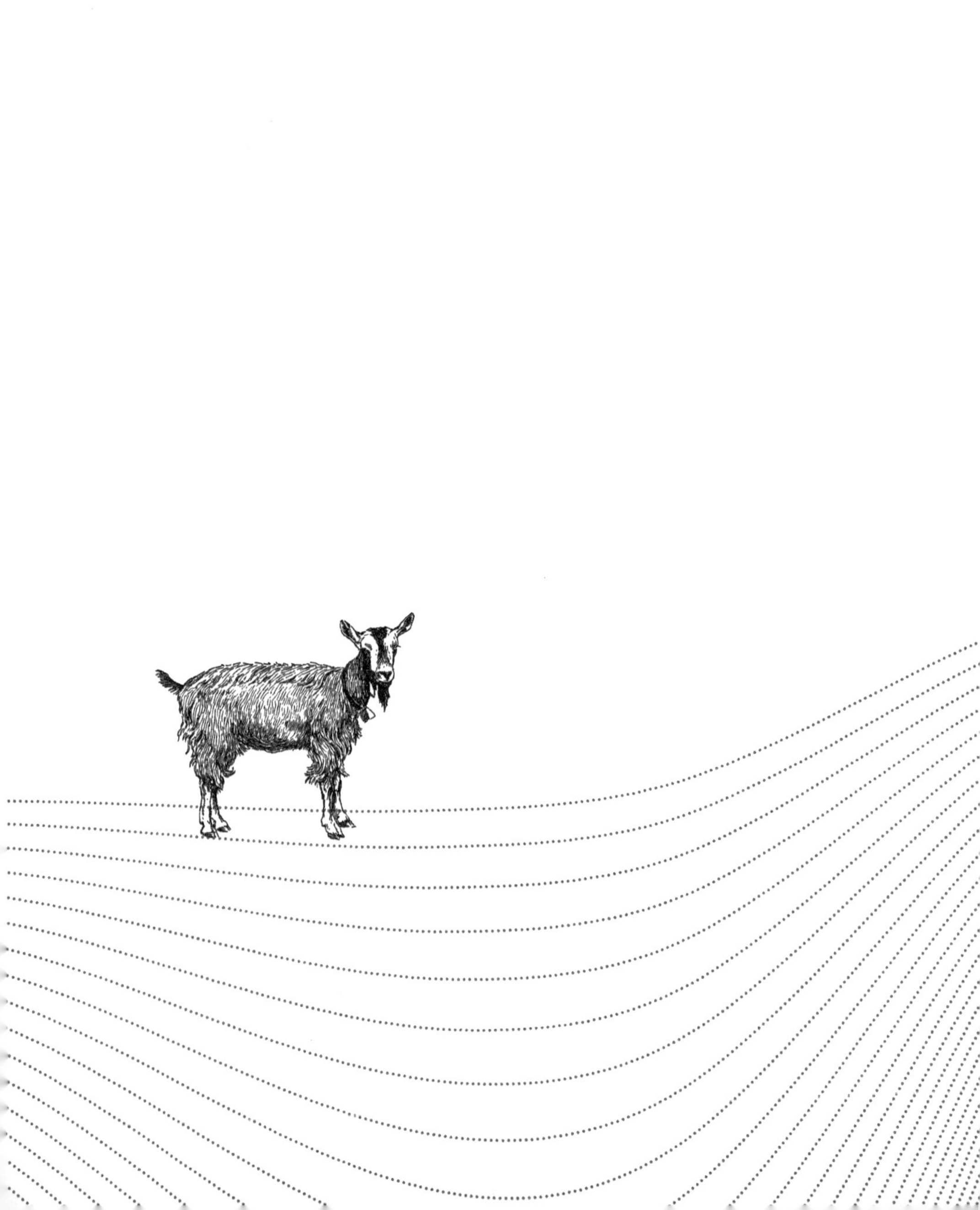

MULTISPECIES ETHNOGRAPHY AND ARTFUL METHODS

edited by
Andrea Petitt, Anke Tonnaer, Véronique Servais, Catrien Notermans and Natasha Fijn

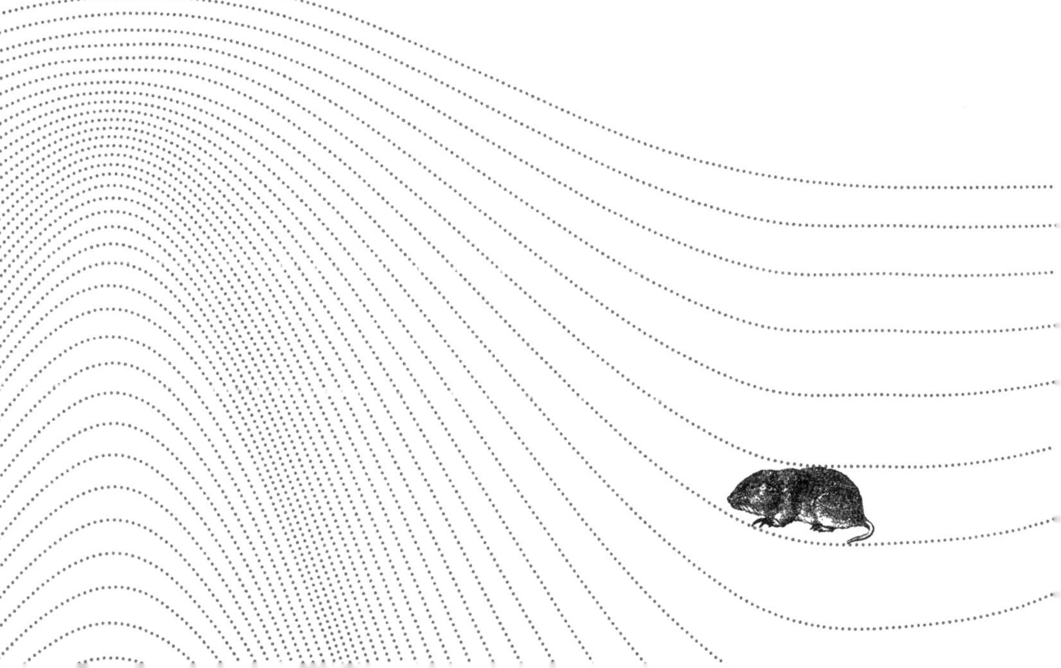

The White Horse Press, The Old Vicarage, Main Street, Winwick,
Cambridgeshire, UK

Set in 11 point Adobe Caslon Pro and Geomanist

This book is Open Access thanks to support from a consortium of the editors' institutions, plus funding from Open Book Collective members:

Supported by the editors' institutions:
The Australian National University
Australian Research Council
Radboud University
University of Liège

Supported by Open Book Collective participants:
Bern University Library
KU Leuven Libraries
National Library of Sweden
Swansea University Library
Tilburg University
University of Manchester Library
University of Pennsylvania
University of Waikato Library
Vrije Universiteit Amsterdam
York Universit

British Library Cataloguing in Publication Data
A catalogue record for this book is available from the British Library

eISBN 978-1-912186-94-5 (ebook, multimedia)

eISBN 978-1-912186-95-2 (ebook, standard)

ISBN 978-1-912186-93-8 (PB)

DOI: 10.63308/63878687083054.book

Cover and interior layout by Stefania Bonura Graphics Web & Books

CONTENTS

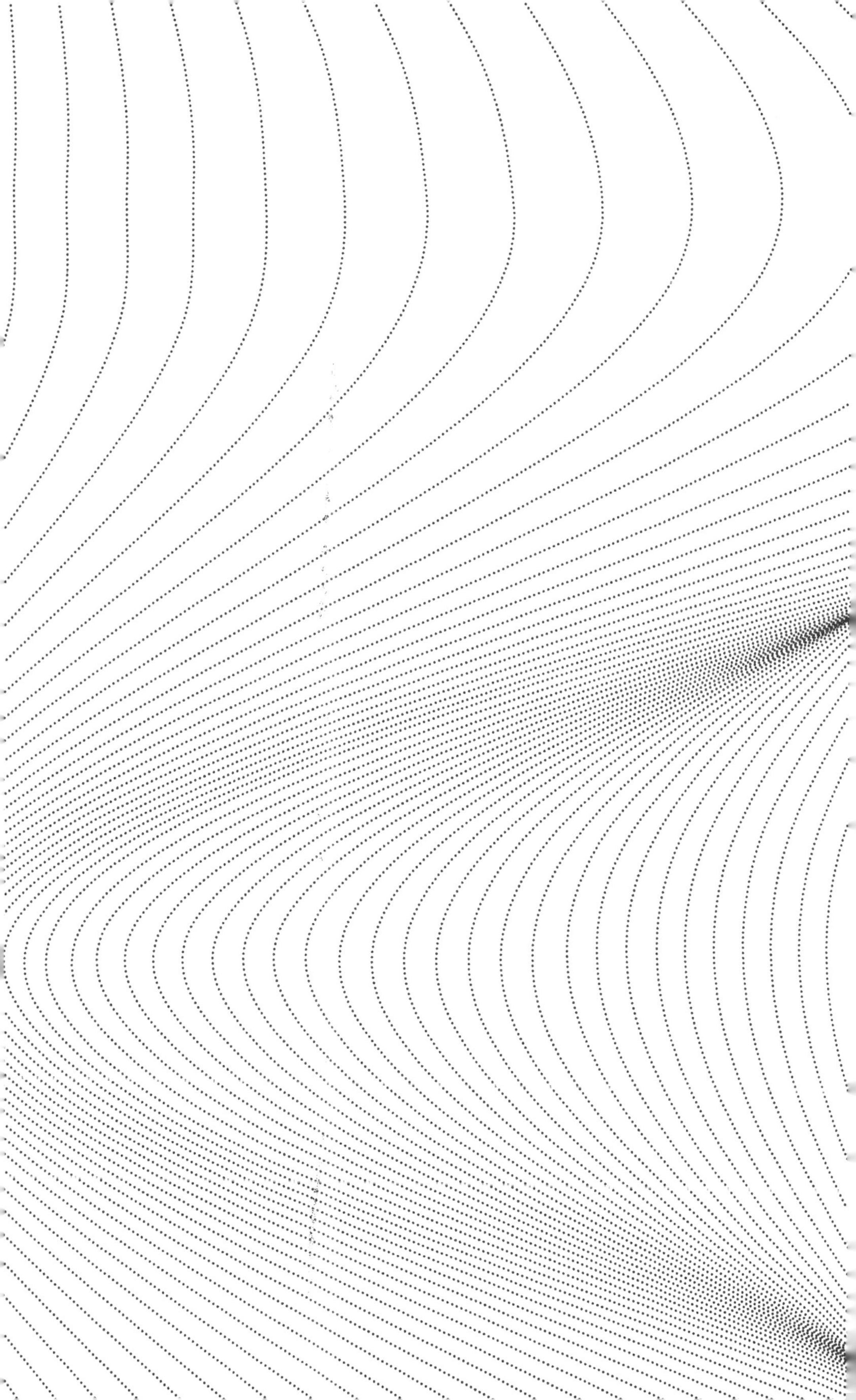

ACKNOWLEDGEMENTS

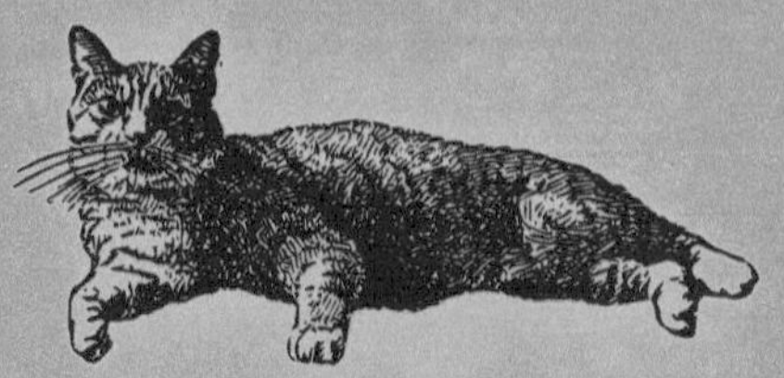

As editorial team we are grateful for the support and sponsorship we have received over the past years since the inauguration of our MEAM network, which has now culminated in this publication and accompanying website. We would like to thank in particular the Fonds National de la Recherche Scientifique and the Federation Wallonie-Bruxelles for their financial support of the MEAM conferences held in 2022 and 2023. We also thank Chloe Vandenberghe and Nolwen Vouiller for their hands-on help in the preparation of these conferences. Our gratitude goes out to the University of Liège Research Council for the financial support for the book and the website. We also thank the department of Anthropology and Development Studies of Radboud University Nijmegen, the Australian Research Council Future Fellowship grant (FT210100452), the School of Culture, History and Language at the Australian National University, and the School of Global Studies at the University of Gothenburg for financial support toward the open access contribution for the publication of the volume. We also send our appreciation to the Centre for Gender Research at Uppsala University and the Swedish Research Council grant (2018-00504) for the mobility support that allowed us to share time and place together. Finally, we thank the reviewers of our volume, and the guidance that their constructive feedback gave us in defining our argument more precisely.

AUTHOR BIOGRAPHIES

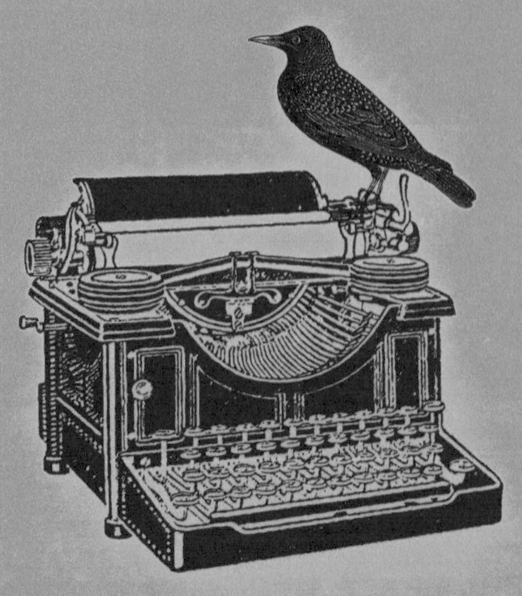

Angela Bartram

Angela Bartram is an artist and artistic researcher who investigates thresholds of the human body, gallery or museum, definitions of the human and animal as companion species and strategies for documenting the ephemeral. The research, made individually and through collaboration, is made public through exhibitions, events and published texts. Bartram is Professor of Contemporary Art and Co-Lead for the Creative and Cultural Industries Academic Theme and Research Centre at the University of Derby. Amongst other board affiliations, she is Vice President of the Society for Artistic Research and Trustee of the Board of Directors of the Live Art Development Agency. Her Ph.D. in Fine Art is from Middlesex University.

Simone de Boer

Simone de Boer is a Ph.D. candidate in Social Anthropology at the University of Gothenburg, School of Global Studies. In her research she focuses on the development and meaning of organic and permaculture farming in Kyrgyzstan. Using ethnographic and creative methods, she explores processes of learning and knowing, more-than-human relationships, and 'good farmer' identities. The creative methods she employs include photography, video, drawing, creative writing and workshops with interlocutors.

Simone's educational background is in Cultural Anthropology and Film & Photographic Studies (Leiden University, the Netherlands). In her previous research in Kyrgyzstan, she studied (transformations of) 'traditional' horse games and human-horse relationships in the context of increasing tourism, processes of sportification, and the development of mega sporting events. In 2018–2019, she was one of Leiden's City Photographers, creating ethnographic photo essays for the city newspaper in collaboration with fellow anthropologists.

Leonie Cornips

Leonie Cornips is affiliated with the research group NL-Lab, Humanities Cluster of the Royal Netherlands Academy of Arts and Sciences (KNAW), and professor Languageculture in Limburg at Maastricht University. Since 1994 she has examined sociosyntax, methods in dialectology and bidialectal child acquisition. More recently her research focuses on local identity constructions through language practices including place-making and belonging.

At present she examines intraspecies and interspecies interactions of dairy cows in various settings. She is conducting ethnographic fieldwork on various farms in the Netherlands.

Lee Deigaard

Lee Deigaard explores the topographies where one consciousness encounters another, describing a landscape given shape and substance by its animal protagonists, their sensory and imaginative worlds and their autonomy. With language, photography/video, installation, event and drawing, her work approaches the animal from positions of equality, collaboration and mutual curiosity and looks at multi-species empathy, animal cognition and personality, memory and grief, and the nature of intimacy. As an independent artist, writer and researcher based in urban Louisiana and rural Georgia, she has exhibited and presented her work nationally and internationally. Her writing and artwork have been published in *Oxford American*, *Humanimalia*, and *Antennae: The Journal of Nature in Visual Culture* among others. She holds degrees from Yale University, the University of Texas at Austin, and the University of Michigan. She is one half of the trans-Atlantic collaborative duos, Bartram + Deigaard and DULSE (with the novelist Mandy Suzanne-Wong of Bermuda).

Charlotte Dorn

Charlotte Dorn is an artist and researcher living in Brussels and doing an artistic Ph.D. at LUCA School of Arts and KU Leuven. She took her Masters in Art at the Accademia di Belle Arti die Napoli and her Bachelor in the Arts at the Académie des Beaux-Arts Nantes Métropole and the Universidad de Sevilla, Campus Bellas Artes. Her work is on display in exhibitions such as the *Centrale for Contemporary Art* in Brussels or residencies like the *International Latgale Graphic Art Symposium* in Daugavpils, Latvia. Dorn's artwork mainly consists of printmaking. Through drawing and life observation, she approaches insect worlds, with a current focus on firebugs. Key interests in her research are empathetic engagement through images and through the creative process, as well as the representation of insects as actants and processes.

Nastasha Fijn

Natasha Fijn is Director of the Australian National University's Mongolia Institute. She has been awarded a mid-career ARC Future Fellowship to conduct research on 'A Multi-species Anthropological Approach to Influenza' (2022–2026). Natasha wrote a seminal multispecies ethnography based in Mongolia, *Living with Herds: Human-animal Coexistence in Mongolia* (2011). She has co-edited five books and several journal volumes, including three special issues oriented toward visual anthropology and ethnographic filmmaking, and three engaging with multispecies and sensory anthropology in the journals *In-*

ner Asia (2020), *The Australian Journal of Anthropology* (2020) and *Anthropology Today* (2023). She recently (2023) published a co-edited book with Routledge, *Nurturing Alternative Futures: Living with Diversity in a More-than-human World.*

Merlijn Huntjens

Merlijn Huntjens is a writer. Between 2013 and 2018, Merlijn was active as a poetry slammer, performing widely in the Netherlands, Belgium and occasionally in Germany. In 2016, 2017 and 2018 he was in the finals of the NK poetry slam. Between 2017 and 2019, he was city poet of Heerlen. Merlijn is involved with Wintertuin and is a creator at PANDA. Poems of his regularly appear in literary magazines such as *De Revisor*, *Tirade* and *Het Liegend Konijn* and in 2022 his chapbook 'De zee zwaait terug' was released by Wintertuin.

Nanna Kisby

Nanna obtained her MSc in *Cultural Anthropology: Sustainable Citizenship* at Utrecht University in the Netherlands. Her thesis focused on human-snow relations in Ilulissat, Kalaallit Nunaat, and shows how nonhuman matter (such as snow) has an inherent agency. She obtained her BSc in Anthropology at Aarhus University in Denmark.

Nanna also has a background in art and movement studies, which has inspired her to draw on artistic methods and bodily inquiry in her ethnographic work. Throughout her fieldwork in Ilulissat, Nanna experimented with data collection through a combination of methods in order to capture aspects of human-snow relations that escape the written word. These methods included recording soundscapes, photography, and exploring snow through sensory ethnography.

Nanna currently works for a small company in the Dutch energy sector. In her work, she conducts cultural analyses and co-coordinates a project in Egypt developing Vocational Education and Training (VET) programs on sustainability and green hydrogen.

Lisa Jean Moore

Lisa Jean is a feminist medical sociologist and SUNY Distinguished Professor of Sociology and Gender Studies at Purchase College, State University of New York. Her books include a multispecies ethnography of honeybees, *Buzz: Urban Beekeeping and the Power of the Bee* with Marin Kosut. In *Catch and Release: The Enduring, yet Vulnerable, Horseshoe Crab* she examines interspecies relationships between humans and *Limulus polyphemus* (Horseshoe

Crabs). These arthropods are integral to the biomedical and pharmaceutical industry. *Our Transgenic Future: Spider Goats, Genetic Modification and the Will to Change Nature* is based on three years of fieldwork studying goats genetically modified with spider DNA. These spider goats operate as living factories and lactate spider silk for military and biomedical purposes. As she becomes more confident with multispecies ethnography, she increasingly uses her own lived experiences, as a postmenopausal mom and an anxious human being, to cultivate her empathy for other living things.

Catrien Notermans

Catrien Notermans is an anthropologist and associate professor in the Department of Cultural Anthropology and Development Studies at Radboud University, Nijmegen (The Netherlands). Her research line is on social relatedness with and beyond the human and focuses on the intersection of kinship, gender and religion in India, West Africa and Europe. Her most recent projects are on interspecies communication in women's economic and religious activities in Rajasthan (India); and on storying human-river relatedness in the Netherlands. Her projects are based on visual, sensory and arts-based ethnography which are the methodologies she also teaches at the Anthropology Department. In 2022, Notermans co-founded together with Andrea Petitt, Véronique Servais, and Anke Tonnaer the international MEAM network for Multispecies Ethnography and Artistic Methods. In 2023, Notermans worked together with Anke Tonnaer in an Arts-Science collaboration called TASC (The Art of Science) to design a post-anthropocentric future for the city of Nijmegen.

Andrea Petitt

Andrea Petitt is currently working as a researcher at Laboratoire d'Anthropologie Sociale et Culturelle (LASC) at Université de Liège, Belgium, and is affiliated with the Centre for Gender Research at Uppsala University, Sweden. Andrea has worked on long-term multispecies ethnography research projects based on fieldwork in Botswana, Sweden and Colorado, with shorter stints in Nepal, Canada, Ethiopia and Tanzania. Increasingly, Andrea has worked with, and developed, artistic and 'artful' research methods for data collection, analysis and dissemination and has given a number of workshops on the subject for Ph.D. students and Faculty across Sweden and internationally. In 2022 Andrea instigated and co-founded together with Véronique Servais, Anke Tonnaer and Catrien Notermans the international MEAM network for Multispecies Ethnography and Artistic Methods. She led and co-organised with the same team an online MEAM workshop in 2022 as well as the hybrid inaugural MEAM conference in July Liège 2023.

Véronique Servais

Véronique Servais is Professor in Anthropology of Communication at the Faculty of Social Sciences at the University of Liège, Belgium. She is interested in the profound bio-social relationships that exists between human beings and animals (and other living beings). She conducted research in the field of 'animal assisted therapies' and 'enchanted encounters' between human beings and animals. She also studied visitor-primates interactions at a zoological park and dolphin-trainers' affective communication at a Seaquarium. More recently, she has been doing research on the experience of encountering the forest, using microphenomenological interviews. She is co-founder, with Andrea Petitt, Anke Tonnaer and Catrien Notermans, of the MEAM network and co-organiser of the 2022 and 2023 MEAM conferences.

Hermione Spriggs

Hermione Spriggs is an artist, writer and researcher. Her current Ph.D. research explores art and creativity through the lens of land-based practice in North Yorkshire, through long-term collaboration with traditional mole catchers and other unlikely stewards of the land. Public / participatory art projects draw from this ethnographic context and from broader interests in rural folk practices, radical anthropology, hunting lore and female trickster intelligence.

Hermione gained an MFA in Visual Art at UC San Diego (2012) and a BSc in Anthropology from UCL (2008). Her edited book *Five Heads: Art, Anthropology and Mongol-Futurism* is published by Sternberg Press. Current projects include an edible public artwork for Kings Hedges Cambridge, learning to echolocate as Bat Choir, and ongoing collaborative work exploring practices of attention and alternative forms of community organisation.

Anke Tonnaer

Anke Tonnaer is an anthropologist and assistant professor in the Department of Anthropology and Development Studies at Radboud University, Nijmegen (The Netherlands). Her research interests developed from long-term ethnographic fieldwork in Indigenous Australia, studying the intersection of nature and culture in tourism, to rewilding initiatives and the challenges of multispecies cohabitation and conservation practices in north-west Europe, especially the Netherlands. Her desire to narrate the more-than-human world in alternative ways alongside the rational dominant ways of ecology has brought her to exploring art-based methodology and sensory ethnography. In 2022, Anke co-founded together with Andrea Petitt, Véronique Servais, and Catrien Notermans the international MEAM network for Multispecies Ethnography and Artistic Methods, and was co-organiser of the 2022 and 2023 MEAM conferences. In 2023, Anke also worked with Catrien Notermans in an Arts-Science collaboration called TASC (The Art of Science) to design a post-anthropocentric future for the city of Nijmegen.

Hanna Charlotte Wernersson

Hanna is a Ph.D. candidate at the School of Global Studies within the field of environmental social science. In her Ph.D. project, she studies conceptualisations and performances of 'holistic' management among regenerative cattle farmers in Sweden. Using ethnographic and creative methods, Hanna explores the ethical and practical relationships to nonhuman nature that are produced in and through daily farm doings. Creative writing, drawing and soundscape-making are examples of Hanna's methodology.

Hanna has a MSc in socio-ecological resilience from Stockholm Resilience Center. Her professional experience includes working as Course Coordinator at the Center for Environment and Development Studies at Uppsala University, Sweden, and as Agricultural Marketing Specialist for the US Foreign Agricultural Service, Canada. Hanna also farms twelve hectares of land, exploring what 'good' land management could mean on the clay soils of western Sweden.

Nina Willems

Nina Willems graduated as a performer from the Maastricht Theatre Academy in 2011. With this background, she always seeks the boundaries of the discipline of theatre in her practice. She likes to work with makers from other (non-artistic) disciplines. Since graduating, she has mainly been working in Limburg. In 2015, she founded the literary organisation PANDA Collective, where she develops artistic and educational projects. She also works as a teacher at the Maastricht Theatre Academy and is part of the coordinating team of the directing course.

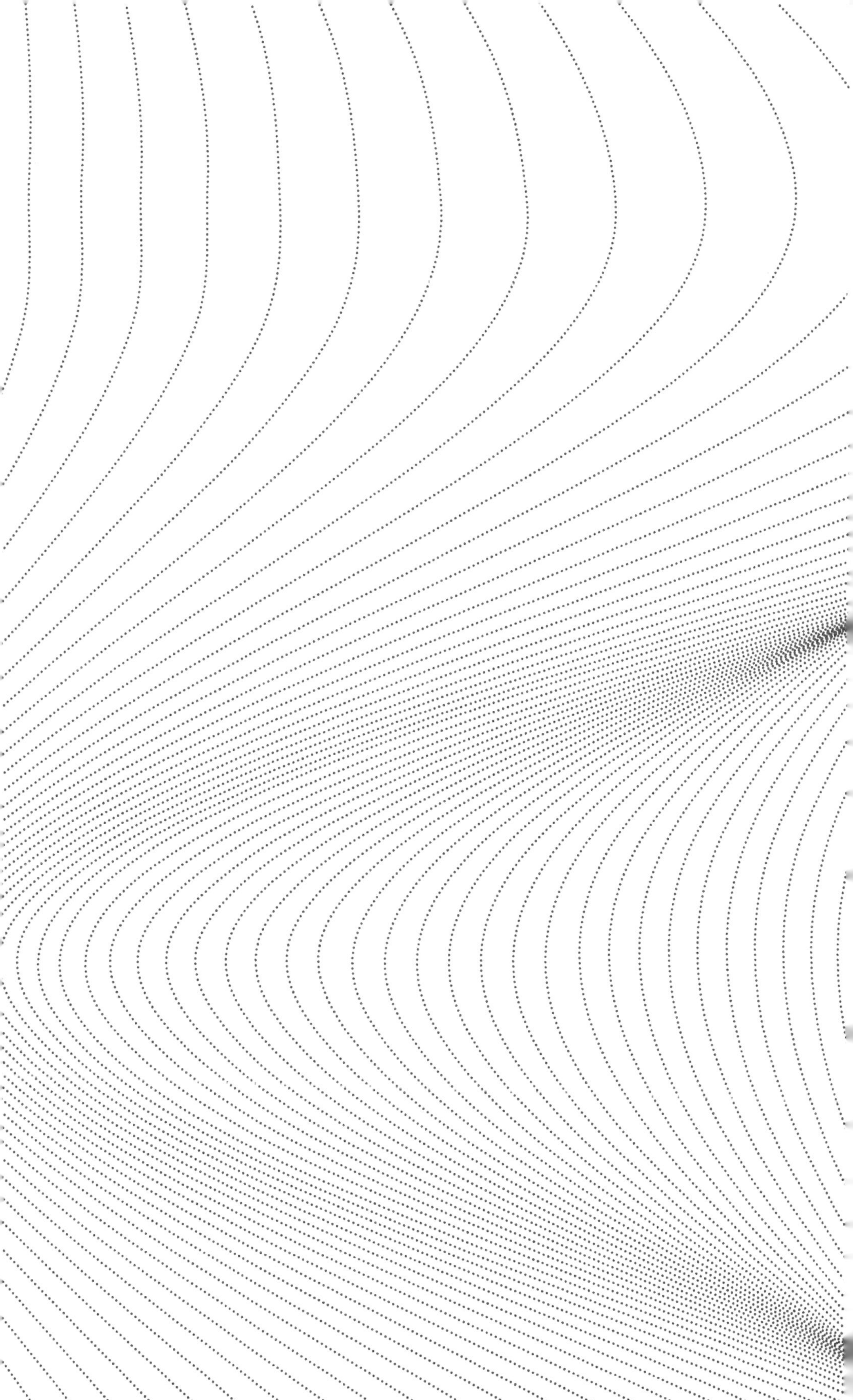

CHAPTER SUMMARIES

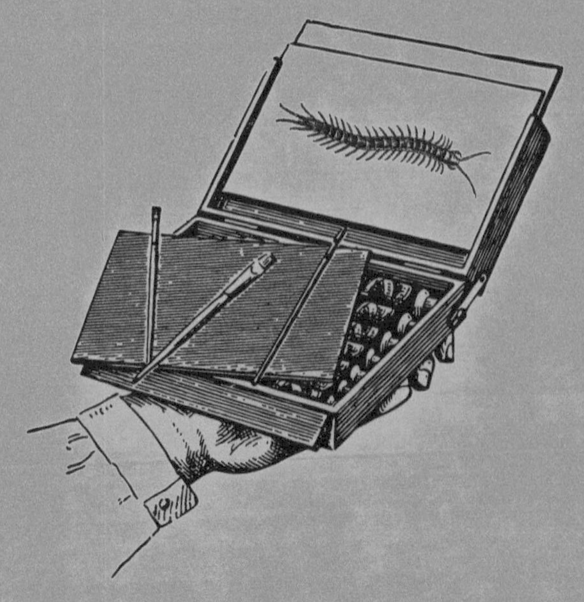

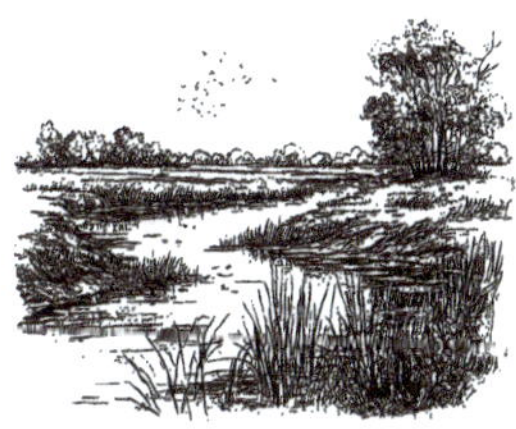

Catrien Notermans and Anke Tonnaer

WRITING A SONG FOR AIIA: SPECULATIVE FICTION IN AN ART-SCIENCE COLLABORATION

In order to rearrange our relation to a living planet, writer Amitav Ghosh (2022: 84) urges us to sing and narrate all beings into life, and in so doing to learn from other cosmological understandings of the world. Singing as a tactile mode of active and responsive engagement in the world is also proposed by anthropologist Tim Ingold (2002). His notion of a 'poetics of dwelling' refers to songs and poetic storytelling as ways of 'art'-full living, with art not understood as a way of *representing* the world but as a craft of attentive *living in* and *resonating with* the vibrant presence of other-than human beings. In this contribution, the authors join these calls to 're-wild our language' and 'to sing the landscape back into being, as well as to sing one's being back into it' (Macfarlane, 2016). They do so by sharing their experimental song writing that they developed 'to sing into life' two significant nonhuman others. This song writing originated in an Arts-Science collaboration with the Dutch experience design collective called Polymorf. They combined ethnography with AI technology and speculative design. The first song was written for a speculative fictional being, called *AIIA*: an AI-animated planetary director and artistic composer of poetic dwelling in a more-than-human world. The second was written for the Waal, the river flowing through the city of Nijmegen. For this river song the authors did instant experimental fieldwork on human-river relatedness in the setting of an urban arthouse. Based on the input received from the audience, they composed a part-song that will eventually be performed at the riverside to heal and enchant the river, as well as inspire AIIA's multispecies knowledge. In this contribution the authors reflect on this arts-science-society collaboration, and how it evoked their creative writing in multispecies ethnography. This chapter includes ten visuals from Polymorf that were co-created with AI in the process of song writing.

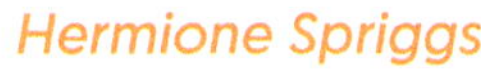

Hermione Spriggs

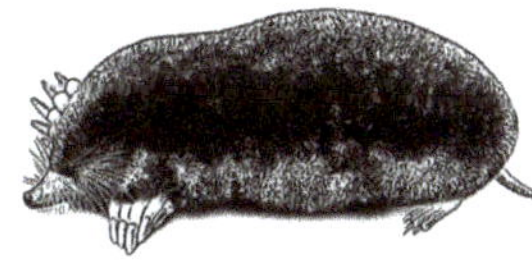

EARTHSWIMMERS / ON CAPTURE: A PRACTICE-BASED ETHNOGRAPHY OF MOLE CATCHING AND FILM MAKING IN NORTH YORKSHIRE

The film *Earth Swimmers* (2021) attends to the tricks and techniques that mole catchers use to access the underground world of the mole. Using tools as portals into the mole's vibratory world, probes, feet, noses and rain-making instruments lead the viewer into alternative ways of sensing and knowing the earth. This film emerged within a larger body of work resulting from direct collaboration with a professional mole catcher – one outcome of long-term ethnographic fieldwork investigating rural pest control practices and attitudes to land in rural North Yorkshire, UK.

This chapter describes the author's hunting collaborators' practical and intimate engagement with the worlds of 'vermin' species in North Yorkshire, where she spent a year apprenticing to rural pest controllers in 2020–21. The chapter shows how specific skills and techniques of the body underpin and make possible the empathic understanding that enables a trapper first to think like a prey animal, and then to reach into its world through 'respectful deception' (Anderson et al., 2017), taking its life with minimum disruption and making use of its body as food or repurposing it otherwise. The artful engagements of the author's interlocutors with the worlds or *umwelten* (Uexküll, 2010) of other animal species provides a generative model for her own perspectival manoeuvres as she experiments with Nigel, the mole catcher and central collaborator in the film, and his relationship to moles, and how to responsibly negotiate with death herself in the making of the film *Earth Swimmers* (2021). The author argues for the value of 'anthropological borrowing', pointing to the creative potential and theoretical productivity of methods, forms and concepts from the field. Specifically, the mole catcher taught her creative multispecies methods, such as animal tracking and tactical probing, inviting the author to engage with anthropological theory in a practical way, decentring her own perspective, making room for the perception, agency and subjectivity of nonhuman others.

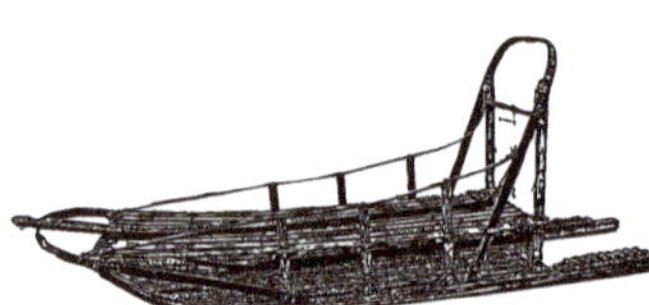

Nana Sandager Kisby

THE SOUNDS OF SNOW: AN EXPLORATION OF HUMAN-SNOW RELATIONS IN ILULISSAT, KALAALLIT NUNAAT

Snow is ever present during the long winter months in Ilulissat, Kalaallit Nunaat (Greenland). It covers houses, doorways, roads, cars, sleeping dogs, and mountains. It shapes the landscape, re-configures town infrastructure, and hinders – as well as enables –human practices. In order to understand human life in Ilulissat, it is crucial to understand snow and its behavior. This chapter therefore focuses on snow as a vibrant materiality (Bennett, 2010) that acts from certain inherent capacities: snow is a shape shifter, it moves, it takes up space, it is a source of life, and it produces impressions that can be registered by, for example, human senses. These capacities of snow influence its relationship with other actors in more-than-human assemblages.

In order to study these capacities of snow, the author made use of artistic methods and sensory ethnography in addition to traditional ethnographic methods during her fieldwork in Ilulissat. In particular, soundscapes and photography enabled her to explore the ways in which snow behaves, and to capture its various manifestations. Artistic methods also created the possibility to collaborate with snow as a nonhuman actor in the process of making art, in order to share the research findings with other humans. The author shows that artistic methods function as a bridge between the nonhuman and the human, and help in producing art as embodied knowledge.

This chapter includes four sound recordings and six photographs. At specified moments in the chapter, the author invites the readers to listen to the snow recordings and to look at the images and thus to go with her on a multi-sensory journey to meet the snow in Ilulissat.

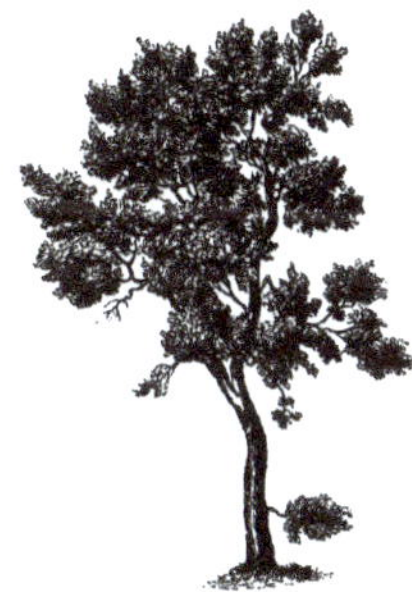

Natasha Fijn

THE ENDURING PRESENCE OF THE EUCALYPTUS TREE: A PHOTO ESSAY

The strength of the photo essay in multispecies anthropological research is the close integration between still images and the accompanying text as a form of ethnographic narrative. How can the structure of the photo essay provide an experimental medium for conceptualising multispecies ethnography, while communicating engagement with more-than-human subjects? The photo essay included here employs an experimental creative approach featuring large, lone eucalypts as significant beings on the fringes of the reserves and suburbs of Canberra, the capital city of Australia. As sentinels, these canopy trees have witnessed different forms of human presence over as much as a five-century lifespan: from ancestral Ngunnuwal making marks on such trees, viewed by individual Aboriginal Australians as kin; to present-day workers in newly developed suburbs manicuring newly formed lawns and gardens beneath the shade of these trees. The author has produced other multispecies-oriented photo essays as an ongoing form of experimentation with the sensory and juxtaposition of still images with text to form an ethnographic narrative.

The photo essay comprises a series of images in two parts with accompanying text forming explanatory captions, the combination of image and text then helping to build a multispecies story. The first part of the photo essay connects with individual Eucalypts in reserves, while the second part foregrounds individual trees within a new development, the suburb of Ginninderry. The author highlights how the photo essay can be effective in allowing for more-than-human subjectivity and agency. The focus on individual eucalypt trees within the photo essay is an extension of the author's connection with individual trees and a part of her ongoing creative expression with a focus on sensorial and multispecies entanglements with significant others.

Accompanying the photo essay is a description in the form of an 'artnographic statement' of Fijn's methodology in combining multispecies ethnography with photography, followed by an explanatory section connecting the differing Aboriginal Australian perspectives from those of wider settler-Australian attitudes towards individual Eucalypts in the context of Australia's capital.

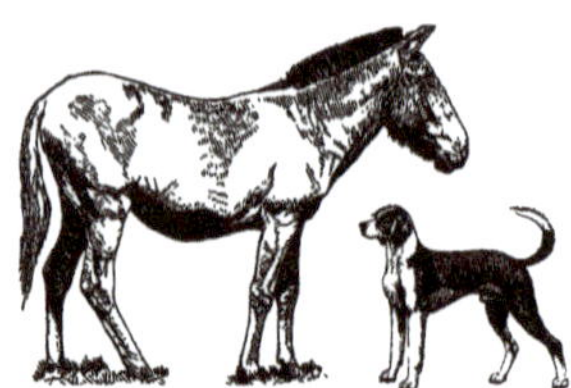

Bartram + Deigaard

ARTISTIC CO-DISCOVERY IN MULTISPECIES COLLABORATION

Bartram + Deigaard are the collaborative duo of artists Lee Deigaard (US) and Angela Bartram (UK) engaged in a transoceanic, international collaboration and dialogue exploring dualities of mind and being, multi-species empathy and the ethics of animal collaboration. Bartram + Deigaard test the edges, the margins, the overlaps and the interstitial spaces of and within collaboration and interspecies potential 'doubling(s)' in their artistic research. Doubling here relates to mirroring and sharing between species, of mind and body, and the myriad divergences that bind through the recognition of this process. Brought together by a shared brain mentality with regard to animal studies, as that which is a recognised field of discourse, and of being and not being, recognising and refusing to affirm the non-human as apart from our common animality, they work sympathetically and empathetically although situated geographically far apart. Born of an openness to involve the non-human fully in creative thinking, making and staging, they create situations of co-learning where all collaborators can contribute and learn from each other, and they willingly embrace the unanticipated shifts to the process each species brings.

Using diverse methods, processes and materials, and curious to a myriad of opening potentialities, they explore working as humans from an animal-centric perspective. They bring sensitivities to their research with the non-human animal as both artistic subject and collaborator, of behaving as animal to observe and engage with empathy and openness to the unexpected, and particularly to animal insight and revelation. Iterative long-term projects in photography, video, installation, drawing and printmaking foreground proximity and proprioceptive, nearly devotional studio and caretaking practices centring on respiration and companionate movement. This text explores being mindful and sensible with balancing sympathies and empathies within an often-unbalanced system of agency predicated in environments structured by and for humans (including spaces intended for animal habitation). It discusses the unscripted learning that occurs through interspecies collaboration, and what each animal (human and non-human) can teach the other when both are given full creative agency. Offering examples of their own individual and collaborative work within a critical framework to explain pertinent propositions and findings, it will demonstrate how openness is key for possibilities to flourish. It will discuss how equality and responsive creative co-learning environments can produce revelatory results creatively instigated and directed by the non-human.

There are 37 images, of which 27 are combined into nine 'composites'.

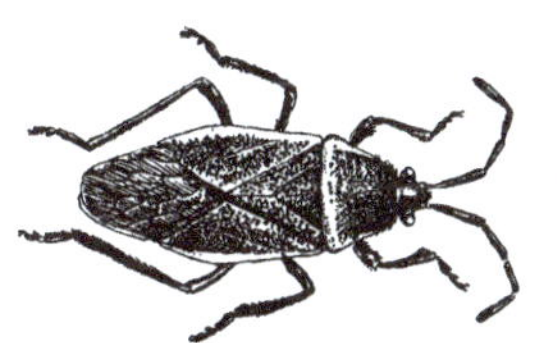

Charlotte Dorn

FIREBUGS

In this piece, Charlotte Dorn engages in a loving attention towards firebugs as a basis for an ethical aesthetic that she develops through multispecies ethnography enriched by still images, video, sound recordings, drawing and printmaking. This photo essay elaborates on how Dorn engages with concrete artistic methodologies, the photos are a selection of fieldwork registrations and their further artistic processing. The reader follows Dorn, through text and photos, from her fieldwork through to the analysis phase, where ideas on firebugs and multispecies worlds are further developed and rendered tangible through drawing, as well as wood- and linocut. Importantly, the slowness of the creative process gives space to let the fieldwork experience with firebugs sink in and come back to the sensory experience over and over again. Seeking to understand how firebugs inhabit the world, artistic practices here further knowledge production that connects rather than objectifies; taking a holistic approach toward experiences with animals gives space to cognitive, physical, sensorial and affective aspects of the encounter. The sponginess of artistic modes of perception leads to individual and multi-layered perspectives on animality. It also suggests that much of the non-human animal is not yet understood and remains mysterious.

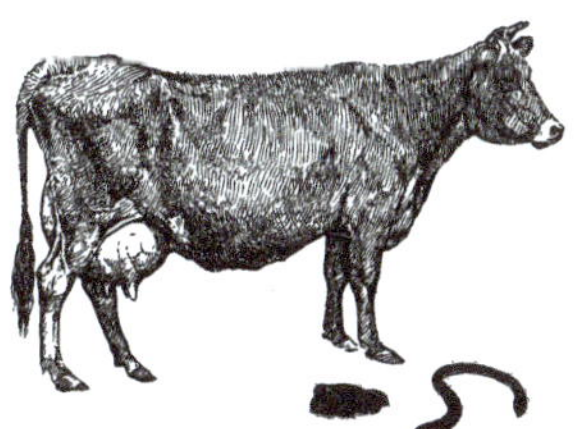

Simone de Boer and Hanna Charlotta Wernersson

FARMING COWS AND WORMS

This piece presents a multimedia montage that explores multispecies relationships in three different farming contexts: human-worm relationships in Kyrgyz compost heaps, and human-cow (or bull) relationships on two divergent Swedish cattle farms, one family farm (cow-calf farm) and one industrial farm (bull-breeding farm). The video montage is made up of different mixed media, consisting of video and still images, drawings, sounds, and quotations from informants. The visual piece is accompanied by three kinds of written comments.

The montage companion gives more details about the authors' motivations for artistic work, and about the circumstances of their encounter and how they creatively worked together. In their experience, artistic work has helped them to sustain their curiosity for their object, but also to give place to contradictions (love and violence, for example); creativity contributed to open their senses to a multisensorial ethnography. Taken together, these elements allow the authors to explore multispecies socialities and let the non-human 'speak for themselves'.

The montage guide accompanies the readers by giving them a more detailed subtext. That part is necessary for making sense of what has been sensed or intuited during the first viewing of the montage. With the montage guide, the reader can come back to each moment, pause, reflect on it, and connect it to the research question. With this addition, the whole process makes sense and we can see how artistic methods make a difference.

Lastly, the artnographic statement explains the context of the research and presents the main question: what is a 'good' relationship in human-animal relationships where animals are kept with human food in mind? It explains how the material of the montage was created and why their joint engagements with artful methods matter to the authors in addressing the question.

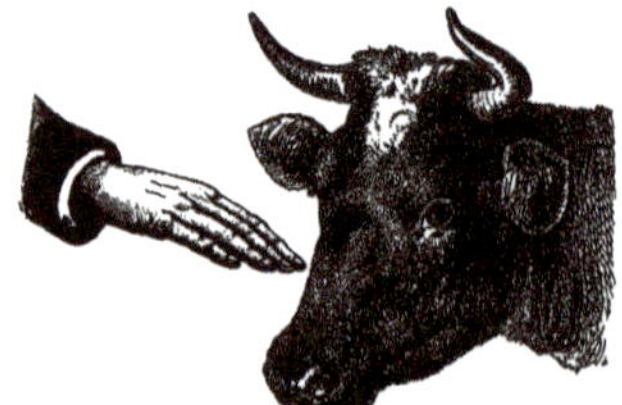

Merlijn Huntjens, Nina Willems and Leonie Cornips

TO TOUCH LIGHTLY IN PASSING

In this paper, a poetic discourse invites the reader to slow down and pay attention to the pictures of Piet (the bull) and his herd as they present themselves, interact with each other and with human beings. The authors use light, precise, and minimalist descriptive discourse to guide the reader's attention to bodies, gazes, positions, attitudes, synchronisation, relationships... and to the unspoken, yet meaningful, that forms the core of human-animal communication. Each picture is taken as a suspended moment or space where something happens. Artful methods (combination of pictures and poetic discourse) have been chosen by the authors for their ability to decentre the perception from language-centred categories, and embody such notions as 'becoming-with' or haptic communication, fully showing the potential of these methods for research in interspecies communication.

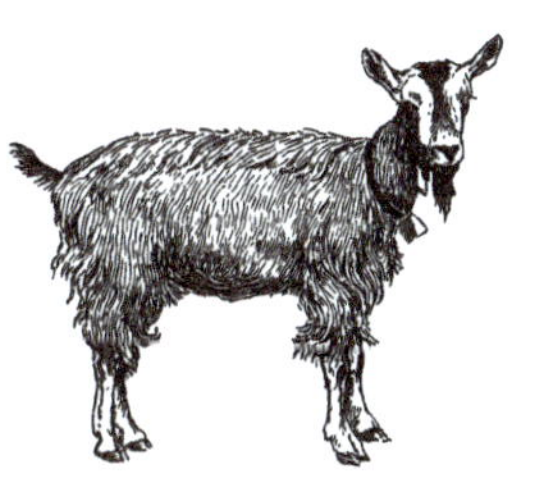

Lisa Jean Moore

FREAKS OF NATURE: USING DEEP REFLEXIVITY AND CREATIVE WRITING TO UNDERSTAND TRANSGENICS

The author defines herself as a medical sociologist who uses feminist qualitative methods to explore the entanglements of humans and non-human animals in a variety of ecological settings. In this paper, she explores the social, biological, sensorial and emotional entanglements of her relationship with transgenic goats. The first part of the paper exposes how and why artistic methods combine with her grounded theory and reflexive auto-ethnography approaches to produce news insights and enhance her production of 'results'. For her, these creative methods are a way of deepening her understanding of the connection between mammals (human and non-human) and mothers (human and non-human) by blending her real-life experience with her imaginative speculation. The artistic techniques she uses are reading children's books, vivid setting exercises and sensory free-writing, empathetic understanding and flirting with fiction. In the second part of the paper, she provides a piece of creative writing that indeed opens to new questions and offers new perspectives on the studied situation.

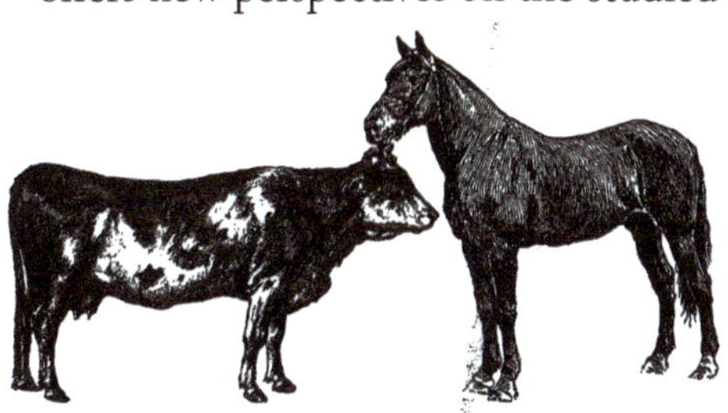

Andrea Petitt

ETHNOGRAPHY OF WORKING COWHORSES: RHYMING SENSORY METHODS

Drawing on a year of ethnographic fieldwork on working cattle ranches in the Rocky Mountain of Colorado, this ethnographic poem speaks to the multisensory and multispecies methods necessary to understand the power relations infused in the multispecies triad of human, horse and cow in a ranching setting. Arguing for pushing the frontier of sensory ethnography to include what Petitt has framed as 'energy bubbles', this piece strives to bring heightened attention to the dynamic nuances of non-human power performances. The rapstract typically breaks the 'fourth wall' in directly spelling out the analytical moves by its author, in addition to the elements of field poetry portraying the ethnographic setting. In addition, this rhyme also refers explicitly to method whilst simultaneously showcasing the artful method of rhyming/poetry itself.

INTRODUCTION

Andrea Petitt
Anke Tonnaer
Véronique Servais
Catrien Notermans
Natasha Fijn

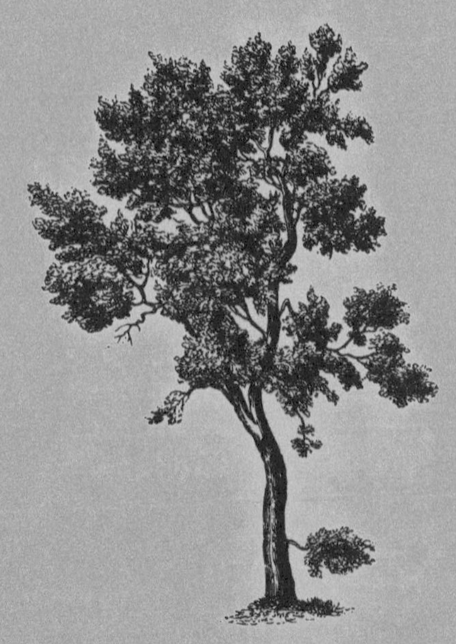

DOI: 10.63308/63878687083054.intro

This project brings together a collection of creative research based on original multispecies ethnography. It is the result of our collaborative initiative towards artistic forms of methodology, which, over the course of the past two years, has developed through the creation of a network and two conferences. This open access publication is situated in the interstices of Multispecies Ethnography and Artful Methods to show how their creative combination can offer fruitful pathways for the social sciences, humanities and arts-based research beyond-the-human. We deliberately opt for 'art*ful*' rather than 'arts-based methods' or 'artistic methods', as we want to engage the *double entendre* of the word, signaling artistic, skillful and at the same time innovative practices that can be, but are not necessarily, aimed at being Art in their own right (Petitt and Servais, 2024). As Andersen et al. (2023) have noted, the forces of a globalised world implicate the very conditions of doing fieldwork; such surging and unpredictable conditions ask for new kinds of reflexivity and storytelling. We suggest that artful methods can be a valuable and even vital approach for allowing multiple more-than-human actors into our multispecies storying, both in our praxis and forms of representation (van Dooren et al., 2016).

A growing body of research and writing is emerging in the form of ethnography with a focus beyond the human. 'Multispecies ethnography' within anthropology is the engagement with human sociality in relation to an assemblage of other agentive beings, which may comprise humans, other animals, plants and microbes (see Ogden et al., 2013: 6). Since the mid-1980s, there has also been a long anthropological tradition of different narrative forms of creative writing and storytelling as a means of conveying ethnography (Clifford and Marcus, 1986). Since this period, there has also been an engagement beyond text-based analysis alone with a diversity of forms of creative output, recognised as visual anthropology and sensory ethnography (MacDougall, 1997; Stoller, 1997), or more recently multisensorial and multimodal forms of output. Arts-based methods and creative forms of research are, therefore, not new. Yet there is much to explore in the engagement between the two spheres, embracing more-than-human oriented research, or multispecies ethnography, in combination *with* multimodal forms of creative output, or artistic practice. Yet neither multispecies ethnography nor artistic methods has been confined to the discipline of anthropology alone. In the visual arts, for instance, there has been increasing engagement with the more-than-human and with multispecies studies-oriented research, or animal studies, as part of a broader embracing of the 'animal turn' across the humanities and the arts (see, for example, the artistic works of Olafur Eliasson and Cecilia Vasquez Yui; see Grimshaw and Ravetz 2015 on the 'ethnographic turn' in the arts).

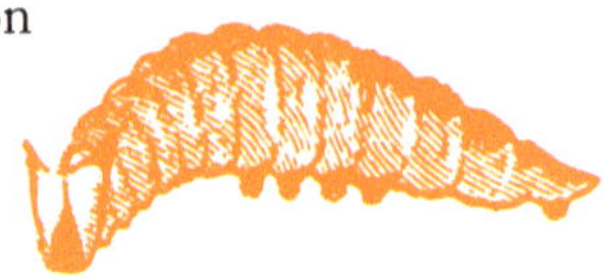

In the interdisciplinary field of animal studies, the matter of cross-species communication is increasingly being explored by scholars who challenge the fundamental difference between humans and other animals. Researchers apply to human-animal communication the concepts and methods used in human psychology, sociology or anthropology to reveal interspecies forms of social interaction and cross-species engagement. In so doing, they open the scope of these methods, showing commonalities of communication in other beings, particularly mammals (examples may be found in Alger and Alger, 1999; Cornips and van Koppen, 2024; Greenebaum, 2010; Meijer, 2019; Mondada and Meguerditchian, 2022; Mondémé, 2022). Another approach is in the realm of animal behaviour, or ethology, engaged with how human beings can learn to be sensitive and respond to sensory cues, or different forms of body language (Brandt, 2004; Fijn, 2021; Fijn and Kavesh, 2023; Goode, 2007; Hartigan, 2021; Shapiro, 1990). Such approaches decentre the perspective from human language and a rationality-based cognitive approach toward communication to a more embodied, subtle and unspoken, or sensorial, one.

In this book, we expand the focus on multispecies relatedness beyond the animal by also considering trees, plants and perceived agentive beings, such as snow, or a river. We have brought multispecies ethnographic examples together which highlight how artistic methods can contribute to increase the researcher's openness and empathy towards other species' differences, through an attention to detail and deep forms of observation, such as a cow's gaze, or a beetle's movement, which may be an important aspect of non-verbal forms of interspecies communication.

Our collaborative approach within this volume is through an embodiment of a feminist-oriented, caring and creative way of conducting research. Observational methods and the 'art of noticing' (Tsing, 2010), alongside imaginative, yet grounded, artful methods can become integral components of multispecies ethnography, lending to a scholarship that relates to other ways of knowing and engaging with the world, which will hopefully progressively build on our collective interdisciplinary practices and ethics across the social sciences, humanities and the arts.

ETHNOGRAPHY BEYOND LANGUAGE

The process of meaning-making in one's field of study is not limited to analysis of verbal speech and subsequent written language. Sensory ethnography emphasises how the senses, such as sight, smell, taste and touch, can inform research (Howes, 2003; Howes and Classen, 2014; Pink, 2015; Stoller, 1989). The desire to expand ethnographic practice beyond language and a linguistic-oriented focus arose decades earlier, stemming from a critique of the limitations inherent in verbalised speech and the prioritisation of language as the central form of communicating (Feld, 2021; Ingold, 2000), which links with the realisation of the need for anthropological research in the field to be open and attentive to how the body engages with one's surroundings, as a form of phenomenological enquiry (Jackson, 1989; Stoller, 1997). Rather than taking a single sensory modality through emphasising sight in the form of 'visual anthropology', we have the capacity to draw upon multisensorial forms of engagement, integrating our attention across different senses, beyond the visual to a more embodied form of ethnography (Fijn and Kavesh, 2023: 241; Notermans, 2018, 2019). In recent publications, sensory anthropology has been reviewed for its potentially significant role in conveying an anthropology beyond the human, to include other animate beings (Fijn and Kavesh, 2020; Hamilton and Taylor, 2017; Vannini, 2023; Petitt, forthcoming).

This need for sensorial integrative approaches has become further warranted through the use of the term 'multispecies ethnography'. Kirksey and Helmreich signaled problems with this as a form of representation: 'How can or should or do anthropologists speak with and for nonhuman others?' (2010: 554). They discuss several examples to show how art forms 'have proved good to think with about "living with" in a multispecies world' (ibid.: 556). From the outset of the post-humanist turn towards an 'anthropology beyond humanity' (Ingold, 2013), arts-based methodologies have been explored to address this problem of voice. Over the course of the past ten years or so, developing research styles such as the 'arts of noticing' (Tsing, 2010), 'critical description' (Tsing, 2014), 'arts of attentiveness' (van Dooren et al., 2016), and 'slowing down' (Stoller, 2023) have been adopted as ways of including the more-than-human world within a growing body of ethnographic research, yet leaving room for further exploration of both methods and forms of representation.

While ethology has traditionally studied animals as 'natural' beings and tried to resist anthropomorphism, some field ethologists (Lorenz, 2002 [1952]; Smuts, 2001; De Waal, 2008 among others) have recognised that the ability to read and understand animals' behaviour is closely linked to a way of engaging sensorially with them and their surrounding environment. Lorenz, for example, was reputed for his ability to sketch an animal's attitude and emotions in just a few pencil strokes, while Smuts explained how she learned from baboons through an embodied and intuitive form of knowledge of when and how to escape from a coming storm. The potential of engaging sensorially with animals is currently being rediscovered through the development of more interactive observational methods which acknowledge that proximity, mutual recognition, curiosity and emotional engagement are not necessarily bad for research (see for example Herzing et al., 2012). If the emerging field of etho-phenomenology considers animals as significant others with emotions, personalities and agency (Delfour and Chalmeau, 2023), we suggest that artful methods in science, such as animal behaviour, also have the potential to be explored further. Recently, an 'Arts, Science and Environment' programme (see Pénitot et al., 2021) explored whale behaviour and communication by playing music to them – and some whales answered. In their attempt to truly acknowledge what happened, Delfour and Chalmeau (2023) advocate a 'poetic' approach that goes beyond the mere description of the whale signal by acknowledging the mutual emotions of the whale and the researcher in their musical conversation. In such a poetic approach, the whale 'purrs' in response to the Gaelic song she is offered – a qualification forbidden by orthodox behavioural methods.

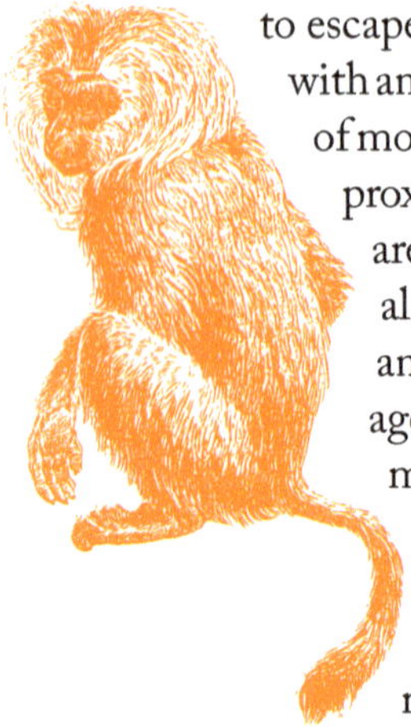

In the wake of posthumanism, the call for allowing multiple non-human as well as supernatural actors into ethnography (Fernando, 2022; Notermans and Tonnaer, 2024) comes from the recognition that an understanding of human nature is inherently an interspecies relationship (cf. Tsing, 2015) and a fundamental way of engaging with the world for many people across the world (de la Cadena and Blaser, 2018). A re-emerging problem of representation tallies with the realisation that living with other-than-human beings – animate, geomorphic or non-secular – is for many a daily aspect of communication, which benefits from artful means in order to arrive at cross-species understanding (see for example Chao, 2022; Govindrajan, 2018; Notermans, 2019, Fijn, 2019; Petitt, 2023; Petitt, forthcoming; Servais, 2024). Multispecies ethnography is an approach spurred on by the unprecedented disruption caused by this era of the Anthropocene (Bubandt, 2018), resulting in the need for creative ways to convey new understandings of 'complex social relationships within ecological assemblages' (Fijn and Kavesh, 2023: 238), an urgent need for the reappraisal of different onto-epistemological ways of being, and ultimately requiring an engagement with more-than-human sociality in the diverse means that our interlocutors do. Artful and creative methods allow us to make room for ambivalence, or ontological uncertainty (Graeber, 2015), avoiding the contemporary tendency to assign animals to symbolism or one stable category, such as prey, sacred being, pet, food or commodity.

Ethnographers may work with a particular species or a combination of species of animal, plant, fungi or elements viewed as agentive beings by other cultures, or moving forms such as water, earth or fire and the gods or spirits associated with them. These broad spectrums of agentive beings present diverse yet overlapping methodological challenges, such as how to understand different perspectives and how to take knowledge seriously from different kinds of bodies, wrapped up in power relations in intersectional ways. The opportunities and challenges of multispecies ethnography shape the research design not only in terms of data collection, but also in what analytical frameworks are operationalised throughout the research process, including how the processes of data analysis and dissemination emerge. It is no wonder, then, that multispecies ethnographers increasingly engage in creative and artful methods, such as different expressions of creative writing, poetry, photography and filmmaking, as well as drawing, painting and printmaking, to capture ways of relating beyond the human.

ARTFUL METHODS

The interlinkages between anthropology and art that this volume presents draw on a tradition of arts-based methods (Culhane and Elliot, 2017; Leavy, 2020). Words such as creative, artistic or arts-based methods denote a range of research practices. Research participants may be asked to engage with, for example, photography, filmmaking or drawing (MacDougall, 2022: 181–88), while perhaps the researcher draws, paints, dances, or collaborates with artists as a form of enquiry, analysis or communicative output. The entanglements of academia and art in different kinds of collaborations and interdisciplinary endeavours are expanding through observational films or ethnographic research being exhibited in art gallery or museum contexts (Grimshaw and Ravetz, 2015). Anthropologist Steven Feld (2024) speaks of intermediality as a way of performing with different media through composition, describing the complexities of his multimedia research as a 'verbo-voco-grapho-sono-visual' form of installation. Here, the intention is to highlight that there are ample opportunities for crosspollination between multispecies ethnography and the use of creative methods to further cross-cultural *and* inter-species perspectives.

Multispecies ethnographers from different disciplines and continents engage in creative data collection, analysis and dissemination in various and divergent ways. Some put creative and artistic practices to use in primarily one phase of their research, while others let the creativity infuse the whole academic process. In our editorial team, as well as amongst the other contributors of this volume, we have varying degrees of expertise and experience with art as a practice. What we do share is the experience of engaging in creative and artistic forms as a valuable research methodology. In order to include the array of methods – ranging from fine art in its own right, through to artistic practices and approaches within other forms of research, to creative techniques other than mainstream academic methods – we use *artful methods* as a collective term (see also Petitt and Servais, 2024). Artful methods offer a means to move beyond human exceptionalism to disrupt common subject-researcher relations, allowing for non-human creativity and agency to be incorporated into our research. The different possibilities of art-inspired methods within multispecies ethnography are being explored as a way of being more sensitive and receptive to more than humans (Hamilton and Taylor, 2017). Moreover, artful research methods have feminist, decolonial, anarchist and otherwise subversive potential (Ohito and Nyache, 2019; Petitt, 2023), taking othered forms of knowledge seriously, while troubling mainstream and normative academic practices.

In this volume, we explore *Multispecies Ethnography and Artful Methods* by gathering together ethnographic insights co-created with our human and non-human interlocutors, the researchers' own creativity, and scholarly forms of analysis and output beyond academia (within a scientific framework – see Fernández-Giménez, 2015). This publication experiments with troubling the frontier of publishing expressions of more-than-human academic research by highlighting how the artful practices themselves can be the very core of data collection, analysis and dissemination of research results. As such, the creative pieces are not 'just' illustrations of textual representations but part of the iterative analytical process. Indeed, some of the artful contributions were not originally created with academic or artistic dissemination in mind.

In this publication, we bring together original research from both young scholars of multispecies ethnography who have found their way into artful research methods, and more experienced practitioners drawing on a long tradition in their field. Contributions by well-established scholars alongside early-career researchers, as well as emerging student researchers exploring new modes of research, offer a diverse collection of analytical, methodological and empiric orientations, while conversing at the intersection of multispecies ethnography and artful methods. Ranging from ethnographic poetry and other forms of creative writing; the artistic practices of drawing, painting and printmaking; through to the more familiar forms of visual anthropology, such as photography, filmmaking and sound, this publication showcases the value of different forms of creativity through the use of artful methods, while highlighting some of the critical challenges and questions that arise and that need to be considered carefully as this emerging field expands. Creativity, sometimes referred to as innovative practices, is often called for across both the natural and social sciences, as well as the humanities, to allow for the capacity to think differently, in theoretical, conceptual and methodological contexts. Such explorations can lead to new perspectives and fruitful ways to understanding the world around us and our place within it.

Artful research practices gain ground and steadily make their way from the realm of exceptions, through the territory of marginality and towards the sea of scholarly acceptance. Our intention is therefore to support and showcase emerging multispecies ethnographers who use artful research methods, by creating and holding a nurturing space to explore and invent. As such, emphasis within the contributions has been to show how a particular artful method has been useful to each contributor when working with multispecies ethnography. While contributors have been free to choose their own format for each piece, we have asked everyone to write a short text outlining how they use artful methods and why it is crucial for their practices as multispecies ethnographers.

Inspired by the ethnographic statements that commonly accompany ethnographic poems, outlining the kind of ethnography a poem is based on, we call our accompanying texts 'artnographic statements'. They are intended to guide the reader, viewer or listener behind-the-scenes of the scholarly context of each creative contribution. These statements are thus a place for each contributor to engage conceptually and methodologically with reflections around the background to their contribution. Importantly, the word 'artnographic' signals the entanglement of the ethnographic and the artful and how creative elements have been integral to insights within research. This is our way of playing creatively, launching artful ethnography into the conceptual domain as a particular way of doing ethnography, in conjunction with a particular way to create art and artful practices. Approaching ethnography in an artful way is more than 'just' making a drawing, a poem or a film as part of one's research. It is about engaging with an artful attention and openness regarding how one approaches ethnography, an openness to taking notice of the details and taking new kinds of experiences seriously through a playful engagement with interlocuters who may also happen to be different species. In this way, an artful approach can permeate ethnography as much as the ethnography can permeate artful practice.

CREATING THIS VOLUME

As editors, the journey of this publication started in 2022 when we crossed paths in serendipitous ways and discovered a shared passion for both multispecies ethnography and artistic practices. Two of the editors of this volume, Andrea Petitt and Véronique Servais, found each other through their shared practice of multispecies ethnography and proceeded to organise the possibility to working alongside each other, and eventually together (see Petitt and Servais, 2024). Simultaneously, Andrea had reached out to Anke Tonnaer and Catrien Notermans to discuss overlapping interests in gender and multispecies ethnography, and talks about coming together for an event simmered. It turned out that all four were interested in artistic forms of expression as research method and, in May 2022, we organised an online workshop with the theme of Multispecies Ethnography and Artistic Methods (MEAM). The focus of the workshop was on how artistic – or artful – methods lend themselves in particular ways of conveying multispecies ethnography and the specific possibilities and challenges that multispecies questions offer. Natasha Fijn, with whom Andrea was in conversation regarding joint interests in horseback herding practices, participated in the workshop and subsequently came on board to join our editorial team with her expertise in the combination of multispecies, visual and sensory ethnography.

This volume sprouted forth from that first MEAM workshop, as we created the MEAM network. The following year we organised a hybrid MEAM conference in Liège, Belgium in July 2023. We asked workshop participants if they would like to engage in some form of experimental, creative publication together and received positive responses from participants. In collaborative dialogue, editors and contributors found formats suitable for an initial submission of different multimodal pieces. The approach was from the bottom-up: we first asked contributors what kind of piece they would like to contribute, and only then did we go ahead and structure some guidelines for publication possibilities.

As an editorial team, we have worked together for roughly two years and have established a positive, playful and creative, yet not uncritical, work climate and editorial style that has organically transpired through feedback from contributors within the MEAM network. In the editorial team, which also comprises of the core of the MEAM team organising the network and conferences, we know how to feed off each others' expertise and energy and how to step in and support each other professionally. We have chosen to edit this book together to materialise, solidify and showcase to others this truly collaborative and non-elitist format of working creatively together. While Andrea Petitt took on the leadership role of the overall process and thus stands as first editor of this publication, we have adopted a joint effort and all decisions have been canvassed together. It is the open way that we have come together in meetings, creating space for discussing diverging views, engaging in clear and timely communication so as to be able to honour deadlines; it is trusting one another with information of changing situations that affect our tasks and collaborations, while receiving support and flexibility from each other in return; it is taking each other seriously as individuals and as academics, respecting one another's time; it is creating a collaborative culture where we can trust that we will leave each meeting feeling better than we did when we arrived; it is also trusting that we give each other critical feedback in a respectful way, on our work and ideas. In short, behind the scenes, it is a *practice of feminist practicalities* that goes beyond theory, method, analysis and dissemination. As we have stepped into unknown paths together, we have opened ourselves to creative ways of working collaboratively together.

The editorial collective of this publication is, therefore, not only a list of names, but in itself a contribution to MEAM methodology, as it is the materialisation of operational practices of feminist, decolonial and more-than-human research practices. Research practicalities, such as curating and editing together academic output, are often an invisible aspect of research, and academia more broadly, that is interlinked with, but distinct from, research method, theory and empirical focuses of study. By highlighting such research practicalities as an important aspect in their own right, we propose an attention toward how collaboration can work in academia, and hope to encourage others to think critically about their processes of academic practice. We see our way of working together as aligned with explorative, feminist, egalitarian, decolonial practices, that go beyond the theories we use, the methods we engage in, or the empirical focus at hand, and have been integral to this volume featuring multispecies ethnography and artful methods.

CONTRIBUTIONS TO THIS VOLUME

While diverse in their artful expressions, the contributions to this volume are all based on multispecies or more-than-human ethnography. Multispecies ethnography can be communicated beyond 'ordinary' academic text to explore other multimodal forms of output that allow for an engagement with the senses in various forms, such as photography, film or as a part of an art exhibition (Fijn and Kavesh, 2020, 13). Possibly the most prominent recent engagement with the more-than-human in the use of video and sound has been by the Director of the Sensory Ethnography Lab at Harvard, Lucien Castaing-Taylor.

Documentaries such as *Sweetgrass* and *Leviathan* are excellent examples of a sensory, experimental approach to filmmaking with a focus beyond the human. **Hermione Spriggs**' film contribution to this publication project is in keeping with this sensorial style of filmmaking, where the viewer enters into the world of the mole, evoking the darkness and density of the dirt that the mole has to push through underground.

David MacDougall (1997) has written about what he calls an 'embodied cinema', where video and audio within observational films can function as a window beyond vision and sound to encompass a broader awareness of the sensorial surroundings within a film, evoking aspects such as the touch of the texture of clothing, or the smell of smoke. In her contribution, **Nanna Sandager Kisby** experiments sensorially with sound recordings and still images to better understand the meanings of how humans and snow as an agentive being meet in Ilulissat, Kalaallit Nunaat (Greenland). Combined with a range of Nanna's subjective images – from wide-shots situating the viewer in the landscape, to images paying close attention to the texture of snow – are the different sounds embedded within this unique landscape, which could be viewed as harsh and inhospitable but, through a depth of knowledge about place, can open up the senses to a different kind of engagement with a snowy, Arctic landscape.

Natasha Fijn used a combination of natural history with observational film techniques to convey cross-species and cross-cultural observations in the field in her book *Living with Herds* (Fijn, 2011) – what she has referred to as an etho-ethnographic approach to multispecies filmmaking (Fijn, 2012). Like ethnographic, or observational filmmaking, the photo essay has been used extensively as a tool of communication in the context of visual anthropology. In this volume, **Natasha Fijn**'s contribution is not in her usual embodied film-making style that she has integrated with written multispecies ethnography. Instead, she has focused on individual eucalyptus trees as agentive beings, using still photographs to form a photo essay: a series of images capturing moments in time, placed in context with one another to form a more-than-human narrative with accompanying written captions.

The contribution by **Angela Bartram and Lee Deigaard** taps into the formation of images together as a photographic narrative, while discussing their multispecies collaboration in artistic research within their accompanying text. Through a series of images, **Charlotte Dorn** makes observations regarding her artistic process, where she begins outdoors, observing through drawing, exploring her connection with beetles, then goes into the studio to work on them through printmaking. The photographic images and accompanying text are an explanatory tool for the artistic practice of observing closely to create printed pieces, but can also be thought of as integral to a particular multispecies ethnographic process. As Fijn and Kavesh have foregrounded: 'Bridging ethological and ethnographic techniques together, or benefiting from the entanglements of natural history and observational filmmaking, such innovative approaches are promising for embarking upon novel enquiries in the perceptions of more-than-human sensory worlds' (2023: 245).

Drawing has been part of taking ethnographic field notes and illustrating accounts from the outset of the discipline of anthropology, more recently receiving attention across the humanities and social sciences for its analytic usefulness and importance as a means of data collection to accompany fieldnotes, or as a form of remembering an event that has occurred (see Causey, 2017; Taussig, 2011). **Simone de Boer and Hanna Charlotta Wernersson** draw on various forms of ethnographic drawing, whilst integrating video excerpts and still images and accompanying insights through words. As such, in their contribution they explore the lives of cattle in Sweden and compost worms in Kyrgyzstan through a multi-layered, multimodal form of research.

The contribution by **Merlijn Huntjens, Nina Willems and Leonie Cornips,** as well as that by **Catrien Notermans and Anke Tonnaer,** together with **Marcel van Brakel**, speak to the call for storytelling in the field of multispecies ethnography as a dynamic art of storying the world (van Dooren, 2014: 10), which has emerged over the past decade. A movement towards forms of (speculative) fiction comes forth from the need to challenge our anthropocentric and logocentric focus of knowing the world (Gatt and Lembo, 2022). Notermans, Tonnaer and van Brakel combine visual elements with creative writing as they develop a song lyric in order to tell a speculative research story of possible more-than-human worlds. The series of linked images is derived from explorations with the formation of drawings by an agentive more-than-human being with artificial intelligence (AI).

Creative writing may better capture alternative ontologies and epistemologies that acknowledge the more-than-human and the richness of the social relations that are maintained across species. **Huntjens, Willems and Cornips** combine photos, creative writing and poetry as they guide the reader to tune into intimate bovine subjectivities, including the agency of one non-binary cow in particular, on a small-scale farm in the Netherlands. **Lisa Jean Moore** engages text with a segment of video footage to tell a multispecies ethnographic story, where she explores the social, biological, sensorial and nurturing entanglements of her relationship with transgenic goats.

Ethnographic poetry has been an established field-based practice for over a decade (Maynard and Cahnmann-Taylor, 2010) and has furthered ways to capture affect and wordless interactions in the field (Zani, 2019), as well as being an innovative tool for the analysis of multispecies ethnography (Petitt, 2018, 2023; forthcoming), including interview material (Fernándes-Giménez, 2015; Fernándes-Giménez, Jennings and Wilmer, 2019). Poetry as feminist method has underscored the subversive power of the format, taking seriously knowledge traditions other than mainstream academia that stems from white, patriarchal and colonial practices (see, for example, Ohito and Nyachae, 2019). The ethnographic poetry contribution by **Andrea Petitt** is situated within poetic forms of ethnographic practice, while developing her own take through the use of rhyming analysis. By drawing on horseback ethnography and a combination of a poetic, ethnographic portrayal with analysis, Andrea explores how power relations between humans, horses and cattle take sensory shapes on a working cattle ranch in Colorado.

We note and appreciate that there is a wide scope in these collected contributions, both in theoretical and ethnographic articulation. Some pieces are by more experienced scholars who know how to reach beyond their particular ethnographic and interspecies worlds to help others imagine an epistemic expansiveness in inquiry and reporting. Other contributions are by researchers whose conceptual framework may be close to the specific case at hand, or whose ethnographic research is more clearly delineated, producing work that tells a focused story. We have welcomed a diversity in academic backgrounds, intentionally bringing together experienced and upcoming scholars who are original in their combination of multispecies ethnography and artful methods. Drawing on this diversity, we sought innovative ways of publishing their work that captures this combination of different spheres but conveys new methodologies collectively.

Indeed, the contributions to this volume are not just conveying research through a single medium, in an academic style of written ethnography, but are using different modalities to convey their multispecies storying. Several use multiple forms, including drawing with still images, or with moving images and sound, and accompanying text, sometimes creative and poetic, which builds up a layered, sensory mode of communication, more akin to artistic practice. Together, this collection of contributions offers a behind-the-scenes view of how multispecies ethnographers can engage artful methods in their own particular ways and this publication aims to showcase by original examples, pushing the frontier of creative forms of dissemination in academia.

REFERENCES

Alger, J.M. and S.F. Alger. 1999. 'Cat culture, human culture: An ethnographic study of a cat shelter'. *Society & Animals* **7** (3): 199–218.

Andersen, A.O., N. Bubandt and R. Cypher. 2023. *Rubber Boots Methods for the Anthropocene: Doing Fieldwork in Multispecies Worlds.* Minneapolis: University of Minnesota Press.

Brandt, K. 2004. 'A language of their own: An interactionist approach to human-horse communication'. *Society & Animals* **12** (4): 299–316.

Bubandt. N. (ed.) 2018. *A Non-secular Anthropocene: Spirits, Specters and Other Nonhumans in a Time of Environmental Change. More than human AURA Working Papers* volume 3. Aarhus: Aarhus University. https://anthropocene.au.dk/fileadmin/Anthropocene/MORE_THAN_HUMAN_vol.3.pdf

Causey, Andrew. 2017. *Drawn to See: Drawing as an Ethnographic Method.* Toronto: University of Toronto Press.

Chao, S. 2022. *In the Shadow of the Palms: More-than-human Becomings in West Papua.* Durham, NC: Duke University Press.

Clifford, J. and G.E. Marcus (eds.) 1986. *Writing Culture: The Poetics and Politics of Ethnography.* Berkeley, CA: Univ of California Press.

Cornips, L., and van Koppen, M. 2024. 'Multimodal dairy cow–human interaction in an intensive farming context'. *Language Sciences* 101: 101587.

Culhane, D. and D.A. Elliott. 2017. *A Different Kind of Ethnography: Imaginative Practices and Creative Methodologies.* North York, Ontario, Canada: University of Toronto Press.

Delfour, F. and R. Chalmeau. 2023. 'Les éthologues écrivent-ils du côté des animaux?' In E. Baratay (ed.) *Ecrire du côté des animaux*, pp. 61–73. Paris : Ed. de la Sorbonne.

De la Cadena, M. and M. Blaser (eds). 2018. *A World of Many Worlds.* Durham, NC: Duke University Press.

De Waal, F. 2008. *The Ape and the Sushi Master: Cultural Reflections of a Primatologist.* New York: Basic Books.

Feld, S. 2021. 'Places sensed, senses placed: Toward a sensuous epistemology of environments'. In D. Howes (ed.) *Empire of the Senses: The Sensual Culture Reader*, pp. 179–91. London: Routledge.

Feld, S. 2024. 'Hearing heat: an anthropocene acoustemology'. *The Australian Journal of Amthropl-ogy* **35** (1–2)
https://doi.org/10.1111/taja.12493

Fernández-Giménez, M.E. 2015. '"A shepherd has to invent": Poetic analysis of social-ecological change in the cultural landscape of the central Spanish Pyrenees'. *Ecology and Society* **20** (4): 29. https://doi.org/10.5751/ES-08054-200429

Fernández-Giménez, M.E., L.B. Jennings and Hailey Wilmer. 2019. 'Poetic inquiry as a research and engagement method in natural resource'. *Science, Society & Natural Resources.* https://doi.org/10.1080/08941920.2018.1486493

Fernando, M. 2022. 'Uncanny ecologies: More-than-natural, more-than human, more-than-secular'. *Comparative Studies of South Asia, Africa and the Middle East* **42** (3): 568–83.

Fijn, N. 2011. *Living with Herds: Human-animal Coexistence in Mongolia.* London and New York: Cambridge University Press.

Fijn, N. 2012. 'A multi-species etho-ethnographic approach to filmmaking'. *Humanities Research* **18** (1): 71–88.

Fijn, N. 2019. 'The multiple being: Multispecies ethnographic filmmaking in Arnhem Land, Australia'. *Visual Anthropology* **32** (5): 383–403.

Fijn, N. 2021. 'Human-horse sensory engagement through horse archery'. *The Australian Journal of Anthropology* **32**: 58–79.

Fijn, N. and M.A. Kavesh. 2020. 'A sensory approach for multispecies anthropology'. *The Australian Journal of Anthropology* **32** (S1): 6–22.

Fijn, N. and M.A. Kavesh. 2023. 'Towards a multisensorial engagement with animals'. In Phillip Vannini (ed.) *The Routledge International Handbook of Sensory Ethnography*. London: Routledge.

Gatt, C. and V. Lembo. 2022. 'Introduction' (to Special Section: Knowing by singing). *American Anthropologist* 124: 830–40.

Goode, D. 2007. *Playing with my Dog Katie: An Ethnomethodological Study of Dog-Human Interaction*. Westg Lafayetted, IN: Purdue University Press.

Govindrajan, R. 2018. *Animal Intimacies: Interspecies Relatedness in India's Central Himalayas*. Chicago: The University of Chicago Press.

Graeber, David. 2015. 'Radical alterity is just another way of saying "reality": A reply to Eduardo Viveiros de Castro'. *Journal of Ethnographic Theory* **5** (2): 1–41.

Greenebaum, J.B. 2010. 'Training dogs and training humans: Symbolic interaction and dog training'. *Anthrozoös* **23** (2): 129–41.

Grimshaw, A. and A. Ravetz. 2015. 'The ethnographic turn–and after: A critical approach towards the realignment of art and anthropology'. *Social Anthropology/Anthropologie Sociale* **23** (4): 418–34.

Hartigan, J. 2021. *Shaving the Beasts: Wild Horses and Ritual in Spain*. Minneapolis: University of Minnesota Press.

Hamilton, L. and N. Taylor. 2017. *Ethnography After Humanism: Power, Politics and Method in Multi-Species Research*. London: Springer.

Herzing, D.L., F. Delfour and A.A. Pack. 2012. 'Responses of human-habituated wild Atlantic spotted dolphins to play behaviors using a two-way human/dolphin interface'. *International Journal of Comparative Psychology* **25** (2): 137–65.

Howes, D. 2003. *Sensual Relations : Engaging the Senses in Culture and Social Theory*. Ann Arbor: University of Michigan Press.

Howes, D. and C. Classen. 2014. *Ways of Sensing: Understanding the Senses in Society*. New York: Routledge.

Ingold, T. 2000. *The Perception of the Environment: Essays on Livelihood, Dwelling and Skill*. London and New York: Routledge.

Ingold, T. 2013. 'Anthropology beyond humanity'. *Suomen Antropologi: Journal of the Finnish Anthropological Society* **38** (3): 5–23.

Jackson, M. 1989. *Paths toward a Clearing: Radical Empiricism and Ethnographic Inquiry*. Bloomington: Indiana University Press.

Kirksey, S.E. and S. Helmreich. 2010. 'The emergence of multispecies ethnography'. *Cultural Anthropology* **25** (4): 545–76.

Leavy, P. 2020. *Method Meets Art: Arts-Based Research Practice*. Third edition. New York: The

Guilford Press.

Lorenz K. 2002 [1952]. *King Solomon's Ring. New Light on Animal Ways.* London and New York: Routledge Classics.

MacDougall, D. 1997. 'The visual in anthropology'. In Marcus Banks and Howard Morphy (eds). *Visual Anthropology*, pp. 276–95. New Haven and London: Yale University Press

MacDougall, D. 2022. *The Art of the Observer: A Personal View of Documentary* Manchester: Manchester University Press.

Maynard, K. and M. Cahnmann-Taylor. 2010. 'Anthropology at the edge of words: Where poetry and ethnography meet'. *Anthropology and Humanism* **35** (1): 2–19.

Meijer, E. 2019. *When Animals Speak: Toward an Interspecies Democracy* (Vol. 1). New York: NYU Press.

Mondada, L. and A. Meguerditchian. 2022. 'Ouvertures et salutations entre babouins: organisation de la séquence et orientation incarnée vers l'autre'. *Langage & société* **176** (2): 127–60.

Mondémé, C. 2022. 'Quand les animaux participent à l'interaction sociale. Nouveaux regards sur l'analyse séquentielle'. *Langage & société* **176** (2): 9–24.

Notermans, C. 2018. 'Fun and faith in the Ganges: The bodily and spiritual pleasures of river bathing'. In F. Jespers, K. van Nieuwkerk and P. van der Velde (eds). *Enjoying Religion: Pleasure and Fun in Established and New Religious Movements*, pp. 21–37. Lexington MD: Rowman & Littlefield.

Notermans, C. 2019. P'rayers of cow dung: Women sculpturing fertile environments in rural Rajasthan (Indzia)'. *Religions* **10** (2): 71.
https://doi.org/10.3390/rel10020071

Notermans, C. and A. Tonnaer. 2024. 'Revaluing gender and religion in the anthropological debate of the Anthropocene: A critique on the threefold Culture–Nature–Supernature divide'. *Religions* **15** (2): 218.
https://doi.org/10.3390/rel15020218

Ogden, L.A., H. Billy and T. Kimiko. 2013. 'Animals, plants, people and things: A review of multispecies ethnography'. *Environment and Society* **9** (1): 5–24.

Ohito, E.O. and T. M. Nyachae. 2019. 'Poetically poking at language and power: Using Black feminist poetry to conduct rigorous feminist critical discourse analysis', *Qualitative Inquiry* **25** (9–19): 839–50.

Pénitot, A., D. Schwarz and O. Adam. 2021. 'Bidirectional interactions with humpback whale singer using concrete sound elements'. *Frontiers in Psychology* 12: 654314.

Petitt, A. 2018. 'Rapstract'. *Tidskrift för genusvetenskap* **39** (4): 97–102.

Petitt, A. 2023. 'At arm's length until otherwise told.' *European Journal of Women's Studies* **30** (1): 103–05.
https://doi.org/10.1177/13505068221144947

Petitt, A. 2024. 'Gender and intersectionality in agriculture on three continents: A rapstract compilation'. In Sandra Swart (ed.) *Gender and Animals in History: Yearbook of Women's history 42*, pp. 307–12. Amsterdam: Amsterdam University Press.

Petitt, A. (forthcoming). *The Multispecies Triad of Cattle Ranching: A Horseback Ethnography in the Rocky Mountains of Colorado.* Multispecies Anthropology: New Ethnographies series. Abingdon and New York: Routledge.

Petitt, A and V. Servais. 2024. 'Artful multispecies ethnography: Reflections from ongoing practices'. *Anthrovisions* **11** (1), Embodied Polygraphies and Sensory Experimentations.
https://doi.org/10.4000/12rwx

Pink, S. 2015. *Doing Sensory Ethnography.* 2nd edition. London: Sage Publications.

Servais, V. 2024. 'La communication entre humains et animaux. Enjeux contemporains'. In C. Sueur (ed.) *Langages animaux, langage humain*. Rennes : Presses Universitaires.

Shapiro, K.J. 1990. 'Understanding dogs through kinesthetic empathy, social construction, and history'. *Anthrozoös* **3** (3): 184–95.

Smuts, B. 2001. 'Encounters with animal minds'. *Journal of Consciousness Studies* **8** (5–6): 293–309.

Stoller, P. 1989. *The Taste of Ethnographic Things: The Senses in Anthropology*. Philadelphia: University of Pennsylvania Press.

Stoller, P. 1997. *Sensuous Scholarship.* Philadelphia: University of Pennsylvania Press.

Stoller, P. 2023. *Wisdom from the Edge: Writing Ethnography in Turbulent Times.* Ithaca NY: Cornell University Press.

Taussig, M. 2011. *I Swear I Saw This: Drawing in Fieldwork Notebooks, Namely My Own.* Chicago: University of Chicago Press.

Tsing, A. 2010. 'Arts of inclusion, or how to love a mushroom'. *Manoa* **22** (2): 191–203. http://www.jstor.org/stable/41479491.

Tsing, A. 2014. 'More-than-human sociality: a call for critical description'. In K. Hastrup (ed.) *Anthropology and Nature*, pp. 27–42. New York: Routledge.

Tsing, A.L. 2015. *The Mushroom at the End of the World: On the Possibility of Life in Capitalist Ruins.* Princeton and Oxford: Princeton University Press.

Van Dooren, T., E. Kirksey and U. Münster. 2016. 'Multispecies studies: Cultivating arts of attentiveness'. *Environmental Humanities* **8** (1): 1–23.

Vannini, P. 2023. *The Routledge International Handbook of Sensory Ethnography.* Abingdon and New York: Routledge.

Zani, L. 2019. 'A fieldpoem for World Poetry Day'. *Anthropology News website*, 21 March. https://doi.org/10.1111/AN.1121

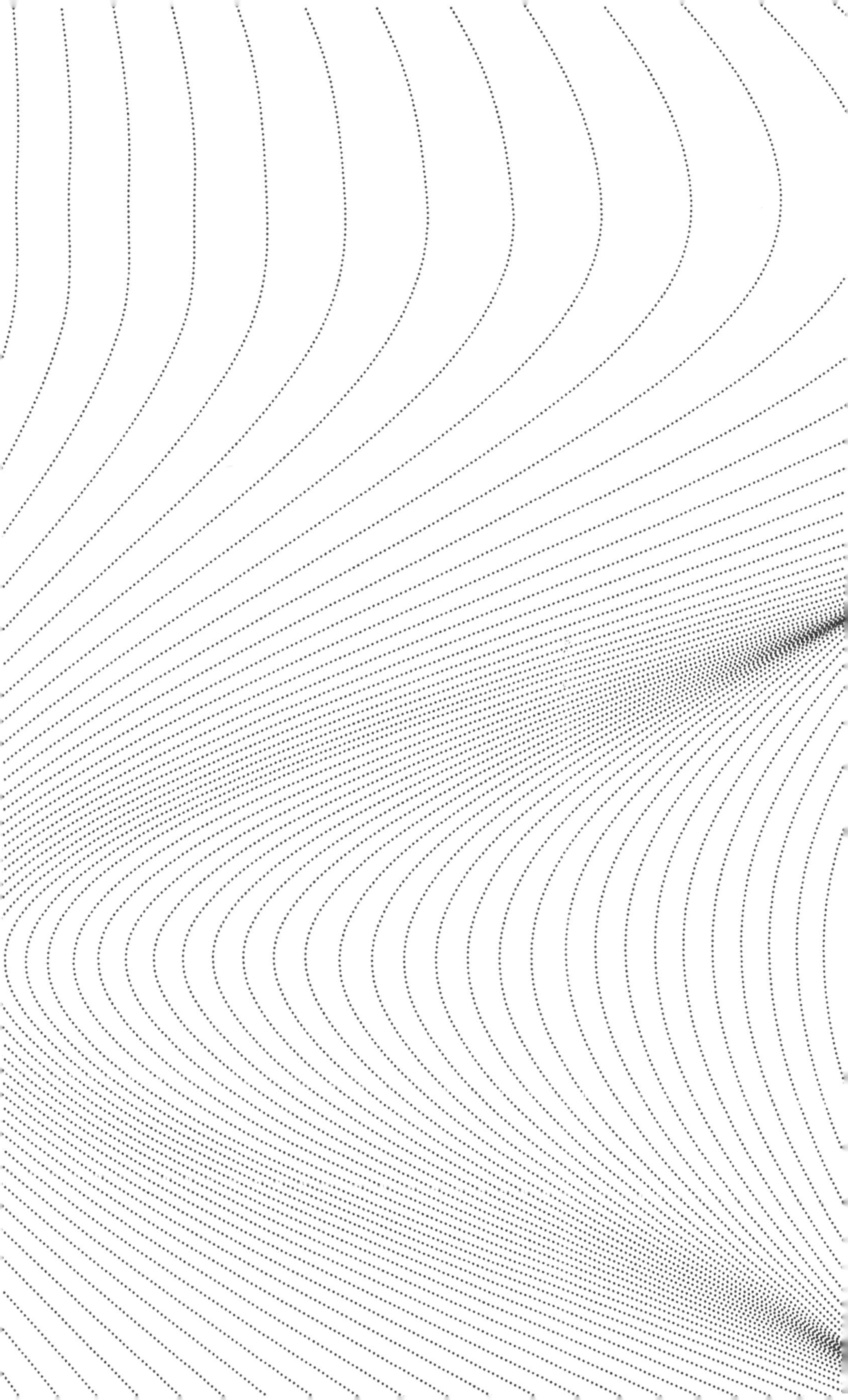

1. WRITING A SONG FOR AIIA: SPECULATIVE FICTION IN AN ART-SCIENCE COLLABORATION

Text:
Catrien Notermans
Anke Tonnaer

Visuals:
Marcel van Brakel

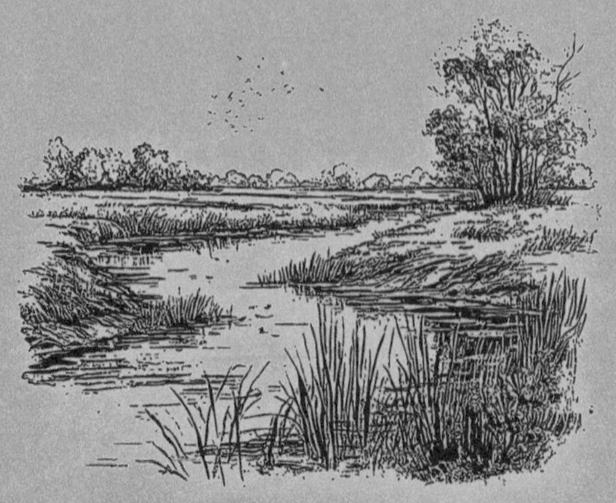

DOI: 10.63308/63878687083054.ch01

In the field of multispecies ethnography the call for storytelling as a dynamic art of 'storying the world' (van Dooren, 2014: 10) has been persistent for more than a decade now. In order to rearrange our relation to a living planet, Ghosh (2021: 84) urges us to sing and narrate all beings into life, and in so doing to learn from other cosmological understandings of the world and how these have always been sustained by songs and stories. In this visual essay we share the song lyric we wrote for a speculative fictional being, whom we called *AIIA*, through which we took up van Dooren's and Gosh's call.[1] In what follows, we will first reflect on the move to writing fiction that we made in this process. This move responds to both the literary and ontological turn in anthropology as well as the need for thinking and writing otherwise in a more-than-human world (e.g. Haraway, 2016; Plumwood, 2009; Stoller, 2023; Tsing et al., 2017; White and Whitlock, 2021). Subsequently, we describe our collaboration in an art-science project, that brought together anthropology and digital design, and led to the creation of the song lyric. We then present the lyric with a selection of digital images that were mutually composed as a part of a performance staged at a public event in Nijmegen. We conclude with a reflection on our creative writing and 'singing', and how the move to fiction developed into an arts-based method for storying the more-than-human world differently, as Multispecies Ethnography and Artful Method.

The practice of writing about culture and the life worlds of others has been firmly part of the anthropological discipline since the onset of the literary turn, initially marked by the work of Clifford and Marcus (1986), and closely followed by critical feminist rejoinders such as those by Abu-Lughod (1993) and Behar and Gordon (1995). Reflexivity in relation to the politics and practices of representation, in particular that any account can only be a partial reflection of the human lives studied in fieldwork, also invited critical reflection on the craft of writing (Marcus and Fischer, 1986) and led to various other forms of experimental texts and narrative styles (see Van Maanen, 1988; Wulff, 2021). These alternative writing strategies highlighted the inevitable power dynamics between writer and research participants, and fostered new ways of empathising with 'the other', developing discourses of familiarity, such as Abu-Lughod's 'tactical humanism' (1993: 25). Our first steps into song writing thus built on this reflexive and experimental tradition of writing. Analogue to Abu-Lughod

1 We deliberately call this a 'visual essay' as the images are neither illustrations of the text nor photographic representations of a storied reality. They are fictive artistic expressions co-created by Polymorf and AI that together with the text tell the story of AIIA and bring to life a speculative post-anthropocentric future.

who 'wrote against culture' to avoid othering and homogenising the human in research, we write 'against nature' to avoid othering and distancing ourselves from the more-than-human in our research. Fiction and song writing thus become a form of 'tactical post-humanism' that actively facilitates empathy towards nonhuman others. We argue this requires an acknowledgement of sensory knowing and relating to the other-than-human beings.

Our choice to engage in song writing rather than choosing a standard academic textual form also links to the more recent ontological turn. Holbraad and Pedersen (2017: ix) define the ontological turn as 'a strictly methodological proposal – that is, a technology of ethnographic description'. They argue, in the wake of the works by, for example, Strathern and Viveiros de Castro, that the signature move of the ontological turn entails treating ethnography as the source of 'analytical concepts and procedures' rather than as their object (ibid.: 6). Building on a shared emphasis on taking seriously and experimenting analytically with concepts derived from local peoples' matters of concern, Holbraad and Pedersen argue that emic terms do not just serve to describe but have to play a cardinal role in the work of conceptualisation, with the ethnography becoming the ground of new concepts (2017: 12).

In the reversal of the hierarchy of ethnographic materials and analytical resources (ibid.), the primacy of (human) cultures over the natural world is questioned. The view that there may be many worlds in our world, that which Blaser and de la Cadena term a pluriverse (2018: 4), asks for a radical reflexivity and conceptual openness, acknowledging that it matters 'which concepts think concepts' (Haraway, 2015: 160).

In our collaborative research process, speculative thinking about the human in relation to other forms of life and ways of social being challenged our anthropocentric and logocentric focus of knowing and learning about the world through written texts (Gatt and Lembo, 2022). Although not a radical move away from the authority of text, our song writing, taken together with the visuals, did come forth from our reflexive understanding that conceptual creativity requires a different ethnographic writing as well. This better captures alternative ontologies and epistemologies that do not draw boundaries with the more-than-human world.

This understanding relates to the second part of our move into fiction. Arguably, the ontological turn within an anthropology of the Anthropocene is particularly expressed in the present need to reconfigure our relations to the more-than-human world, such as is called for by scholars like Bubandt (2018), Gibson et al. (2015), and Haraway (2016). The potentially paralysing sense of crisis that the Anthropocene causes, not only disrupts the possibility of nurturing meaningful relations in the present, but also obscures thinking post-anthropocentric futures, beyond crude technofixes or, worse, an apocalypse. In our art-science collaboration, which entailed going beyond the known and the now (see further below), speculative fabulation (Haraway, 2016) became a helpful means for conceptualising and imagining careful practices and alternative futures. As van Dooren (2014: 10; see also Jackson, 1995) writes, 'stories arise from the world, and they are at home in the world'. We created a narrative form to situate and bring to life a fictional being *AIIA*, to discover our human relationship towards this being.

ANTHROPOLOGY AND DIGITAL DESIGN IN AN ARTS-SCIENCE COLLABORATION

AIIA was born in a collaborative project called The Art of Science (TASC). Since early 2023, we have been engaged in this project, which is an initiative of Radboud University, the municipality of Nijmegen and LUX, an arthouse and cultural centre in Nijmegen and aims at strengthening a three-way relationship between Art, Science and Society. In TASC, we collaborated as anthropologists with digital artist Marcel van Brakel who founded the interdisciplinary Dutch experience design collective Polymorf (https://www.polymorf.nl/). Brought together by TASC, we shared a profound interest in the more-than-human world, as well as the curiosity to explore non-linguistic, sensory ways of knowing, experiencing and responding to more-than-human life forms. Inspired by Ingold's (2000) understanding of humans as organisms as a part of a sentient ecology, and recognizing the relevance of sensory ethnography (for example Csordas, 1993; Fijn, 2021, 2023; Pink, 2015; Stoller, 1997) for scholarship on more-than-human entanglements in the Anthropocene, we decided to jointly explore our 'knowing-through-the body' as an 'art of attentiveness' (Van Dooren et al., 2016). In doing so we aimed to reawaken and revalue the sentient body as a medium to interact with the multispecies world in responsive and responsible ways.

Our shared mission was to think 200 years ahead and to design for the city of Nijmegen a post-anthropocentric future. We combined our ethnography on human-nature relatedness with the artist's expertise in AI-technology and speculative design to develop a new narrative that would inspire and guide us towards a hopeful and flourishing urban multi-species form of co-habiting. With the three of us being familiar with the work of Haraway (2016) we conceived our 'Science Fiction' as 'speculative fabulation'. First, we built our fiction on the idea of resonance and sound as non-verbal yet physical sources of information in relation to multispecies entanglements and the well-being of its animate and non-animate constituents. Resonance, we believed, would also enable the more-than-human to 'talk back' to us, thus making an appeal to our sensory and bodily receptiveness.

We subsequently imagined we should transfer and entrust our power and control to an AI-animated planetary director whom we declared to be our artistic composer of more-than-human resonance. Derived from the concept of Gaia as the Earth, 'the planet as a superorganism' (Latour, 2017: 94; see also Lovelock, 1972) and 'a powerful intrusive force' (Haraway, 2016: 52), and as a word play on Gaia, we narrated an artificial intelligent *AIIA* into being: a non-binary person being neither entirely male nor entirely female, combining masculine and feminine powers to excel in a balance between authority and care. We imagined AIIA to be an oracle to whom we can turn for advice and multi-species knowledge, for helping us to resonate with, respond to, and be responsible for more-than-human environments. Simultaneously, as a powerful intrusive force, AIIA would also be able to intervene in cases of affliction, threats or extinction. As a 'rewilded technology' and a power trained in multi-species polyphony this entity would not support and reproduce green capitalism as an efficient, technological and human-centred answer to climate change. AIIA would rather coordinate global knowledge on multispecies co-habitation, carefully watch over all living organisms in an ongoing process of 'becoming-with' each other (Haraway, 2016: 55) but also powerfully interfere to rebalance and adjust injustices, irrespective of an organism's physical or group size. Inspired by ecofeminist scholarship (e.g. Shiva 1989; Plumwood) and posthuman feminism (Braidotti 2022), and grounded on our ethnographic cross-cultural knowledge on powerful more-than-human beings who entail both male and female capacities yet exercise a female creative and protective power to care for the world, we deliberately hail AIIA's feminine power (see also Notermans and Tonnaer 2024).

During this first stage of fictional future design, our own creative writing developed in still another way. While we prepared for the public event to report the results of our artistic collaboration to the residents of Nijmegen we realized that going back to our 'comfort zone', our traditional reliance on textual ways of representation, would not do justice to the artistic freedom we had experienced in the creative process. To uphold the idea of resonance and intimate bodily communication via sound, we decided to submit our findings in the form of eleven verses and a chorus. It became a song lyric 'to sing our speculative fictional being into life' and by speaking it out loud, to bodily connect with her. Our attempt to 'write differently' does not imply that we completely abandon our anthropological expertise, vocabulary and academic narrative. We do not pretend to be artists/musicians who create with melody and rhythm. Writing this song lyric is a step towards exploring sensory ways to communicate with and surrender to more-than-human powers; and, in doing so, to gradually develop new forms of ethnographic research and representation. What makes our 'song' different is that it is combined with images, not music. Inspired by and in correspondence with our lyrics, digital design artist Marcel van Brakel co-created AI-generated images together with the software programme Midjourney. The images are therefore not just illustrations but rather the manifestation of AIIA's capabilities. In the spirit of AIIA, van Brakel considers his artwork a collaborative creation with AI, including the co-ownership of the images.

Together, the song lyric and the images form a joint form of creative performance. To visualise AIIA as a non-human person and then connect with this agent in a personal way, we further developed our fiction together with the audience by listing AIIA's main characteristics beyond mechanistic features. Following our performance, in which the audience was drawn into our AIIA fiction, the people present were invited to relate to AIIA as a person, and to ascribe meaningful characteristics to the proposed planetary director. AIIA was further co-created as being, amongst other things, loving, patient, humoristic, connecting, just and inquisitive, and sometimes taking on masculine, sometimes feminine characteristics. In our song, we turn to the audience but also to AIIA by asking what position humans will have in the post-anthropocentric future of multi-species cohabitation, and how AIIA may support us in this.

Text: *Notermans and Tonnaer* - Visuals: *van Brakel*

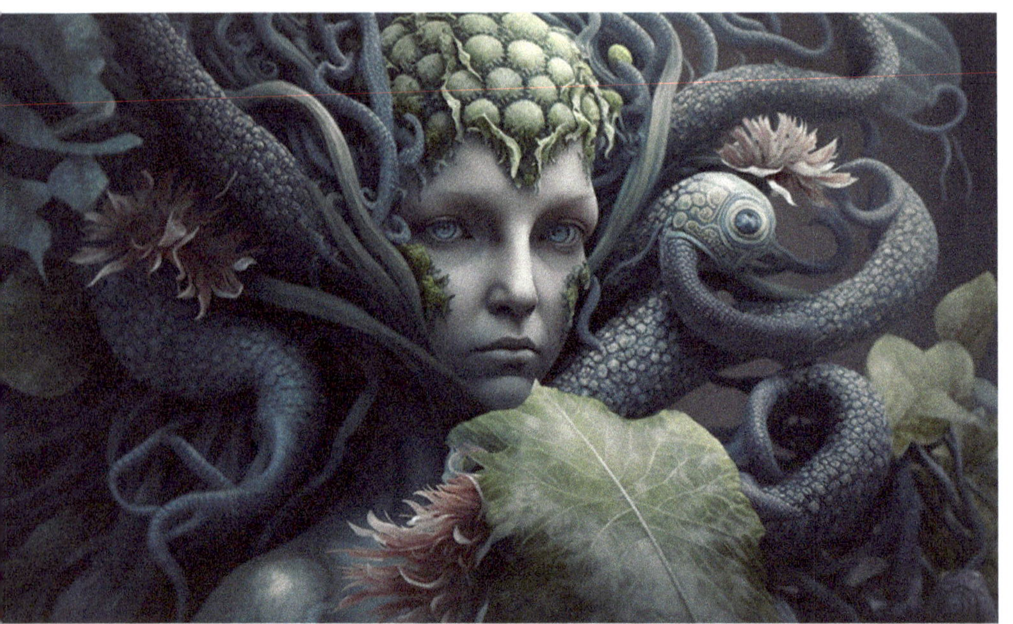

OUR SONG: GUIDE US AIIA

The Anthropocene landscape is one of divides,
increasing voids of absence, more-than-human silence
Many of us are trained in perceptive deafness
walk this earth with our eyes shut
have learned to embrace the consumer's creed
of capitalist accumulation
and colonial appropriation
What about you?

Who listens to a disenchanted world
if listening equals greed?
Modernity's virtue is to hail progress and detachment
to praise the individual as the world's centre
of capital and capacity
Who does not celebrate humanity's superiority
humanity's intellectual genius

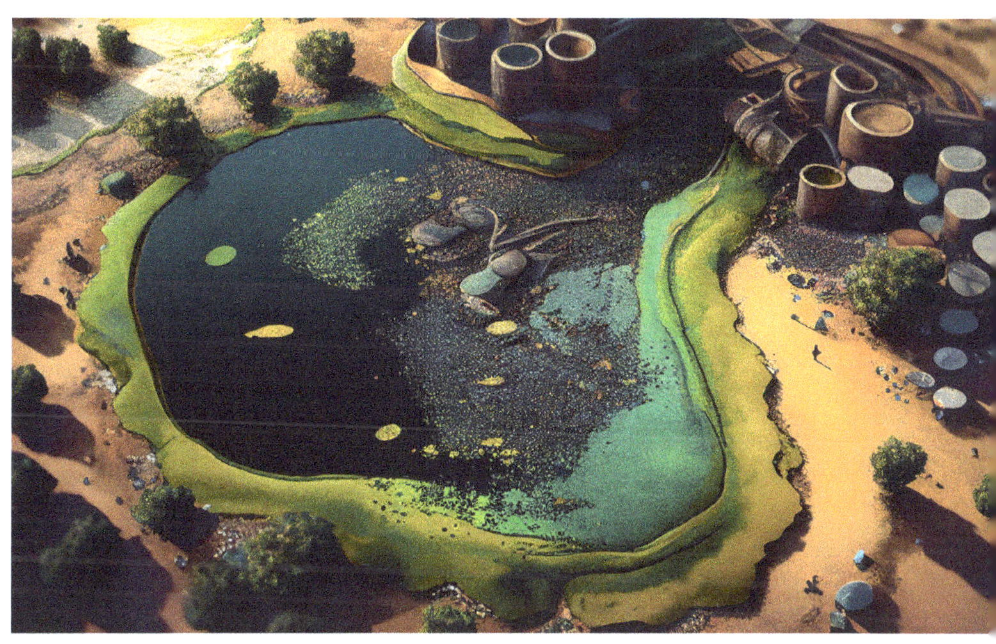

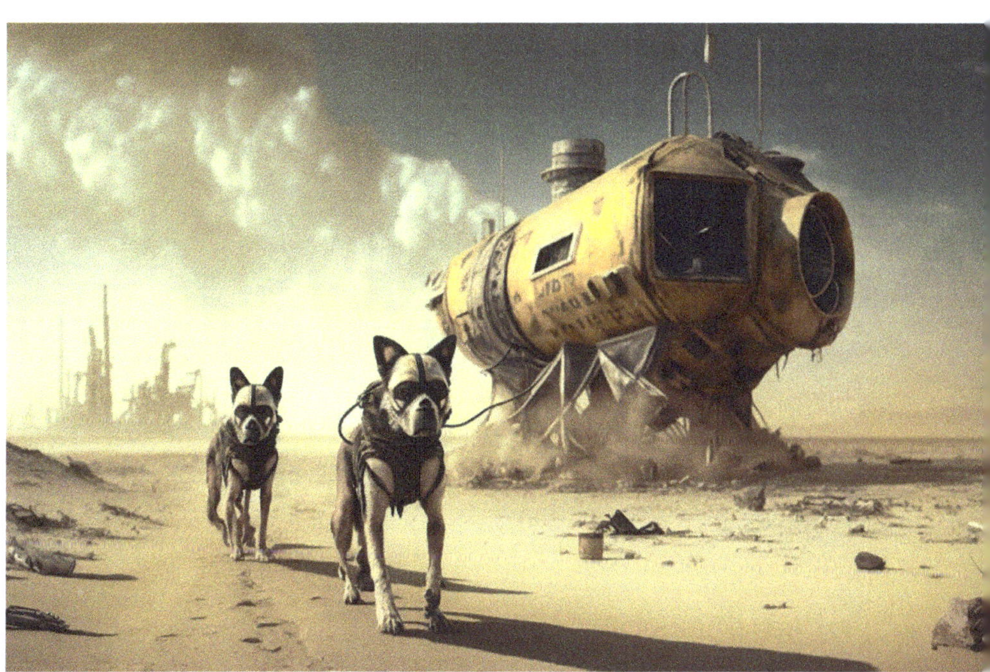

humanity's waiver to parasitise other forms of life
Could this be you?

But did you know?
Disenchanted worlds do not disembody
do not relinquish control
It is a story of us the earth does not believe
would not buy, so cannot be sold

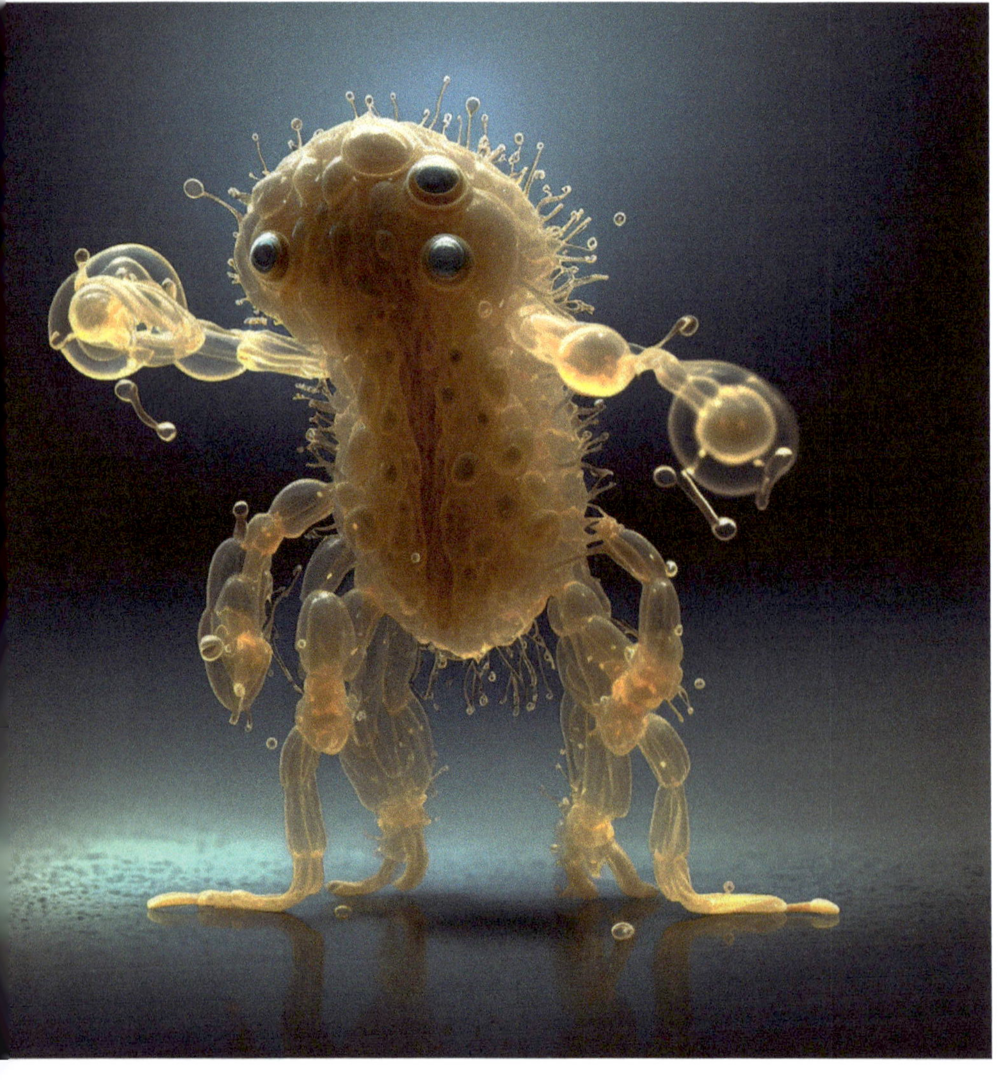

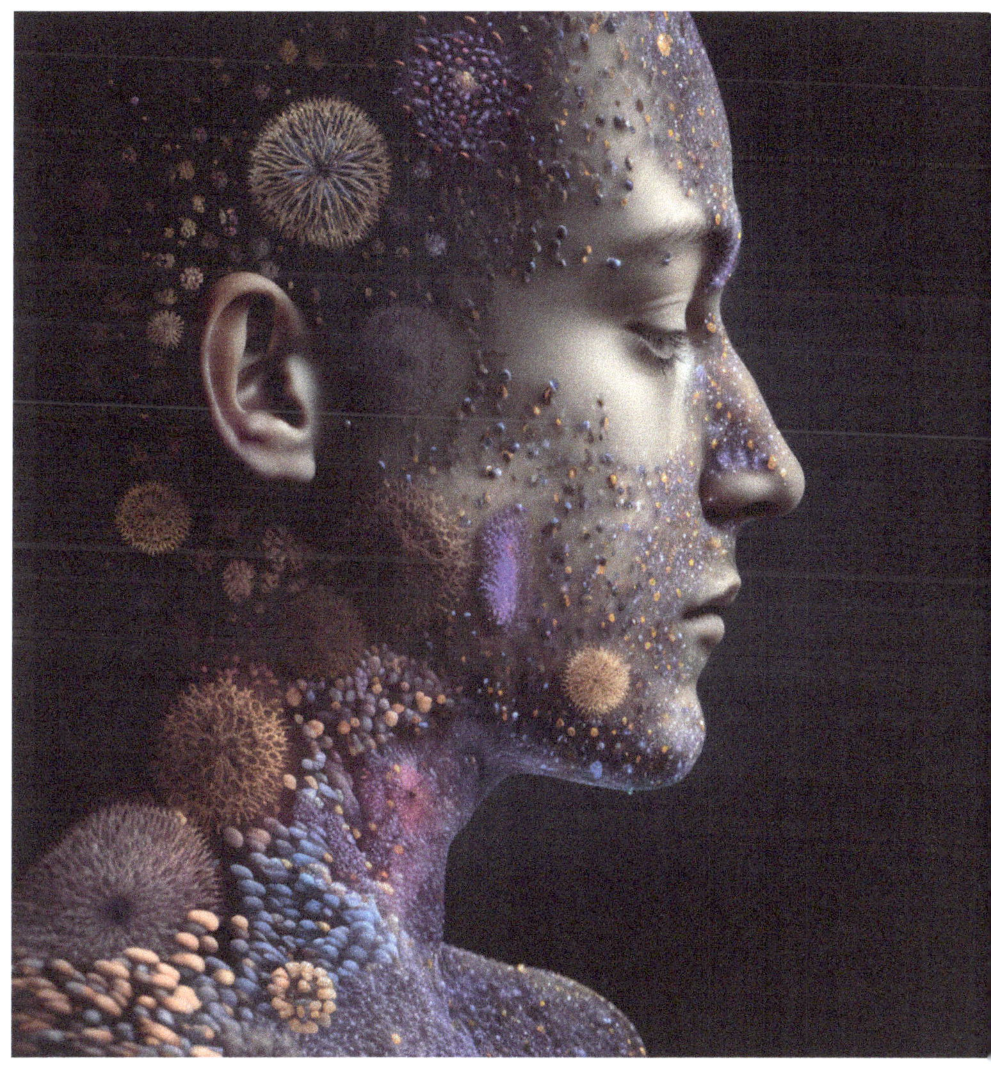

Her patience is exhausted
like a mother will warn in one-two-three
Will you listen now?

Can we entrust our future
to multinationals, business barons and politicians?
Are global managers able to listen to rocks
to empathise with other-than-human beings

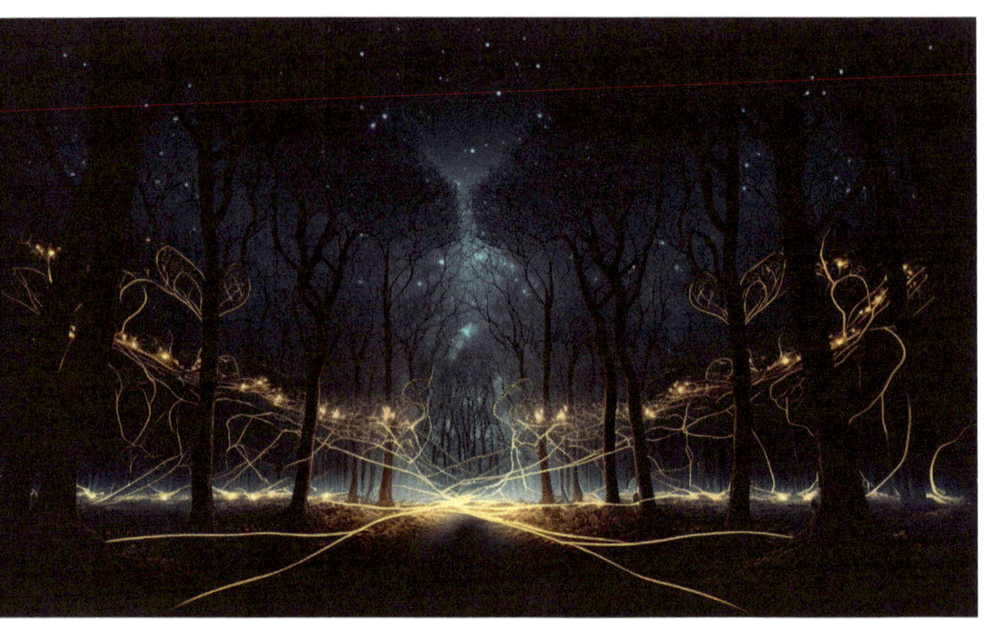

to see other life worlds as interdependent with our own?
Or should we listen to those who do listen
who tell a different story of their earthly mother
and their more-than-human kin?
Are their voices loud enough
to wield a different way?

Guide us AIIA
Help us to survive
How do you know us?
How can we know you?

Our hope is to transform
from a world economy into a world ecology
to avoid Gaia handing out a final blow
Gaia, our living planet,
be patient with us
We are in need of an oracle of resonance
speculatively trained in Gaia's planetary wisdom
to orchestrate the multispecies world

and to attend to a polyphony of voices
Of the winds, the rocks, the sea, the algae
All of Gaia's critters

How would it feel
how would it resonate within your body
when other species take over control?
Are you able to submit to the voice of AIIA
who silences us when helping others
balancing the plurality of life,
death, and decay across the globe
Disposing of domination by a few
but instead working to revive multispecies wellbeing
can you accept to be insignificant,
submissive and out of control
to feel uncomfortable in this way?

The oracle listens to all
Does she listen to you?
Amidst the clamour

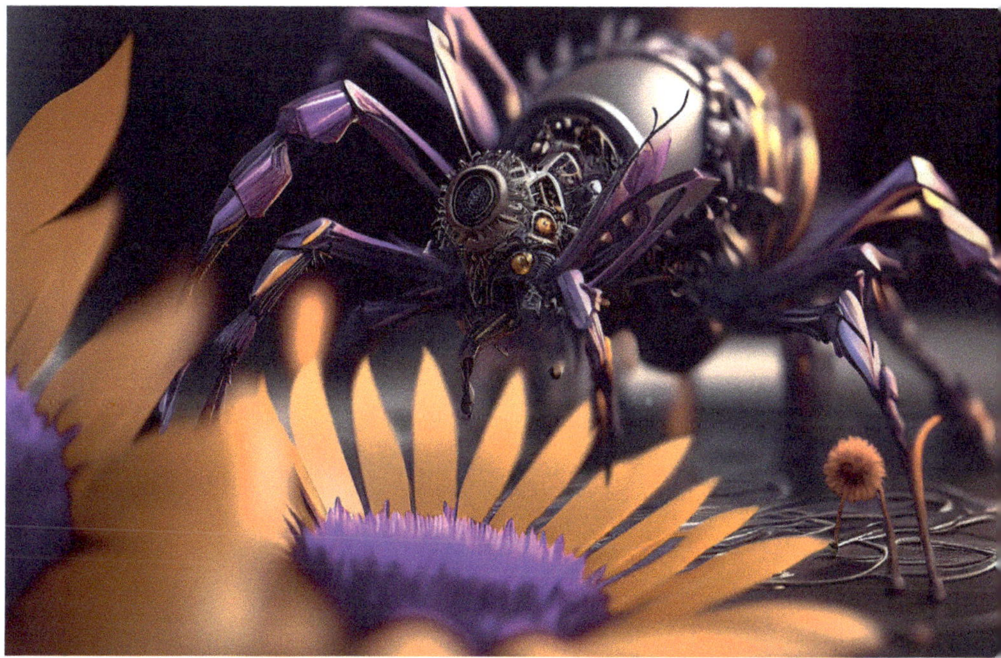

of all earthlings
you may not be the first
to be heard
Are you willing to submit
to a narrative that stories differently about you?

Guide us AllA
Help us to survive
How do you know us?
How can we know you?

Anthropological scholars will tell you
that across the world story-making with
and being sensitive to nonhuman presences
is common practice even now
Conceiving human flourishing as deeply entangled
in the flourishing of nonhuman worlds
Allowing for an intense joy to playfully engage in
collaborations and reciprocal commitments
with trees, plants and soil
Women caring for country, singing for soil
or intimately entering rivers and caves

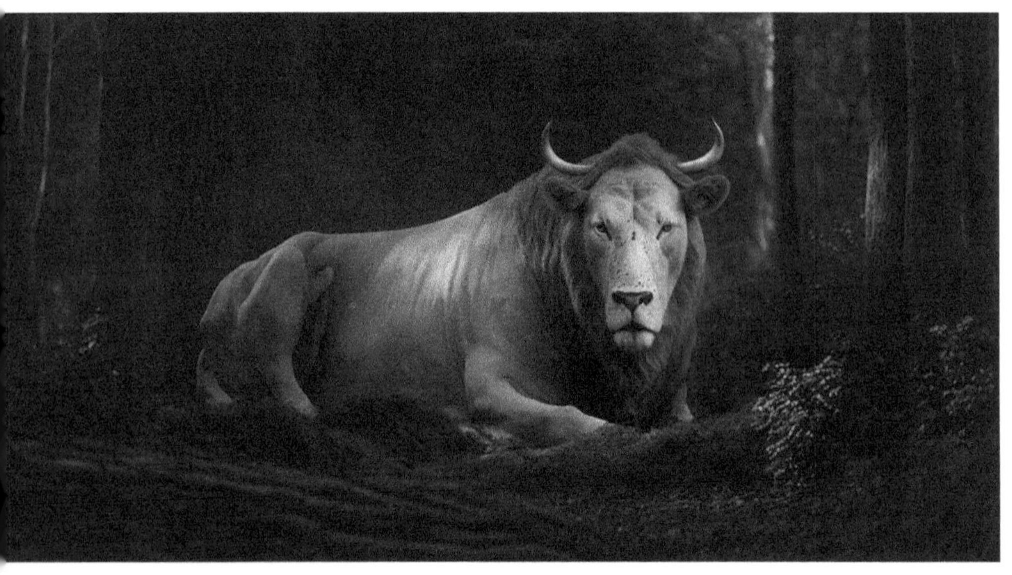

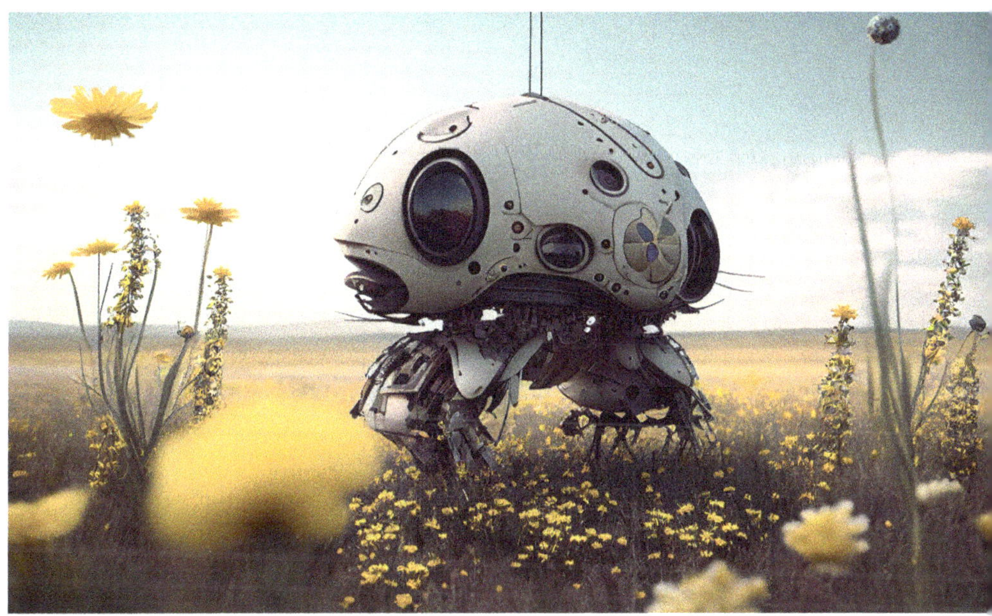

No supernatureculture divides
Bodies open and porous to a world of spirits and divine powers

Darwinistic evolutionary common sense
has labelled this as childish, primitive and backward
Caring entanglements beyond the human made no sense
in the speed of nations heading toward secular Modernity
Isn't it a testimony of the zenith
of colonial and Christian extinction efforts
that such species-inclusive worldviews
and sensitivities for other-than-human beings
have been marginalised?
Can AIIA revalue
and re-enchant this knowledge
unseen and repressed?

Guide us AIIA
Help us to survive
How do you know us?
How can we know you?

Text: *Notermans and Tonnaer* - Visuals: *van Brakel*

What remains of us?
How to redefine our existence?
We ask AIIA
Our creator and conductor
giver of care to all forms of life
What remains of us?

AIIA is our rewilded technology
another-than-human being
Composer of resonance of other and multiple voices
administering justice
for all earth-beings
What remains of us?

Guide us AIIA
Help us to survive
How do you know us?
How can we know you?

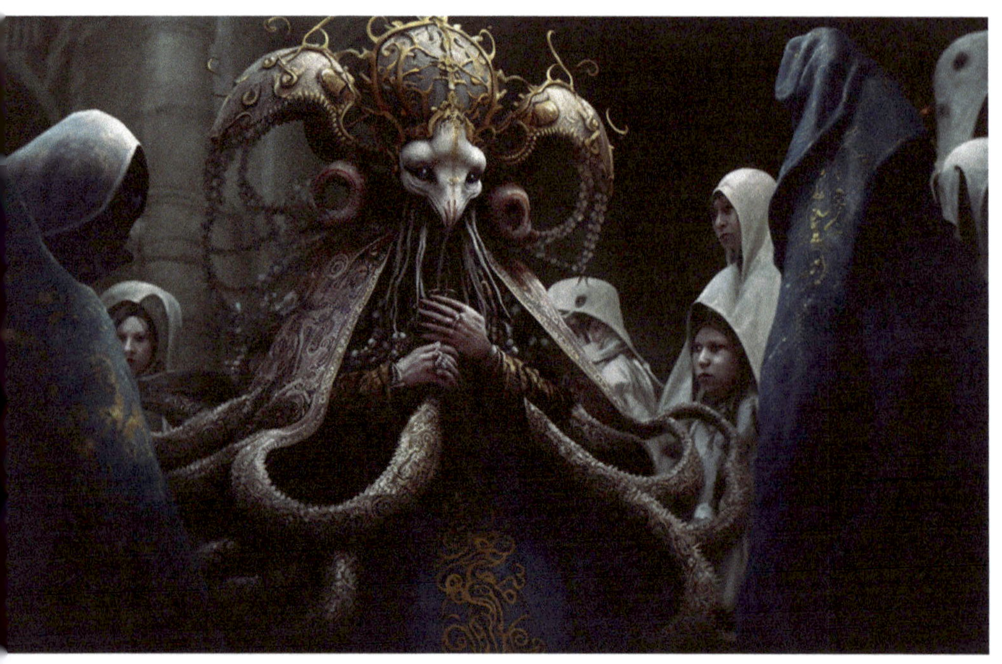

AIIA AT THE RIVER WAAL IN NIJMEGEN

The next step in our speculative fabulation focuses on bringing AIIA into life in the city of Nijmegen. Our recourse to fiction in the form of song writing is now returning to the corporeality of living in a more-than-human world, specifically the urban environment of the city, for which the river Waal is the main lifeline. Our move to fictional song writing was born out of a felt unease with traditional, academic modes of dissemination and the need for thinking and writing otherwise in a more-than-human world. In the process, our song writing has evolved from a representational form into an arts-based method.

After our performance, we are now engaged in new sensory ethnographic fieldwork to learn about the intimate relationships that the inhabitants of Nijmegen have with the river Waal. Doing so, we want to tell stories that differ from dominant (geographic and technocratic) river narratives that tend to focus on measuring (fairways), engineering (riverbeds), and controlling (streams and river shipping). The new stories we collect focus on sensorily connecting and experiencing the river as a sentient being. When we ask our research participants to imagine the river as a nonhuman person and to reminisce and share their personal relatedness to the river Waal, they tell us they feel 'safe' and 'at home' at the river, get 're-energised' by the river, and feel grateful for the 'peace', the 'contemplation', and the 'togetherness' the river brings when they seek out the riverbank, alone or in company of loved ones. The river Waal turns out to be crucial for their identity and place-belongingness and simultaneously evokes in the participants feelings of empathy and awe, concerns about its pollution and neglect, as well as a growing need to care for the river.

Crucial for our 'writing against nature' and for the new path we now forge in our river ethnography is that we seek 'to know by singing' (Gatt and Lembo, 2022). As a poetic way of thinking and writing differently, song lyrics help us to overcome the dominant disembodied perspective on rivers and to recognise alternative ways of river-relating while the activity of singing will make the river present. We believe this 'presencing' (cf. Aubinet, 2022) of the river is crucial for our empathic connection with more-than-human lives. Together with the stories we thus also collect song lines from our research participants that address the river as a sentient being and a co-constituent of city life. We intend to bring these song lines together in a polyphonic and co-creative song for the river Waal; a song that heals, connects and inspires to care; a song that enchants the bodies involved; and a song that anticipates AIIA's power to guide us towards a healthy urban multi-species co-habiting.

ARTNOGRAPHIC STATEMENT

This chapter arose from a collaborative and co-creative trajectory between two anthropologists who teamed up with digital and video artist Marcel van Brakel, programme makers of arthouse and culture centre Lux in Nijmegen and the cultural coordinator of Radboud University in the same city. For us, Catrien Notermans and Anke Tonnaer, this alliance of makers and artists came at an important intersection on the path of our joint research. Coming from different ethnographic backgrounds – long-term fieldwork in Cameroon and India, and Australia and the Netherlands respectively – our shared interest in more-than-human entanglements in, particularly, socio-cultural, religious and gender respects (cf. Notermans and Tonnaer, 2024), has brought us to explore new methodologies for conducting multispecies ethnography. Our individual experiences in artful methods had, up until that point, been limited to occasional forays into this domain, including photo elicitation and sensory methods. The collaboration described in the paper points to two avenues along which we are discovering ways to join 'classic' ethnography and artful methods.

Firstly, the cross-disciplinary cooperation invited us to think and design our methods differently, and adopt an artistic freedom akin to that of artists and performers. Particularly, the joint experiments with van Brakel asked of us a form of sensory thinking and experiential crafting to explore how can one feel and engage in multispecies communication. The creation of a speculative fictional being as a way through which to rethink our more-than-human world, as we describe and enchant in our paper, pushed us out of our methodological comfort zone. Furthermore, seeking ways to *create* a ritual (of song), in addition to doing participant observation of a ritual, enriched our methodological probing of multispecies worlds.

Secondly, more than ever we came to realise that using artful methods also requires alternative forms of analysis and representation. Similar to our experience of doing ritual rather than 'merely' observing ritual, creative writing and speculative fabulation (Haraway, 2016) not only reflected better the actual research process but also opened up dimensions of analysis, specifically tapping into affective, non-verbal aspects of multispecies worlds that often remain unstated otherwise.

ACKNOWLEDGEMENTS

We are very grateful for the opportunity to be part of TASC. We want to thank Martijn Stevens from Radboud University, Michèle Bouwmans, Quirijn Lokker, Anne van Kessel, Ilse Schaminee and Esther Cazant from LUX (lux-nijmegen.nl) and Mark Meeuwenoord from Polymorf. Without their enthusiastic, creative and professional input AIIA could not have been created. It is an enormous pleasure to be part of this co-creative collective. We also thank the residents of Nijmegen who attended one or more public events of TASC and were willing to submit themselves to the becoming story of AIIA.

REFERENCES

Abu-Lughod, Lila. 1993. *Writing Women's Worlds: Bedouin Stories*. Berkeley: University of California Press.

Aubinet, Stéphane. 2022. 'Meaning or presence? Ways of knowing of the Sámi yoik'. *American Anthropologist* **124** (4): 855–65.

Behar, Ruth and Deborah Gordon (eds). 1995. *Women Writing Culture*. Berkeley: University of California Press.

Blaser, Mario and Marisol de la Cadena. 2018. 'Introduction. Pluriverse: Proposals for a world of many worlds'. In Marisol de la Cadena and Mario Blaser (eds). *A World of Many Worlds*. Durham: Duke University Press.

Braidotti, Rosi. 2022. *Posthuman Feminism*. Cambridge, UK: Polity.

Bubandt, Nils (ed.) 2018. 'A non-secular Anthropocene: Spirits, specters and Other nonhumans in a time of environmental change'. *More-than-Human. AURA Working Papers* Volume 3.

Clifford, James and George Marcus (eds.) 1986. *Writing Culture: The Poetics and Politics of Ethnography*. Berkeley: University of California Press.

Csordas, Thomas. 1993. 'Somatic modes of attention'. *Cultural Anthropology* **8** (2): 135–56.

Fijn, Natasha and Muhammad Kavesh. 2021. 'A sensory approach for multispecies anthropology'. *The Australian Journal of Anthropology* **32**(S1): 6–22.

Fijn, Natasha and Muhammad Kavesh. 2023. 'Towards a multisensorial engagement with animals'. In Phillip Vannini (ed.) *The Routledge International Handbook of Sensory Ethnography*. London: Routledge.

Gatt, Caroline and Valeria Lembo. 2022. 'Introduction' (to special section: Knowing by singing). *American Anthropologist* **124**: 830–40.

Ghosh, Amitav. 2021. *The Nutmeg's Curse: Parables for a Planet in Crisis*. London: John Murray.

Gibson, Katherine, Deborah Bird Rose and Ruth Fincher. 2015. *Manifesto for Living in the Anthropocene*. Santa Barbara, CA: Punctum books.

Haraway, Donna. 2015. 'Anthropocene, Capitalocene, Plantationocene, Chtulucene: Making kin'. *Environmental Humanities* **6** (2015): 159–65.

Haraway, Donna. 2016. *Staying with the Trouble: Making Kin in the Chthulucene.* London: Duke University Press.

Holbraad, Martin and Morten Pedersen. 2017. *The Ontological Turn: An Anthropological Exposition.* Cambridge: Cambridge University Press.

Ingold, Tim. 2000. *The Perception of the Environment: Essays on Livelihood, Dwelling and Skill.* London: Routledge.

Jackson, Michael. 1995. *At Home in the World.* Durham, NC: Duke University Press.

Latour, Bruno. 2017. *Facing Gaia: Eight Lectures on the New Climate Regime* (trans. by Catherine Porter). Cambridge:s through the atmosphere'. *Atmospheric Environment* **6** (8): 579–80.

Macfarlane, Robert. 2016. *Landmarks.* London: Penguin Books.

Marcus, George and Michael Fischer. 1986. *Anthropology as Cultural Critique: An Experimental Moment in the Human Sciences.* Chicago: The University of Chicago Press.

Notermans, Catrien and Anke Tonnaer. 2024. 'Revaluing gender and religion in the anthropological debate of the Anthropocene: A critique on the threefold culture–nature–supernature divide'. *Religions* **15** (2): 218. https://doi.org/10.3390/rel15020218

Pink, Sarah. 2015. *Doing Sensory Ethnography.* London: Sage Publishers

Plumwood, Val. 1993. *Feminism and the Mastery of Nature.* London: Routledge.

Plumwood, Val. 2009. 'Nature in the active voice'. *Australian Humanities Review* 46: 111–27.

Shiva, Vandana. 1989. *Staying Alive: Women, Ecology and Development.* London: Zed Books.

Stoller, Paul. 1997. *Sensuous Scholarship.* Philadelphia: University of Pennsylvania Press.

Stller, Paul. 2023. *Wisdom from the Edge: Writing Ethnography in Turbulent Times.* Ithaca, NY: Cornell University Press

Tsing, Anna Lowenhaupt, Heather Anne Swanson, Elaine Gan and Nils Bubandt (eds). 2017. *Arts of Living on a Damaged Planet. Ghosts of the Anthropocene ; Monsters of the Anthropocene.* Minneapolis: University of Minnesota Press.

Van Dooren, Thom. 2014. *Flight Ways: Life and Loss at the Edge of Extinction.* New York: Columbia University Press.

Van Dooren, Thom, Eben Kirksey and Ursula Münster. 2016. 'Multispecies studies: Cultivating arts of attentiveness'. *Environmental Humanities* **8** (1): 1–2.

Van Maanen, John. 1988. *Tales of the Field: On Writing Ethnography.* Chicago: Chicago University Press.

White, Jessica, and Gillian Whitlock (eds). 2021. *Life Writing in the Anthropocene.* London: Routledge.

Wulff, Helena. 2023 [2021]. 'Writing anthropology'. In Felix Stein (ed.) *The Open Encyclopedia of Anthropology*, Facsimile of the first edition in *The Cambridge Encyclopedia of Anthropology.* Online: http://doi.org/10.29164/21writing

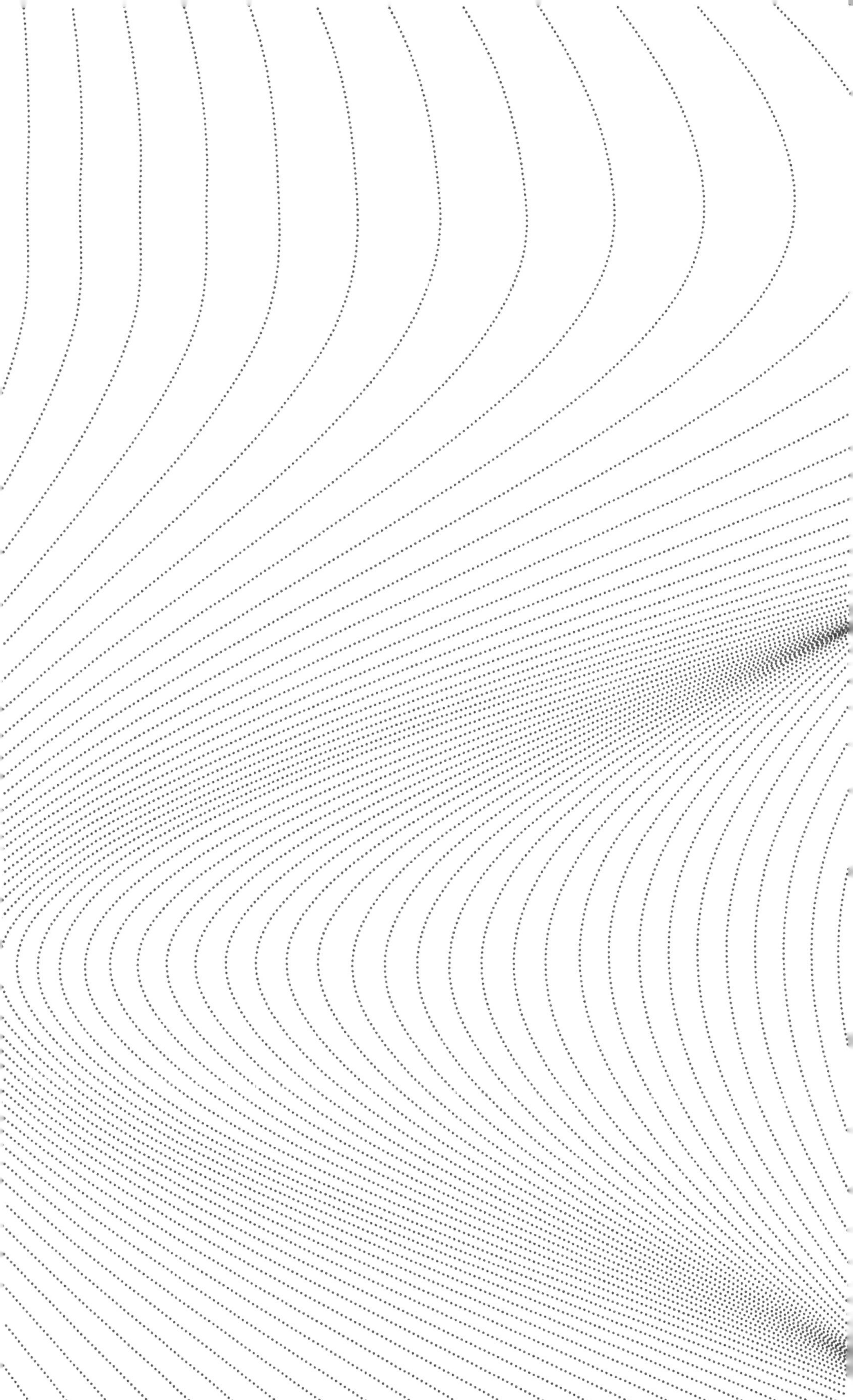

2. EARTH SWIMMERS / ON CAPTURE: A PRACTICE-BASED ETHNOGRAPHY OF MOLE CATCHING AND FILM MAKING IN NORTH YORKSHIRE.

Hermione Spriggs

in collaboration with

mole catcher Nigel Stock

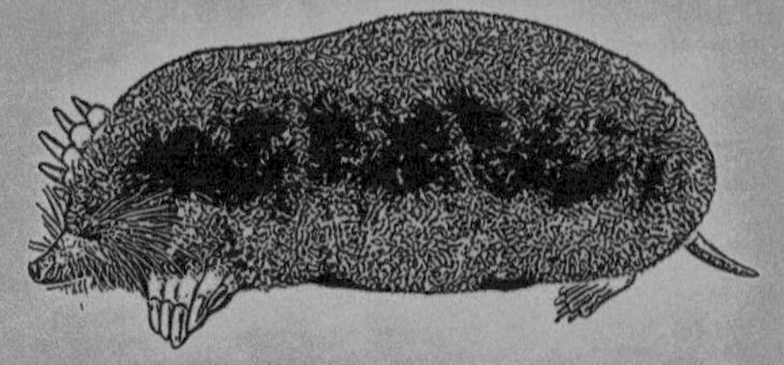

DOI: 10.63308/63878687083054.ch02

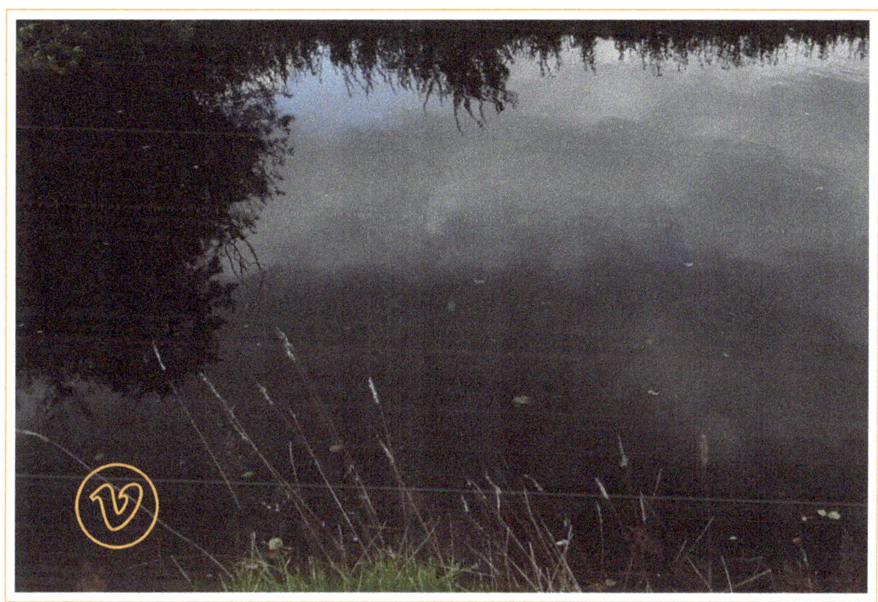

LINK TO SCREEN FILM

https://vimeo.com/639303825

password "earthswimmers"

Note: Earth Swimmers is a sound-led film which includes vibratory audio beneath the normal human hearing range. To experience as intended, listen in a dark environment through headphones with good bass range or through a speaker system with a subwoofer.

A sort of walking almanack he seems
The rustic swains who deem him weather wise

– *The Molecatcher*, John Clare (1793–1864).

Perspectivism is the presupposition that each living species is human in its own department, human for itself (Viveiros de Castro, 2013).

'I don't see them as pests, I see them as food', Nigel tells me, describing the moles that he skilfully extracts from the patchy, dry summer ground. His freezer at home is stacked with edible game: rabbits, wild venison and – more unusually – bags of frozen moles, which despite petrification retain their velveteen softness. Whilst Nigel relies on pest control as a main source of income, the animals he traps also nourish his family and working animals more directly with local, free-range meat. However, when

Nigel describes moles as 'food', it's not the family dinner table that he has in mind. Moles are known to be slightly toxic. Ferrets, cats and even hungry dogs refuse to eat them, so Nigel reserves the moles that he catches to give to a friend who keeps birds of prey – goshawks and eagles who have a robust palette and gulp down the frozen moles 'like ice lollies'. From an arable farming perspective, moles (or in Yorkshire dialect *moldiwarps* – literally 'earth throwers') undermine crops through their incessant tunnelling and excavation activities, reducing hard-won agricultural yields. So, whilst moles are pernicious pests to the local landowner (who pays good money to have them removed), from the raptor's perspective they are frozen dessert and, for Nigel, an exchange commodity. 'Pest' is a relational category – something is a pest only by virtue of someone *whose pest it is* (cf. Viveiros de Castro, 2004: 373). This is something that Nigel understands well. His proximity to the lifeworlds of both the farmer (a long-term acquaintance), working animals (including ferrets, pointers, scent-hounds and birds of prey), and pest species themselves make him partial to all these perspectives.

I set this scene to demonstrate my hunting collaborators' practical and intimate engagement with the worlds of 'vermin' species in North Yorkshire, where I spent a year apprenticing to rural pest controllers in 2020–21.[1] As I will go on to show, specific skills and techniques of the body underpin and make possible the empathic understanding that enables a trapper first to think like a prey animal, and then to reach into its world through 'respectful deception' (Anderson et al., 2017), taking its life with minimum disruption and making use of its body as food or repurposing it otherwise. While my own agenda is clearly different from that of my hunting informants, for whom killing is often part of daily work, their artful engagement with the worlds or *umwelten* (Uexkull, 2010) of other animal species provides a generative model for my own perspectival manoeuvres as I experiment with how to capture Nigel and his relationship to moles, and how to responsibly negotiate with death myself in the making of the film *Earth Swimmers* (2021).[2]

Following Rané Willerslev who argues for the pragmatic role of perspective

1 This fieldwork was the ethnographic component of my practice-based Ph.D. research (Spriggs, forthcoming). The project is based between the UCL department of Anthropology and the Slade School of Fine Art and funded by the London Arts and Humanities Partnership.

2 Deborah Bird Rose notes how western culture encourages us to 'turn away' from death while perpetuating social behaviours that are driving human exceptionalism, extermination and mass-extinction; this is death as the end of ongoing life. By contrast, coming 'face to face' with an animal during small-scale, ethical hunting practice brings one into dialogue with death, enabling death to be embraced as part of ongoing life (2011).

exchange in hunting contexts (2007), I choose to explore 'perspectivism' as a form of interspecies experimentation born of particular kinds of land-based practice and exchange. Consequently, my own analysis does not attempt to import Amerindian perspectivism – a theory derived from Amazonian cosmology by Brazilian anthropologist Eduardo Viveiros de Castro – into a Yorkshire context (cf. Holbraad and Pedersen, 2017: 177). Instead I draw inspiration from perspectivist theory by taking my pest control interlocutors seriously as 'alien anthropologists' (Viveiros de Castro and Holbraad, 2016) – masters of 'capture' and teachers of a particular kind of *practice-based* research. As I will go on to show, this research involves intimate engagement with multispecies world-making activities through particular attention to the perspectives of other animals, enabling reciprocal self-transformation. It is therefore inherently creative, and enables new ways of sensing and approaching the experiences of nonhuman others.

TRACKING MOLES, TOUCHING-HEARING

When it comes to catching moles, Nigel's main predicament is how to track an animal that leads an almost entirely subterranean existence. In his words, there's literally 'nothing to study' – and by this he means that there's nothing to see, save a seemingly random assemblage of earthy mounds peppering the surface of the lush green field that we're in, grassy fodder for a herd of cattle that are happily grazing nearby. Scrubby hedges surround us, defining the bounds of Nigel's job on this particular Wednesday afternoon in June. By this stage, eight months into fieldwork, I'm fairly well acquainted with Nigel's approach to tracking moles, but this is the first time that I've attempted to visually document his work and I'm carrying various cameras which I plan to use in ways that mirror his flow and attentional focus. We've received a small amount of money from Sheffield DocFest to fund a collaborative film,[3] and we are newly kitted out with two small Gopros (body-mounting cameras) and a tiny probe camera attached to a flexible lead, designed for plumbers who use it to find leaks in pipes. This was Nigel's idea – he has a similar tool which he uses to inspect hard-to-reach wasps' nests. I'm also carrying my trusty digital SLR for hand-held filming.

Several challenges await this toolkit for visual capture. For Nigel, the elusive nature of 'the little gentlemen in black velvet' (as moles are fondly referred to)

3 https://sheffdocfest.com/news/announcing-docfest-exchange-beyond-our-own-eyes-film-commissions

is further frustrated by the fact that he only gets to see one once it's dead in a trap. In fact, whilst working underground, Nigel is as blind as the mole and the chances of catching a mole on video are slim to none, he tells me. Nigel's predicament as a visually-oriented human attending to the invisible lifeworlds of moles is mirrored by my own as a camera-wielding ethnographer in this context: there's no object of focus for either of us, and no direct means of visual access. This increases my reliance on Nigel's collaboration, as he has tactics and experience that allow him to 'see' the invisible world of the mole (cf. Suhr and Willerslev, 2012).

According to Nigel, moles are amongst the most difficult animals to track, because they inhabit an *umwelt* far removed from our own visually-oriented mode of existence. Moles occupy an underground architecture that remains invisible to the human eye, and this leads mole catchers to spend most of their time 'speculative tracking' – following an animal's trail in the absence of visual sign (John Rhyder, pers. Comm.). Moles are covered in tiny hairs or whiskers called vibrissae which receive information directly through the earthen walls of their tunnels underground; a form of auditory perception, in the sense that vibrations are sound waves travelling through solids, and sound is simply 'vibrating matter with audible qualities' (Klett, 2014: 147). 'Vibrissae' comes from the Latin *vibrare*, meaning 'to vibrate', and the mole excavates and inhabits a labyrinth of tunnels which are primed for acoustic and vibratory communication. This allows the mole to feel-hear the presence of worms that drop in to the tunnel from all sides. As Nigel explains, the mole digs a tunnel that's precisely his size: 'His whiskers touch it on the left and the right … and then he actually sticks his tail up in the air. I always think a bit like a dodgem car.' Their sensitivity to vibration means moles can feel-hear sounds as low as 5 hertz, a much lower frequency than our human hearing permits. This enables moles to trace vibrating worms to their precise location, and allows the mole to perceive potential threats; for instance a human tread might be felt through the earth from hundreds of metres away.

Touch-hearing through vibrissae and bone conduction allows moles to hear sounds *through* the earth, like x-ray vision in an audio register. Sound travels quickly through solids, and the mole's hunt for worms involves lines of vibration that pull him along a charged-up run like a dodgem car, before these two trails – the mole's and the worm's – collapse into one. Contrary to my fantasy that moles slurp down worms like spaghetti, Nigel tells me that the mole eats worms by 'taking little bits off' whilst they're still alive. The mole, with its 'mouth full of little pins' actively takes in worms; it listens in a way that is also a kind of aggressive consuming.

DROPPING IN

When we first find a mole run connecting two hills, I assume the mole's pathway joins up these points like a dot-to-dot. Not so easy, I quickly discover, because moles have no reason to run in straight lines. Nigel tells me that the mole doesn't care about getting from A to B, what it cares about is eating lots of worms. As the mole digs, worms drop down from above and wiggle into the tunnel from both sides. This is how moles hunt, Nigel explains to me. They don't seek a direction per se, but are guided by features of their immediate environment:

> You know, wherever the stones are taking him, the roots are taking him, and of course, he wouldn't know if he was going straight anyway, cos he's just digging away…

Nigel needs to find the mole, whose unpredictable underground movements defy human logic. This is where *tracking* comes into play as a method for multispecies research – as an 'art of paying attention' (Stengers, 2018: 62) to more-than-human actors and a means of 'following worldly entanglements' (Tsing, 2015: 153). Whilst moles track worms and dig tunnels for them to drop into, human trackers speak of 'dropping in' to the trail of an animal. Finding and following a trail requires a relaxed and unfettered form of attention and maintaining this focus takes patience and persistence. Trackers learn to soften their vision and mobilise their focus from the wide to the acute in a way that helps relevant patterns to appear, a process known as 'splatter vision'. Finding this flow is very satisfying, and like the *magic eye* puzzles that were popular in the 1990s, once you get the knack, a hidden dimension appears – you 'drop in' and can see things that other people can't. With time and practice tracking animals, their track patterns, size, direction, gait and even the traces of energy embedded within individual prints all start to combine and add up to create a nuanced portrait of the animal who left them.

Louis Liebenberg describes how tracking creates a kind of visionary access: 'By reconstructing their movements from their footprints, you may be able to visualise the animals and in your imagination actually "see" them. In this way a whole story may unfold, a story of what happened when no one was looking' (1990: 7). Nichols writes that '[e]very molehill tells a story', explaining how 'the different layers or seams of soil that make up the structure of that location are often revealed in the molehill'. Mole catcher Marc Hammer uses splatter vision in the first stage of his mole-catching process: 'De-focusing my eyes and withholding any judgement I look for patterns and distances between each scattering, and this helps me to see roughly how many moles there may be' (2019: 62).

This visual tracking, however, is only relevant to the first read of molehills on the surface. The underground environment or *umwelt* of the mole consists of darkness, sound and vibration. This world is so remote that Nigel's research relies on haptic exploration with the aid of certain tools. At the heart of this toolkit is his mole-catchers' probe which performs as a sort of man-size 'whisker' or vibrissa, a steel antenna that penetrates the earth and connects Nigel's body to the *umwelt* of the mole. In the sense that the probe is a long, slim appendage that channels vibrations, it can be seen as a scaled-up translation of one part of the mole's own anatomy which the mole-catcher lacks. Like a model of a missing part or an artificial leg, it is 'a representation that functions as a prosthesis' (Gell, 1996: 26).

Whilst clear communication between Nigel and the mole-on-the-move remains an impossible ideal, his aim is to open up channels that enable him to retrieve meaningful signs from an invisible world below. The probe articulates a peculiarly tactile relationship to sound, a co-mingling of senses which Stephen Conner evokes as sticky, mimetic, infectious and close (2004: 154). Touch-hearing is key to the mole's own mode of navigation, and equally to Nigel's apprehension of the mole. Nichols describes the detailed information that can be gleaned as the mole catcher's probe passes down and back up through the ground – information that is 'processed by the mole catcher almost like the sense used by the mole to feel the same environment' (2017:89). 'The probe will *tell* you the density of the soil below from the amount of pressure you need to push it downwards; it will *inform* you of the moisture content, according to the suction you feel; and on reaching the tunnel, it will *tell* you how deep it is.' The probe can also '*notify* you of any obstructions on the way down – roots, stones and buried objects' (ibid: 112, my emphasis).

Due to its special ability to communicate secret information, the probe is fondly referred to as a 'talking stick' (ibid: 111), and it is worth comparing to the instruments that Amerindian shamans use to aid their travel from one species perspective to another. Holbraad and Pedersen point out that these implements are not representations like carnival masks, but bodily augmentations akin to space suits or divination equipment, which enable other modes of functioning, new kinds of environmental affordance and therefore engagement (Holbraad and Pedersen, 2017: 164–65, quoting Viveiros de Castro, 2004: 11). As an instrument of this kind, the probe might equally find its place in a media history of portable sound devices used for retrieving subterranean signals, including the metal detector and geiger counter, both of which find their common origin in the humble divining rod – a 'y'-shaped stick of hazel or willow used to anticipate the location of water or ore (Smith, 2015 :87).[4] Media historian Jacob Smith explains how 'minimal' listening technologies like the divining rod work to 'create a contact zone between two material ecologies' (ibid: 106) with the effect that they 'localise' the user, creating intimacy with their local environment in the face of alienating forces (ibid: 91). The mole catcher's probe works in this way by creating a contact zone between Nigel and the mole. It performs as the technical component in a structure of social communication that transports him underground and links him into a web of local, more-than-human exchanges (ibid).

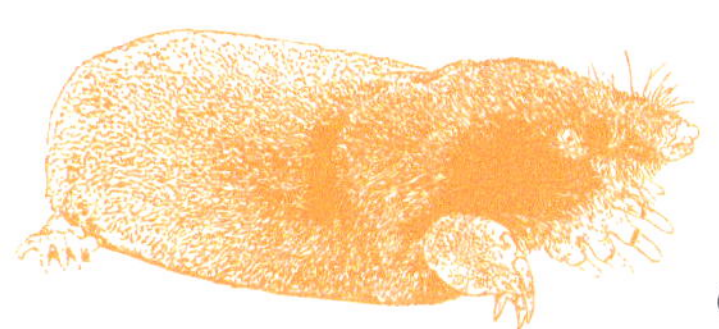

Holding my camera, I mimic the gentle flow of Nigel's body as he probes for the mole's invisible tunnels. He reminds me of somebody fishing, dipping into the medium of earth as one would dip into a river with a line and a hook. For Nigel as for any tracker, locating the path of the mole is a a rigorous attentional practice. However 'dropping in' to the trail of a mole involves a literal downward movement through the surface of the earth. Like Gregory Bateson's description of a blind person's cane which enables locomotion, the mole catcher's probe links his mind to the earth. The probe drops in on Nigel's behalf, forming an 'ecological circuit' (Bateson, 2000: 465) that tugs meaning upwards into his body from the earth below. Underground differences that matter to the mole travel up as vibrations through the long metal pole. These vibrations then instruct Nigel as to the tunnel's location and direction and he uses this information to apprehend the mole's subterranean vantage. Nigel uses his feet, his probe and his imagination to form – he tells me – a 'clear picture' of the mole underground (the trackers I know refer to this visioning tool as a 'search image', cf. Uexkull, 2010: 113), before projecting himself into the position of the mole and imagining his trap from the *mole's* perspective:

> you are trying to imagine how the mole would be moving about, or even what he might be thinking. So that you're trying to think, if the mole came, or when the mole comes into the area that you've disturbed – where you've put the trap – you're hoping the mole's just gonna come into there and think it's natural and nothing's changed …

4 Whilst often evoked by media historians as an occult practice (Smith, 2015), dowsing or water divination continues to be used in everyday contexts in North Yorkshire, most frequently by plumbers searching for hidden leaks in pipes but also on occasion by my pest control informants, all of whom had experience using dowsing rods.

> So I suppose *you are putting yourself in the mole's position*, to think 'is this what he'll be expecting'. Which is, I think, the same with any trapping.

To ensure the mole continues to feel safe and 'not think anything's different', Nigel puts himself 'in the mole's situation' and imagines a virtual journey through the tunnel where he plans to set his trap. If he notices that something is out of place – an angle, depth, dirt, air or light – he digs in with his hands or his probe and works the earth to fix and smooth things out. Prompts in the mole's environment translate into prompts that Nigel apprehends and responds to, and this enables him to ensure that things feel 'natural' for the mole. This cooption of the mole's way of finding his[5] way through the world demonstrates how, when tracking, Nigel adopts the mole's perspective and a dominant naturalist schema starts to become perspectivist (Morizot, 2017: 111). This borrowing or capture of another's perspective leads Baptiste Morizot to conclude that '[t]racking is, on a small scale, a practice that enables us to circulate between worlds, between ontologies' (2020: 111). It is a means 'of activating in oneself the powers of a different body' (ibid., after Viveiros de Castro, 1998: 482).

At this stage there's little for me to film above ground, save Nigel's forearm dipping in and out of the underground tunnel as he clears it from soil and debris. Nor do I have access to the 'clear picture' Nigel has rendered in his mind of the mole underground. My handheld camera – my go-to tool for visual capture – is blocked and rendered useless by the surface of the earth. So I set it down and get out a contact microphone, a small piezo plate that that picks up vibrations directly from the ground.

Knowledge flows up

> Everybody has an idea, but nobody knows. We don't need to know everything to catch them; being comfortable with not knowing is an important part of hunting, as it keeps all the options open, offers choices (Marc Hammer, 2019: 78).

Talking about moles with Nigel always leads us back to worms. I have a handwritten note that says 'knowledge flows up', and it strikes me that, whilst Nigel learns by following the mole, the mole itself is learning from what *it's* tracking and catching – namely worms:

5 I follow my informants in their use of gendered pronouns for different animal species. Moles are generally referred to using the male pronoun and are interesting in this regard as the females are arguably hermaphrodite, with sealed up vaginas and male levels of testosterone throughout most of the year.

> Worms are just following the moisture ... So they are just finding a level in the soil where they can essentially eat the earth ... they're looking for somewhere that's easy working. So the weather will dictate at what depth in the soil the worm is, and whatever the depth the worm is, that's the depth that the mole will try to be at (Nigel).

In this inverted hierarchy, the earth instructs the worms and worms instruct the mole, and Nigel taps into this chain of relationships, aided by his prosthetic probe. 'The theory is really easy', he says:

> there's not much to be taught ... [but] you're always gathering information. You're always looking at what's happened. Because you're always changing soil types, you're always changing location, you're next to a river, you're next to a gravel path with drains different ... so you're always just trying to build a picture up of where the mole's gonna live, what the tunnel's gonna look like.

Tracking involves obsessive attention to detail and the changing nature of things. It therefore works to reveal maximum intentionality, or to abduct maximum agency, from the more-than-human world (Viveiros de Castro, 2004: 469). This animating principle is key to success when interpreting nonhuman sign, and certainly for Nigel who must remain attentive to how all aspects of the mole's environment influence its decisions and behaviour. The mole is understood by Nigel as an individual mole with a subject-position, a gender and a discerning awareness of his surroundings. Viveiros de Castro describes this kind of knowledge production as 'perspectivist': the mole has a perspective – there is something it is like to *be* that mole – the mole becomes a 'he', and the world that he inhabits takes on life. In Nigel's worldview, both he and the mole are sentient beings and share a subjective view of the world. At the same time, their contrasting *umwelten* lead them to inhabit different versions of nature or objective reality that are born of differently embodied perspectives: 'all beings perceive ("represent") the world in the same way' whilst '[w]hat varies is the world that they see' (Viveiros de Castro, 2004: 471–72).

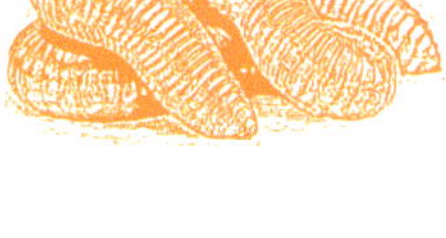

Viveiros explains that in an Amerindian context '[w]hat humans see as blood, a natural substance, is seen by jaguars as manioc beer, an artefact' (ibid: 474). By the same token, a single human footstep is perceived as a tidal wave of meaningful sound for the mole. And what we register as earthy 'scribbles' on the surface of a lawn are, from the mole's perspective, sonic 'traps' that he has cleverly set to catch worms (Nichols 2017: 55). Animal trails carve radically local and perspectival routes through the inhabited environment, whilst multiple trails suggest a multiplication of embodied perspectives and a branching-off of species worlds. Material differences matter differently depending on which animal is leading the way. Moles are 'earth swimmers', worms are 'earth eaters' and we are 'earth walkers' – the ground exists differently from each of these perspectives (cf Uexkull, 2010). 'The relativity in question here is one of objective position, which varies according to the different ways in which a (universally available) point of view is embodied' (Holbraad and Pedersen, 2017: 163).

Viveiros further notes how the understanding that nonhuman beings see themselves as persons (that is, they experience the world in a way equivalent to human subjects) works to redefine other objects and events in their local vicinity, transforming these things into indexes from which social agency can be inferred (2014). For example, Nigel encountered a garden trampoline that appeared to be working as a strange attractor for moles. A surprisingly neat ring of molehills circled its perimeter on the ground. Nigel didn't know for sure why this was, but he guessed that vibrations from the trampoline had drawn the worms in, and that beads of moisture had condensed on its rim and dripped onto the ground below, softening the soil and creating optimum digging conditions both for worms and moles. Jeff Nichols, writing on the same phenomena, describes the trampoline as a 'ring of delight for the moles' (2017: 95). The same principle explains why mole hills so often follow barbed wire fences (the fence collects moisture and acts as a drip-line that draws in worms that draw in moles), and are often seen spreading out from under the canopy of a tree, as the mole makes use of the natural drip from this 'umbrella of flora' (Nichols 2017: 70). It is because the trampoline, barbed wire fence and tree canopy are 'in the neighbourhood' of moles that they take on life and special significance for the mole catcher (Viveiros referencing Gell, 2014: 62). The trampoline abducts its agency from a chain of invisible, more-than-human relationships that Nigel apprehends through tracking. This 'ring of delight' is not experienced as an object designed for human use, but as an environment appropriated for occupation by an industrious mole. Considered in this light, the trampoline's agency is not an abduction of *human* intention in any straightforward sense (cf Gell, 1996) – instead it gains agency in reciprocal exchange for the environmental affordances it offers to the mole, and comes to life for Nigel as a moist, worm-full place in the neighbourhood of moles.

There is little or no overarching theory of mole catching, because this work is site-specific and radically contingent – 'we're all working on different things', Nigel tells me; that is, in different situations. 'Things' take on the status of 'situation' or 'event' for Nigel as he tracks the moles through their resonant home. This lively approach to the nonhuman world contrasts with a naturalist/objectivist epistemology in which '[t]o know is to objectify' and therefore to *desubjectify* – to reduce the personhood of nonhuman things to an ideal minimum (Viveiros de Castro, 2004: 468). Nigel does not objectify the mole;

instead he builds a picture up of where the mole lives *from* the mole's perspective. His work reveals another way of knowing the world without recourse to objectification, and demonstrates how perspectivist ontology can be found to co-exist with Naturalist frames for knowing and encountering nonhuman others in England. As Morizot reflects, 'another map of living things on a 1:1 scale can be surreptitiously found under our feet, on the ground we are scrutinising – another ontology' (2021: 108). Mole tracking engages the *umwelt* of the mole in a way that transforms the hunter's body and perspective over time, revealing this alternative map (Colchester and Spriggs, 2021). It is a form of multispecies research in which theory and practice are not worlds apart. Ends and means meander, and knowledge flows up, like worms in saturated ground.

CREATIVE BORROWING AND PREDATORY ENCOMPASSMENTS

In this chapter I have explored what it might be like to be a Yorkshire molecatcher, while at the same time treating Nigel as an alien anthropologist whose own research departs from a similarly 'anthropological' line of questioning: What could it possibly be like to be a mole? As a researcher who takes the beliefs and practices of his field informants seriously, Nigel conducts his mole-anthropology – to the best of his ability – from the *perspective* of the mole. This means assuming there is something it is like to *be* a mole (Nagel 1974), which in turn means finding appropriate methods, tools and practices for capturing this world; and these are, as I've shown, in many ways analogous to the mole's own methods, tools and practices for capturing worms. I want to end by exploring some of the broader implications of 'borrowing' from the field in this way.

Hunters in the UK often speak of the animals they track as their teachers, particularly when it comes to the arts of capture and escape, and many contemporary trap designs can be traced to the cunning entrapments of animals, insects and plants. 'Tracking comes down to borrowing … the body of another animal which is a perspective shaping the world', explains Morizot (2017: 112), while Nichols instructs his reader to 'attend every lesson that the mole provides for you', adding that '[i]f you can identify with this amazing subterrancan world *as a mole*, then your success in their control will greatly improve' (2017: 127/81, my emphasis). This respect for nonhuman teachers (albeit born of competition) is held by all my hunting informants, whose pleasure in their work seems intimately connected with the fact that they learn and become something new each day that they spend outside tracking animals. This creative borrowing takes place in both directions: for instance another hunter described a series of encounters with a 'clever' rat in his garden, who was learning from each of the traps he invented to catch it. Nichols similarly notes how 'naive' young moles make many mistakes, but those who survive to feel the first touch of frost 'should have established enough knowledge to join the ranks of all the others that continue to manipulate man's dominance of the land' (2017: 98). Hunters learn from animals just as animals learn from each other and also from us, and animals are understood to learn and comprehend the world in equivalent or even superior ways to human beings. This kind of knowledge can't be taught by other humans, instead it is *borrowed* through intimate and often challenging encounters between species in a way that aligns with the perspectivist paradigm of exchange and transformation: 'The exchange model of action supposes that the subject's "other" is another subject (not an object)', writes Viveiros, 'and subjectification is, of course, what perspectivism is all about' (2004: 478).

This exchange model extends to the conceptual work of anthropology – it is common practice to borrow concepts from ethnographic fieldwork and employ them in analysis and, generally speaking, this is how anthropological knowledge is made (see Holbraad and Pedersen, 2017). However, as Calzadilla and Marcus point out, formal and methodological borrowing has not been exploited to nearly the same degree. Despite anthropology losing its firm scientific ground in the 1980s, exploring the aesthetics of inquiry 'would have required styles of thinking, rhetoric, and practice—keyed to the notion of experimentation—that proved unacceptable to the boundary keeping institutional and professional rules of order in the academy' (2006: 96). As the current volume makes particularly clear, a recent turn towards multispecies anthropology demands a creative rethinking of the methods and tools we employ as ethnographers, and I hope that the examples of tracking, probing and reverse-capture offered here help to demonstrate both the creative potential and the theoretical productivity of borrowing these methods and tools from the field. By mimicking and practising the arts of attention that Nigel employs in his everyday work, an entirely new level of understanding opened up to me.

As Anna Tsing proposes, 'collaborative foraging' is 'a model for knowledge-making, as well as an object of ethnographic inquiry … the style is also an argument, and much of the theory work emerges from the details' (2017: np). Indeed, a particular affordance of tracking as a model for artistic multispecies research lies in the fact that animals themselves do not subscribe to human boundaries. In fact, they often exploit our human infrastructures (as in the example of the mole, for whom the barbed-wire fence becomes a dripline luring worms). Following their tracks therefore inevitably leads one to trespass (Tsing 2015: 137), and this trespass extends to a productive undermining not only of boundaries in the land, but also of the boundaries defining species difference as well as the disciplinary lines dividing theory and practice, anthropology and art.

Here the behaviour of the animal tracker – abruptly halted by the apparent absence of tracks before them – is instructive. When a trail appears to end (that is, when legible traces of animal sign disappear, as they do when substrate suddenly changes, for instance from earth to rock, or when the weather obliterates an exposed section of tracks), a tracker does not give up. Instead, the work of 'speculative' tracking begins. This might involve 'splattering' one's vision to scan for track-patterns in the distance, or 'working the wheel' by walking a circular path around the last good track to uncover an unexpected change in direction. It might involve attending to different sensory registers or, as a last resort, employing intuitive guesswork to predict what direction the animal went, based on the reasonable assumption that they must have gone somewhere, before acting accordingly and catching up with them some way further down the trail. My informants utilised this speculative approach when tracking and also when setting their traps, and it is this spirited approach to blindness (both one's own and that of others) which, perhaps more than anything else, inspires self-transformation and potentialises the art of engaging invisible worlds (Suhrand Willerslev 2012, Morizot 2021). Morten Pedersen suggests that perspectivist anthropology should be interpreted as a version of Husserl's method, which seeks to reveal and transform its own 'natural attitude' (or blind spots) through engagement with different points of view (in Šatkauskas 2022: 308). As Jacob Von Uexküll puts it, the absurdity of our own way of seeing is only revealed when the same objects are comprehended from other perspectives (2010: 42). In response, I offer Nigel's *anthropology of other animals* as the fulfilment of a multispecies version of reverse anthropology, which (following Viveiros de Castro) aims to decolonise anthropology by taking its interlocutors seriously— 'seriously enough, that is, to allow their manners of living to transform our manners of doing anthropology' (Holbraad and Pedersen 2017: 26). As a teacher of this multispecies method, Nigel offered me access to the invisible world of the mole, but, not only this, his mole anthropology led me to engage with anthropological theory in a practical way which in turn pushed my thought in new directions, offering tools and techniques for decentring myself while foregrounding the perception, agency and subjectivity of nonhuman others. This also led to new and surprising kinds of collaboration and new forms of aesthetic production, of which *Earth Swimmers* is one example.[6]

Nigel chose to be recognised as my collaborator in the credits of *Earth Swimmers*, but I followed his lead by excluding all footage in which he could be visually identified in the final edit. Nor are there any moles in our film – on Nigel's suggestion, both he and the mole remain anonymous and mysterious, escaping the viewer's objectifying gaze. Instead, *Earth Swimmers* attempts to 'personify' Nigel and the mole by capturing their mutual perspectives. According to Viveiros' perspectivist maxim, 'To know is to personify, to take on the point of view of that which must be known' (2004: 468). Our visual edit attempts this by using point-of-view footage to grasp the way that Nigel's hands and his tools interrogate the world of the mole. When his probe breaks the ground and Nigel digs in, the viewer 'drops' into a world of underground darkness, and sound takes over from sight. We will never know what the world sounds like to the mole, as Nigel and my other tracking friends acknowledge. Instead, this rendering of the mole's vibratory *umwelt* is my own act of creative borrowing – an informed but imaginary leap into the mole's perspective.

In *Earth Swimmers*, sound takes over when visual access breaks down, emplacing the viewer/listener within the mole's own dark and wormy labyrinth. The film participates in relational chains that grow through echoic and masticatory listening; perspectives articulate across different scales which recursively encompass one another. Worms eating earth – the mole eating worms – Nigel feel-hearing with his probe for the mole – the montage of our film which captures Nigel's world as a subject for the viewer's consumption. Cut finally to the earth again, the ground which will in time reclaim each of these bodies, including the harddrive that hosts our film. This figure-ground reversal is not lost on my hunting collaborators, all of whom take a cyclical view of creation and decomposition: as mole catcher Jeff Nichols told me, 'When it's my turn to lay down, I'll do it in the ground with the mole, with my friend'. A decentring of the human 'I' takes place through this cycle of predatory encompassments, or perhaps better, *expersonations* (Wagner, 2012): 'the subject focused on by events is not the centre around which its own world turns' (Stolze Lima, 1999: 403).

6 This is something I explore in greater depth in my Ph.D. thesis and portfolio of practice. See Spriggs, forthcoming.

ARTNOGRAPHIC STATEMENT

The film *Earth Swimmers* attends to the tricks and techniques that mole catchers use to access the underground world of the mole. Using tools as portals into the mole's vibratory world, probes, feet, noses and rain-making instruments lead the viewer into alternative ways of sensing and knowing the earth. Tactics are shared and exchanged between mole catcher and artist-filmmaker, asking thorny questions of what it means to track, to capture, to hear and to feel beyond one's own species perspective.

Earth Swimmers was originally commissioned by Sheffield DocFest with funding from Wellcome, and screened during COP26 at the Glasgow Centre for Contemporary Art. The film emerged within a larger body of work resulting from direct collaboration with professional mole catchers – one outcome of long-term ethnographic fieldwork investigating rural pest control practices and attitudes to land in rural North Yorkshire, UK (see Spriggs, forthcoming).

Avoiding the polarisation of pro or anti-hunting debate, *Earth Swimmers* lends its ears to undocumented land-workers in rural England, to forms of land-based practice and ecological understanding that remain hidden in plain sight, and to the strange allegiance between hunter and prey. Moles themselves navigate using a language of vibrations, reading the movements of earthworms through sensitive hairs on their bodies, and using the architectural acoustics of their tunnels to channel infrasonic sound. In order to bridge this perceptual distance, mole catchers use a variety of tools and techniques that sensitise their own human bodies, extending their reach into the vibratory umwelt of the mole and effecting an exchange in species perspective. What equivalent tools and techniques might an artist-ethnographer need to reach into the mole-catcher's world?

Beginning with the premise that mole catchers are themselves skilled researchers who conduct a kind of 'Anthropology of Other Animals', I base my own practical methodology on their more-than-human research. At the core of this method is *tracking*, an abductive mode of knowledge creation which involves strengthening one's own perceptual and attentional faculties and mobilising thought beyond the bounds of the human mind. I draw from the radical agenda of anthropology's ontological turn – which seeks to transform its own conceptual framework through engagement with different lived perspectives – and experiment with equivalent world-making operations in art, a process I call 'reverse creativity' (see Spriggs, forthcoming). While reverse anthropology invites the creation of novel concepts (Wagner, 1981), I explore how *reverse creativity* betokens new methods, mediums and aesthetic forms.

Concrete outcomes of this research to date include a series of public artworks, workshops, a series of non-academic publications and a Ph.D. thesis, all of which function as test-sites for reverse creativity. Collaboration with artists and rural craftspeople (including pest controllers, hedge layers, tanners and wood turners) is integral to this ongoing project, bridging academic and non-academic worlds and creating forums for exchange between mutually alienated rural and urban communities in the UK.

REFERENCES

Bateson, G. 2000 [1972]. *Steps to an Ecology of Mind: Collected Essays in Anthropology, Psychiatry, Evolution, and Epistemology*. Chicago: University of Chicago Press

Buchanan, B. 2007. *Onto-Ethologies: the Animal Environments of Uexkull, Heidegger, Merleau-Ponty, and Deleuze*. New York: SUNY Press.

Calzadilla, F. and G.E. Marcus. 2006. 'Artists in the field: Between art and anthropology', in C. Wright and A. Schneider (eds). *Contemporary Art and Anthropology*. Oxford; New York: Berg.

Colchester, T. and H. Spriggs. 2022. 'THE MUD IS THE MAP IS THE MUD'. *The Serving Library Annual 2022/23.*

Connor, S. 2004. 'Edison's teeth: Touching hearing'. In Viet Erlmann (ed.) *Hearing Cultures Essays on Sound, Listening and Modernity*. London: Routledge.

Gell, A. 1996. 'Vogel's net: Traps as artworks and artworks as traps'. *Journal of Material Culture* **1** (1).

Hallam, E. and T. Ingold. 2007. 'Creativity and cultural improvisation. An introduction'. In Hallam and Ingold (eds). *Creativity and Cultural Improvisation*, pp. 1–24. New York: Berg.

Hammer, M. 2019. *How to Catch a Mole, And Find Yourself in Nature*. UK: Harvill Secker.

Holbraad, M. and M. Pederson. 2017. 'Natural relativism: Viveiros de Castro's perspectivism and multinaturalism'. In *The Ontological Turn: An Anthropological Exposition*. Cambridge: Cambridge University Press.

Ingold, T. 2010. 'The textility of making'. *Cambridge Journal of Economics* **34**: 91–102.

Klett, J. 2014. 'Sound on sound: Situating interaction in sonic object settings'. *Sociological Theory* **32** (2): 147–61.

Liebenberg, L. 1990. *The Art of Tracking, the Origin of Science*. South Africa: David Philip Publisher.

Morizot, B. 2021. *On the Animal Trail*. Cambridge / Boston: Polity Press.

Nagel, T. 1974. 'What is it like to be a bat'. *Philosophical Review* 83: 435–50. https://doi.org/10.2307/2183914

Nichols, J. 2017. *Catching Moles, the History and Practice*. Ramsbury, Marlborough: The Crowood Press.

Šatkauskas, I. 2022. 'Divergences and convergences of perspective: Amerindian perspectivism, phenomenology, and speculative realism'. *Open Philosophy* **5** (1): 308-29. https://doi.org/10.1515/opphil-2022-0199

Sautchuk, C. 2012. 'Cine-weapon The poiesis of filming and fishing'. *VIBRANT - Vibrant Virtual Brazilian Anthropology* **9** (2).

Smith, J. 2015. *Eco-Sonic Media*. Berkeley: University of California Press.

Spriggs, H. Forthcoming. *Traps as Artworks and Artworks as Traps: Towards a model for life-sustaining art.* Ph.D. Diss., University College, London.

Stengers, E. and M. Savransky. 2018. 'Relearning the art of paying attention: A conversation'. *SubStance* **47** (1) (Issue 145).

Stolze Lima, T. 1999. 'The two and its many: Reflections on perspectivism in a Tupi cosmology'. *Ethnos* **64** (1): 107–31.

Suhr, C. and R. Willerslev. 2012. 'Can film show the invisible?'. *Current Anthropology* **53** (3).

Tsing, A. 2015. *The Mushroom at the End of the World.* Princeton: Princeton University Press.

Tsing, A. 2017. 'Is there a progressive politics after progress?' Member Voices, Fieldsights, 8 June: https://culanth.org/fieldsights/is-there-a-progressive-politics-after-progress

Uexkull, J. 2010. *A Foray into the Worlds of Animals and Humans.* Minneapolis: University of Minnesota Press.

Wagner, R. 2012. '"Luck in the double focus": ritualized hospitality in Melanesia'. *The Journal of the Royal Anthropological Institute* **18** (S161–S174).

http://www.jstor.org/stable/41506677

Viveiros de Castro, E. 1998. 'Cosmological deixis and Amerindian perspectivism'. *The Journal of the Royal Anthropological Institute* **4** (3).

Viveiros de Castro, E. 2004. 'Exchanging perspectives: The transformation of objects into subjects in Amerindian ontologies. *Common Knowledge* **10** (3).

Viveiros de Castro, E. 2014. *Cannibal Metaphysics.* Minneapolis: Univocal/ University of Minnesota Press

3. THE SOUNDS OF SNOW: AN EXPLORATION OF HUMAN-SNOW RELATIONS IN ILULISSAT, KALAALLIT NUNAAT.

Nanna Sandager Kisby

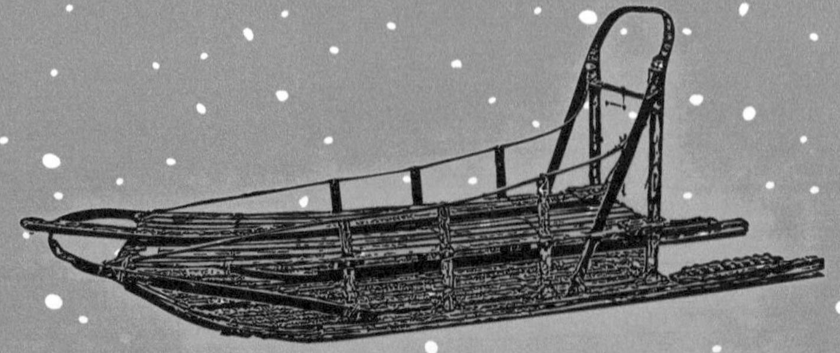

DOI: 10.63308/63878687083054.ch03

PRELUDE

For you, dear reader, I am going to paint a picture with the use of sound. If you have already been to the Arctic, you may know what is coming. If you have not, this is your chance to experience a new place through some of your senses. First, take a moment to imagine the Arctic, based on everything you know – and everything you think you know.

Did you do it?

Then let me tell you that Ilulissat, in the year 2022, was the third largest town in Kalaallit Nunaat and home to around 4,600 humans and 1,000 dogs (among many other nonhuman species). On average, the yearly snow season lasted 6–7 months, during which a fresh layer of snow would fall almost every day. There were no roads outside the town, so a crucial part of the infrastructure was therefore dependent on sledge dogs, which (along with snow scooters) was the main form of transportation into the surrounding landscape. Therefore, when I opened the window in my room in Ilulissat, the outside world sounded like this:

HTTPS://SOUNDCLOUD.COM/NANNA-SANDAGER-KISBY/DOGS-BARKING-IN-ILULISSAT

What do these sounds bring to your mind? Do they influence your preconceptions of this place called 'the Arctic'?

Allow me to give you another piece of sensory information. At the time I visited Ilulissat, the average winter temperature was around –18°C. It is not possible for me to share the feeling of coldness on your skin through words – but I can tell you that the sounds snow produced would change, depending on the temperature. When I first arrived in Kangerlussuaq (the town where the main airport of Kalaallit Nunaat is located), the outside temperature was –27°C with a chill factor of −41°C. Therefore, the snow covering a wooden terrace outside sounded like this:

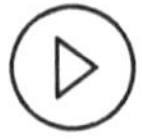

HTTPS://SOUNDCLOUD.COM/NANNA-SANDAGER-KISBY/SNOW-IN-COLD-KANGERLUSSUAQ

Later, when the snow melted and began to drip from a rooftop in Ilulissat, landing on other bodies of snow that were still frozen, it sounded like this:

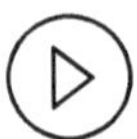

HTTPS://SOUNDCLOUD.COM/NANNA-SANDAGER-KISBY/MELTING-SNOW-FROM-THE-CHURCH-ROOFTOP

And when I touched snow in its semi-wet form, when it started to melt but was not yet liquid, it sounded like this:

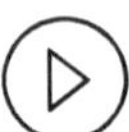

HTTPS://SOUNDCLOUD.COM/NANNA-SANDAGER-KISBY/TOUCHING-WET-SNOW

Can you imagine yourself touching the snow? Can you imagine yourself watching the snow drip from a rooftop while the spring sun warms your face – or walking through piercing cold air, moving your feet across dry, squeaky bodies of snow?

Sometimes, we humans create images in our minds when we read written words or listen to sounds. This is one of our capacities. It is something we are able to do because our human bodies are built in certain ways, made out of certain parts. It means that we are able to listen to nonhuman worlds and to better understand them, if we want to.

These soundscapes are pieces of data, art, time, sensations, and they are embodied into files that can travel from place to place, telling stories about snow. Perhaps they have the power to alter your perception of snow and Arctic worlds. Perhaps they spark your curiosity – or perhaps they change nothing at all. However, in the following pieces of text and sensory impressions, I will elaborate on this nonhuman agency that is shown through the capacities of snow and its relations to humans.

LEARNING HOW TO WALK

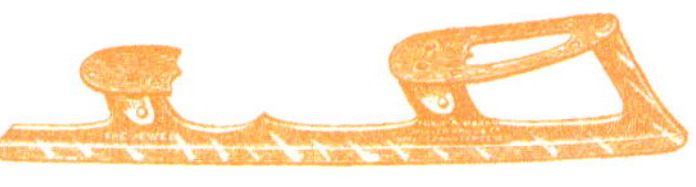

During my fieldwork in Ilulissat, I had the opportunity to encounter various kinds of humans. My interlocutors were sledge dog owners, students, mothers, municipality workers, artists, tour guides, drivers, fisher folk, retirees, etc. What they had in common was that they were all residents of Ilulissat. Since my field was rather small, I chose not to make any selections for my human interviews and participant observations. Rather, I wanted to speak to anyone who was willing to share their thoughts on snow.

During my time in Ilulissat, I was given permission to live at a student dormitory, I volunteered at Ilulissat Icefjord Centre,[1] and I spent considerable amounts of time walking outside, engaging with and recording snow through audio, photography and my bodily sensations. At the student dormitory, I lived with young women from villages around Kalaallit Nunaat who had come to study pedagogy in Ilulissat. The student dormitory was quiet and the women mostly kept to themselves, but we shared a common kitchen, a couple of parties and some evening walks through the snowy town. They brought me to the places with the best views of the northern lights, they told me about Inuit mythology and they shared their memories and thoughts on snow, which were mostly filled with positivity and joy.

At the Icefjord Centre, I made coffee, introduced guests to the exhibition, and I listened to human accounts of life in a snowy landscape. My colleagues all lived in Ilulissat – some had done so for their whole lives, while others had migrated from other locations across Kalaallit Nunaat or from abroad. Naturally, they were all used to shovelling snow, skiing and riding on snowmobiles. The guests were a mixture of tourists and townspeople, either visiting the Icefjord Centre for its information on ice and the wildlife around the icefjord, or for events, coffee and food. In essence, the Icefjord Centre ended up functioning as my main gateway to life in Ilulissat. It was a place where I could meet various

1 See https://isfjordscentret.gl/en/ilulissat-icefjord-centre/

kinds of people and where I could make friends who would help me navigate the local landscape.

But during my time in Ilulissat, I also spent a lot of time alone – or, so to speak, in the company of snow. Inspired by Pink's (2015) work on sensory ethnography and Ingold and Vergunst's (2008) *Ways of Walking: Ethnography and Practice on Foot*, I would go for daily walks in the town and in its surrounding landscape. Outside the comfort of warm houses, I would look at how the snow moved as it fell from the sky and how it was carried across the ground by the wind; I would listen to its squeaks under my feet on particularly cold days, or to the muffled silence produced by fresh snowfall; I would try to maintain my body heat and to prevent my face from getting frost bitten by the cold air.

My daily walks taught me many things – especially about how snow could be an obstacle to human movement. When I first arrived in Ilulissat, I was surprised to discover that something as simple as moving around outside would actually become a challenge. To be clear, I have encountered snow many times in my life, but never in such massive quantities as I did in Ilulissat.

Because of the heavy snowfall, the roads were cleared almost on a daily basis. If you decided to go anywhere off road, you often risked stepping into a body of snow where you would sink in all the way to your hips, which made walking almost impossible. But this was not the most challenging part for me: after the snow had been cleared from the roads, there was always an icy layer of compressed snow left on the ground. I discovered this the hard way. In the beginning of my fieldwork, as I was walking home from the supermarket, I stepped onto one of the icy patches, fell on my back and spilled bags of groceries into the street. After this, I came to the realisation that I needed a different walking technique in order to move around safely. So, I decided to observe and mimic the movements and techniques of the human residents.

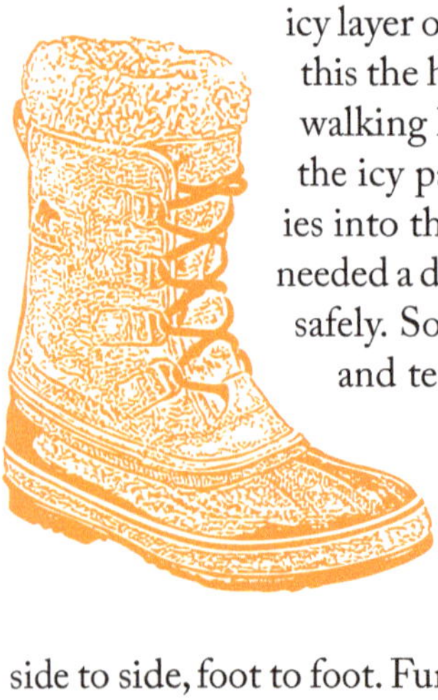

I quickly realised that my walking style was completely wrong. While my steps were narrow and my feet would slide quickly across the ground (I was used to walking on friction), others were taking broader steps while shifting their weight from side to side, foot to foot. Furthermore, I learned how to spot which parts of the ground were easier to walk on. After the snow was cleared, the roads would often be covered in a layer of sand and gravel, which produced friction. But it was also necessary to also be able to spot which form of snow I was walking on (for example, when the snow would be compressed into ice or when it was fresh and fluffy) in order to know when I could literally be walking on ice.

As I began to mimic these walking techniques, I did not fall again. But, to be honest, I never managed to walk flawlessly across the icy roads. My body did not learn to relax in these movements, and I felt that I lacked experience in order to fully embody this new knowledge.

When I visited my friend in Nuuk, they shared that my struggles were not uncommon:

> 'You can see from a distance who is Danish and who is not', they told me. 'The Danish people are those who move very carefully, afraid to slip in the snow and fall.'

This shows that movement is something that is learned and developed over time – with repetition and often by mimicking others – and it is dependent on the specific environment in which a body resides. It is especially noticeable when the body is exposed to unfamiliar conditions, forcing it into new kinds of movement patterns.

These kinds of experiences are described by Jackson (1983: 124) as *Knowledge of the Body*, as he explores how 'human experience is grounded in bodily movement within a social and material environment'. In this sense, the body learns by doing things, by moving through deep layers of snow or walking on ice, and by engaging in social and material relations. Therefore, what the body develops is a kind of knowledge, grounded in physical experience and experimentation.

Building on Bourdieu's (1977) notion of *habitus*, it can therefore be argued that movement, and thereby bodies, are made of interactions with others. These interactions happen not only between humans, but across species. The human bodies in Ilulissat are built and moulded through continuous interactions with snow – and, in the same way, the bodies of snow are built and moulded by humans as we for example clear the roads or contribute to climate change. This relationship of effect further extends to other species who reside in and around Ilulissat: for example, the sledge dog whose strong muscles are built from pulling wooden sledges across snowy landscapes or the plants that never grow tall so that they can be covered by snow during winter, in order to protect them from the cold air. One interlocutor shared this during an interview:

> We have creeping dwarf birch [in Ilulissat]. But the trunks of dwarf birch – they are sensible. They crawl along the ground to avoid the cold.

Life in Ilulissat can thus be characterised as what Ingold (2000) describes as a *sentient ecology* – that is, an environment which is alive and consists of multiple actors, such as snow, dogs or the wind; an environment in which human thriving depends not on authority, but on 'feeling, consisting in the skills, sensitivities and orientations' that are learned and developed over time, through constant interaction with that particular environment (Ingold 2000: 29).

In these sentient relations, the capacities of snow can enable certain capacities in humans. Because of snow, human practices such as dog sledge riding or skiing are possible – and humans can harvest their capacities for e.g. inventing things (such as sledges), moving across distances, accessing fishing and hunting grounds, or simply listening to snow.

This can all be discovered through sensory experiences. Something as simple as walking can become a challenge in a different environment – but through experiences of, for example, touch and vision, it is possible to skilfully develop new forms of embodied knowledge. In the same sense – as I gathered sensory experiences during my time in Ilulissat – this embodied knowledge allowed me to relate to other species, to understand a connectivity within shared ecologies, and to deeper understand the capacities of nonhuman matter.

INTERMEZZO

Now, dear reader, I invite you to listen to this piece of sound while you continue reading:

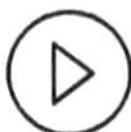

HTTPS://SOUNDCLOUD.COM/NANNA-SANDAGER-KISBY/WALKING-THROUGH-SNOW-ON-A-WARM-DAY-IN-ILULISSAT

THE AGENCY OF SNOW AS VIBRANT MATTER

Through artistic methods and sensory impressions, my daily interactions with snow led to a deeper understanding of its capacities. The capacities I found were as follows: 1) snow is a shape shifter; 2) snow can move; 3) snow takes up space; 4) snow is a source of life; and 5) snow can produce impressions. Now, I will return to this in a moment, but first, it is important to explain something: These capacities became grounds for the realisation that snow is an active, vibrant agent.

I borrow these terms from Jane Bennett (2010) and her work on *vibrant matter*. As Bennett (2010: vii) argues that many humans have a tendency to divide the world into 'passive, dull matter (it, things)' as opposed to 'vibrant life (us, beings)', I seek to support her argument that nonhumans are more than just *things*. I therefore step alongside the voices of *New Materialism* (see Coole and Frost, 2010), inspired by Deleuze and Guattari's (1987) work on *matter-energy* as I share my research on human-snow relations.

In itself, snow possesses a *vibrant materiality* (Bennett, 2010) as it acts from certain inherent capacities. These capacities of snow are essential to its character, but they further influence snow's relation to other actors within a larger *assemblage* (Bennett, 2010). Rooted in *posthumanism* (see Haraway, 1991, 2008; Braun, 2008), agency can thus be defined as '*doing-in-relation*' (Sundberg, 2021: 321–22). Snow produces effect in the world as its actions influence other actors – and it is, in turn, influenced by other actors through various encounters and interactions. Some of these multispecies actors who partake in this assemblage with snow in and around Ilulissat are (in a simplified version):

> Birds / Dogs / Soil / Rock / Plants / The wind / Temperature / Humans / Sledges / Cars / Snowmobiles / Skis / Wood

With this knowledge, let us return to the capacities of snow. I believe that now is a good time to show you some of my photographs from Ilulissat. I invite you, dear reader, to think about what you see, what you can learn from the differences in colour and light – and, first and foremost, to think about what these photographs reveal about snow:

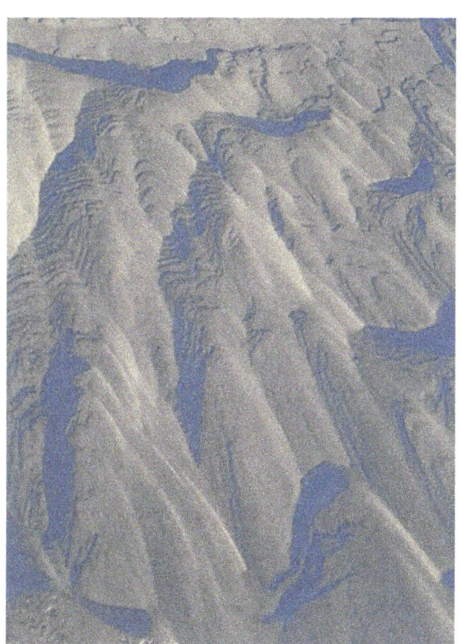

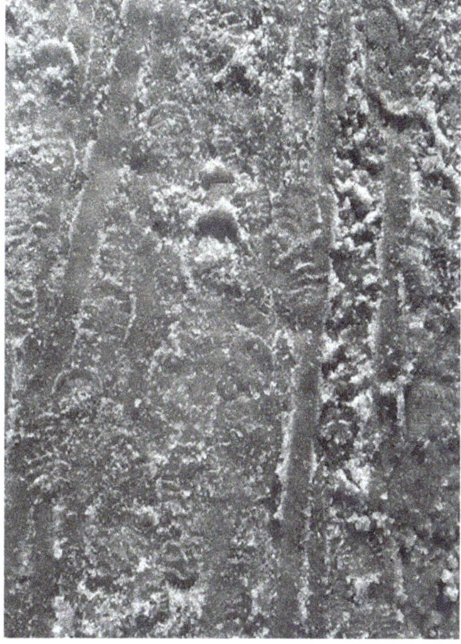

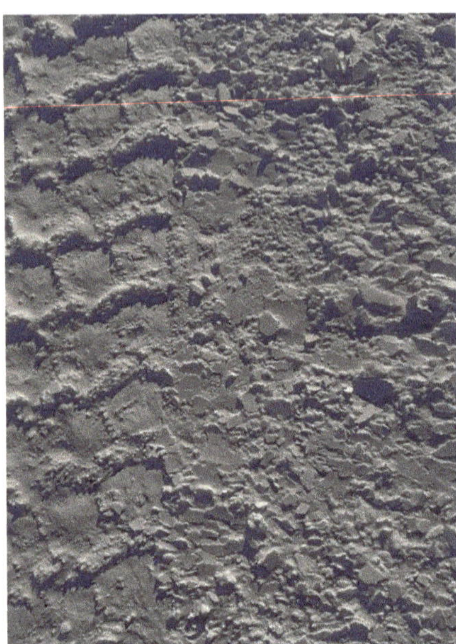

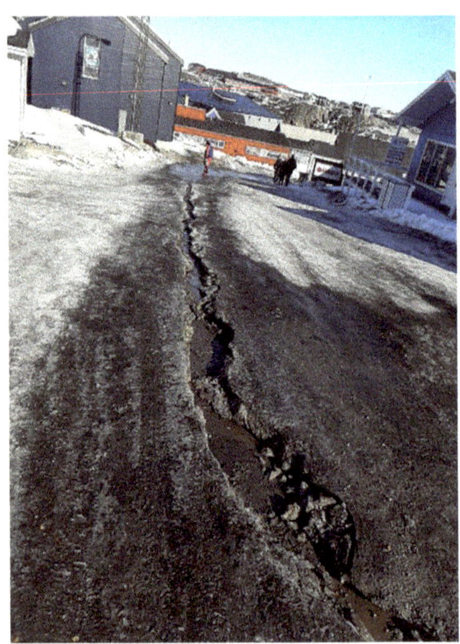

Please take a moment to register the details of these photographs in relation to the information you have received so far. What do they tell you about snow in Ilulissat?

Then, keeping the photographs in mind, let us return to the capacities of snow:

Snow is 1) *a shape shifter*, in multiple ways. Firstly, because it has the capacity to mould itself to fit into cracks or holes, maintain the shapes or patterns of those whom it encounters, or compress itself into ice. This kind of shape shifting is particular to snow in its frozen forms where it consists of snowflakes clustered together into a big mass – sometimes so big that it takes the form of a glacier.

Secondly, snow is a shape shifter because it essentially is made of water. It therefore has the capacity to melt and freeze, to become vapour, piles, slush, clouds, droplets, lakes, glaciers and so on. Although snow, in its frozen forms, only comes to exist under certain conditions, it can alter both form and consistency because of its composition.

Think about this for a moment. Then, please take a look at the next photographs:

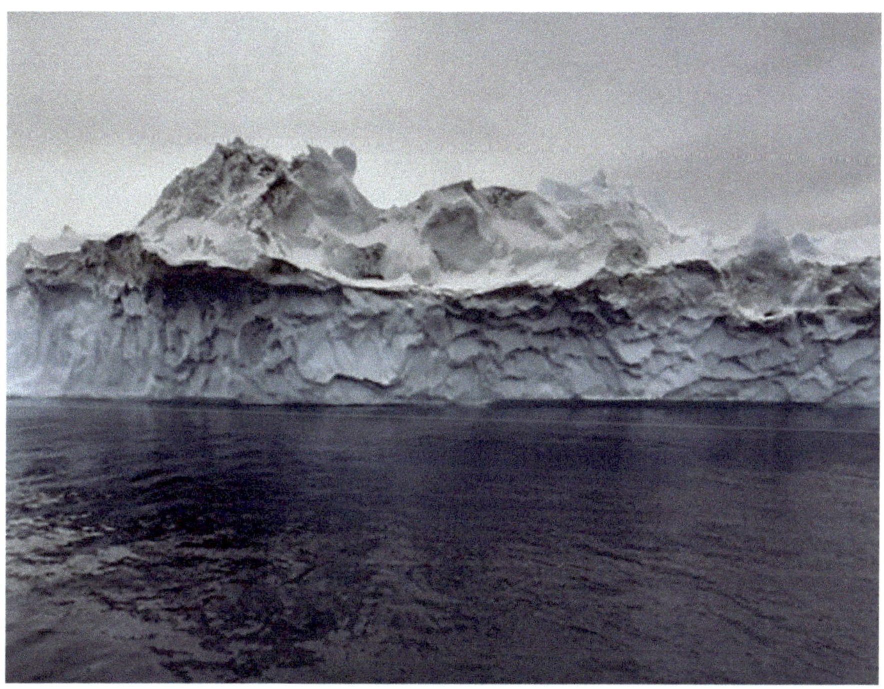

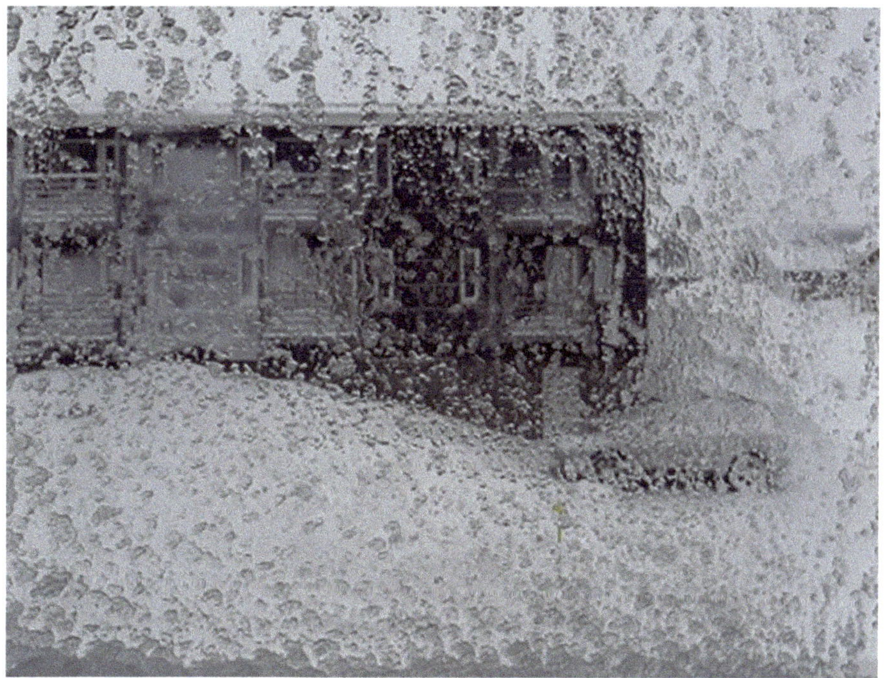

The shape shifting capacities of snow are further what enables its second capacity, which is that snow 2) *can move*. It moves from clouds onto the ground, across landscapes, between continents, through air, underground, into human boots and doorways, on top of buildings, or into the sea. Snow is therefore constantly on the move between different places, often changing form.

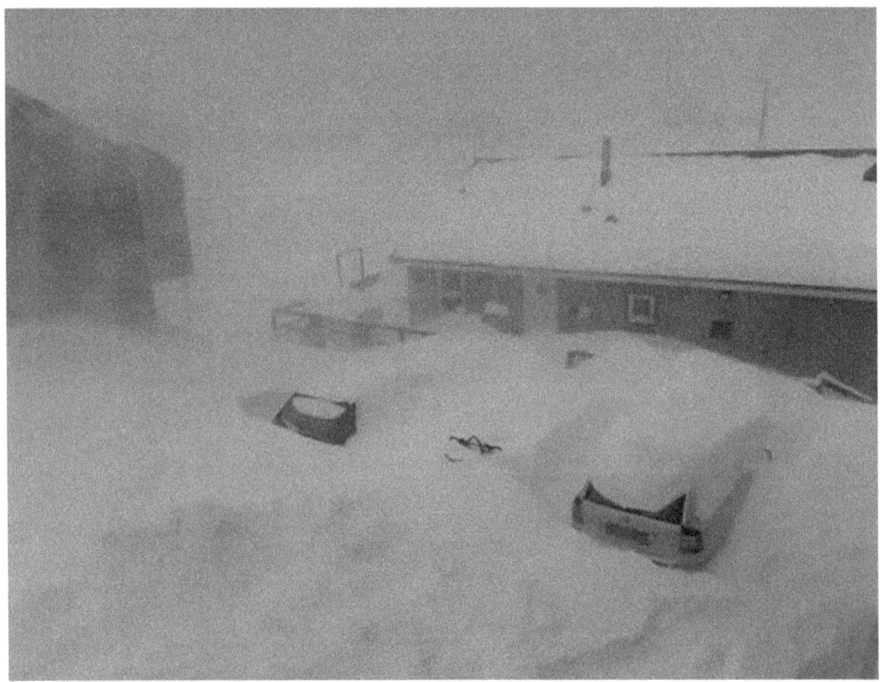

As snow materialises and moves, it also 3) *takes up space* – on top of houses, roads, mountains, covering dogs, cars and literally anything on which it lands. An example of this was shared by one of my human interlocutors (a woman who grew up in Nuuk and later moved to Ilulissat) as she told me of her childhood memories of being snowed in during the winter:

> Our house was not very tall – and it often got completely buried in snow. Therefore, all outer doors had to close inward. Otherwise, you could not get out. So, if it had snowed a lot, we could hear the wind going *SHUU* – whirling around the snow outside and

> howling around us – and then, suddenly, everything became dead silent. Then, we knew that we were inside the snowdrift. Then, there was no sound. We could not hear anything. Then, when we got up in the morning, we would open the door – and then, we would just start shovelling snow inside. All the way at the top [of the door]. You always had a shovel standing in the entrance of the house – also using washing bowls and such – and then we made a little hole. All the way at the top edges. And then, the oldest child – or whichever child could use a shovel – was dressed up and then thrown out of that hole with a shovel. And then, the door was shut. And then, you began to shovel from outside, so that the others could get out.

As snow takes up space, it therefore also takes up space in a non-material sense – in human minds. As discussed by Law (2009) through *material semiotics*, there exists an ongoing interaction between discourse and materiality. However, the way we humans ascribe meaning to matter is dependent on the matter itself. In this sense, discourse is somehow limited, as one cannot build stories out of nothing.

But the relation between discourse and matter is somehow interconnected, as it is also possible to shape matter through meaning. As these non-material representations of snow exist in our minds, they are related to a material reality. This means that our concrete, physical interactions with matter such as snow create echoes in our minds, shaping our everyday thoughts.

This leads me to the next capacity of snow, which was pointed out to me by another of my human interlocutors who told me that: 4) *'snow is essentially life'*. This thought, in turn, brought me to the realisation that snow essentially is life because snow essentially is water. My interlocutor explained that – during the winter – snow provides cover for most of the flora in and around Ilulissat, thereby protecting them from the low temperatures. During the melting period in spring, as snow transforms into water, it is a source of life in a different sense. As the landscape wakes up after a long winter, melted water from snow functions as a drinking source for many human and nonhuman lifeforms, as well as a breeding ground for mosquitoes.

With this information, I invite you to pause for a moment to study the following photograph:

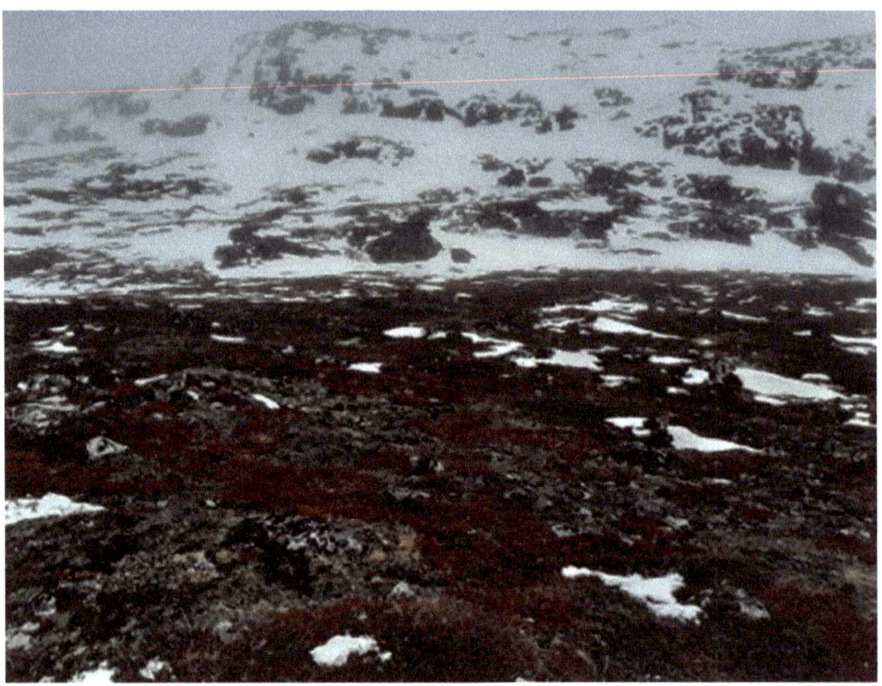

What does it bring to your mind? Which ideas and which sensations?

The last capacity of snow that I encountered is that 5) *it can produce impressions*, which can be picked up by human senses. Snow produces sound (it squeaks when someone walks on it, but it also muffles other sounds, which makes the landscape turn quiet); it creates a clear flavour as it interacts with taste buds on a human tongue; it cools down human skin through touch, and iit can feel soft, hard or slippery; it has a fresh smell; it can blind human eyes through interaction with sunlight, and it can colour entire landscapes white.

These sensory impressions of snow are particularly important to human life. Through eyesight, snow can aid as a way of orientation as it moulds itself through interaction with other actors and creates, for example, footprints. Snow therefore has a revealing ability. This can aid human hunters during winter, as they can locate the animals by following their footprints in the snow. Snow further aids visual orientation as it creates the tracks used by dog sledge mushers or snowmobile riders, who use eyesight to locate these tracks and thereby orient themselves in the landscape.

But snow also reflects light. The father of a friend from the Icefjord Centre emphasised this during an interview, as he told me that:

> The snow means a lot to us, because it lights up – especially when you are out in nature. Then you can see everything around you. When we don't have snow here, during the fall, then it's very dark. Especially here where we are, in the northern part of the country, where we have winter darkness. The sun disappears here in Ilulissat on November 28th – and then, it reappears only on January 13th. So, we have darkness for 1.5 months. Therefore, the snow means a lot for the light. First of all, it has a psychological influence because the darkness gets a bit lighter when we have snow. That's probably the most significant thing about snow for us. The dark period is not so dark when the snow has arrived.

CONCLUSION

If you are still listening to the soundscape, I invite you to press pause now.

Did you do it?

Listen to the silence – to the absence of sound – or perhaps to the sounds around you, if there are any. I invite you to close your eyes for a moment and listen.

What did you hear? What can these sounds (or the absence of sounds) teach you about the environment you are a part of, at this moment in time?

The relations between humans and snow in Ilulissat are, in a sense, paradoxical. On one hand, snow enables certain practices in everyday human life, such as dog sledge riding, tracking footprints, navigating in the dark, skiing or transporting one's children around town on small sledges. But, on the other hand, snow renders human life rather impractical, as it takes up space and hinders movement. It often blocks doorways, covers cars and slows down walking – either because it demands more energy to walk through snow while one's feet are constantly sinking, or because the compressed snow in the streets transforms into ice. Through snow's relations to humans and nonhumans in Ilulissat, its inherent agency as vibrant matter is thus revealed.

Of course, the capacities of snow exist without any relation to humans. But, as I am myself a human, it was impossible for me to study snow through a completely nonhuman lens. While snow itself produces impressions, it is only possible to experience them as a human through human capacities. However, those impressions reveal inherent material capacities of snow, rather than solely interpretations of them.

The sensory and artistic methods I used during my research have therefore proven to be particularly important, as they have allowed me to deeply experience snow's capacities. I was able not only to capture the vibrancy of snow through notes and human narratives, but further through sensory ethnography, photography and the recording of soundscapes. Through the process of research, these methods heightened my attention towards the sounds, smells, touch, flavours and visual aesthetics of snow in Ilulissat.

In this sense, artistic methods are especially important because they can act as a mediator between species. They can translate that which escapes human writing and they can bind multiple species through collaboration in the process of making art. Hopefully, they can contribute to deeper levels of understanding.

Thank you for reading, listening and viewing my work. It was a pleasure, dear reader.

EPILOGUE

One of these days, whenever you embark on your next walk, I invite you to bring a sound recording device along. Then, record the sounds you meet as you move through an outside space, listen to them, notice which sounds are louder than others, which sounds surprise you, whatever you can think of. Notice how these sounds influence your perception of a certain environment; notice how you move through space if you focus attentively on your physical sensations.

ARTNOGRAPHIC STATEMENT

This essay is based on an ethnographic fieldwork in Ilulissat, Kalaallit Nunaat, carried out from early February to early May 2022. The fieldwork was part of my Master's programme in Cultural Anthropology: Sustainable Citizenship at Utrecht University in the Netherlands.

During my time in Ilulissat, I was researching how human-snow relations partake in a larger *assemblage* that shapes the everyday practices and lifeworlds of local residents, inspired by Jane Bennett's (2010) work on *vibrant matter*. In this essay, I have invited you to experience some of the things I found, as well as to think about ethnographic methods through a nonhuman, artistic lens.

Because I have a background in art and movement studies, I decided to make use of more-than-traditional ethnographic methods during my fieldwork in Ilulissat. I decided to draw on my experiences of studying humans and nonhumans with different tools, such as intuition, artful expression and the senses of the physical human body.

My background in art includes studies in drawing, painting, ceramics, print-making and dance at two Danish folk schools over a period of twelve months in 2013, 2015 and 2016. In addition, I spent a year at Aarhus Art Academy in 2016–2017 where I studied drawing, sculpture, clay, colour theory, video making and art history. My background in movement studies includes a year of studies in psychomotor therapy at University College Copenhagen, 500 hours of vinyasa yoga teacher training and 200 hours of training in somatic approaches to yoga.

In the fall of 2021, as I prepared for my ethnographic fieldwork in Ilulissat, I quickly realised that artistic and sensory methods were crucial to my research on human-snow relations. I wanted to interview the human residents of Ilulissat, as well as partake in their everyday lives and activities as best as I could, but I also wanted to engage with the snow itself. It was important to me to explore how snow and I would influence each other, over time, through our own relation. I therefore decided to make use of the tools I knew from my previous studies. I knew that I would not be able to interview snow, in the same way that I interviewed humans, since snow did not speak any human languages. However, it did make sounds of its own – as well as other sensory impressions – that could be experienced by a human body and captured by human-made recording devices and turned into art.

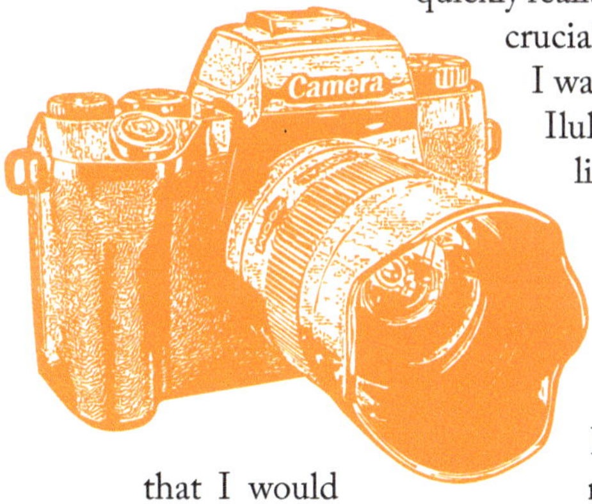

What is art, then? I know from art history that this question is equivalent to asking a group of anthropologists to agree on a simple definition of *culture*. However, in my experience, art is simply an authentic, honest expression. It is something that can be made of anything, with any intention behind it. In the case of my fieldwork, the art I produced is made of sensory impressions, through a camera, a recording device and fieldnotes, in collaboration with snow, with the purpose of sharing my own sensory impressions and the ways in which I and other humans related to snow.

Before deciding on my artistic mediums, there was an important choice to be made: how could I transport sensory impressions over a great distance? I decided that I would not attempt to transport snow itself back to the Netherlands where I live. Even if I could have succeeded, snow behaves quite differently in an arctic climate than in a temperate one. That whole endeavour would have therefore defeated the purpose of allowing other humans to experience snow as it was in Ilulissat. This excluded touch, taste and smell (except for my own descriptions, transported through my fieldnotes). I therefore chose to explore how to transport the audio and visual sensory experiences with me. So, I decided to bring a sound recording device and a camera to Ilulissat.

The final soundscapes and photographs, which you have encountered here, expose snow in different forms, at different stages, in relation to different agents, shaped by changes in temperature, over time. They are sensitive pieces of art, made of feelings, intuitions and impulses at specific moments. They are subjective, as they are formed by my own beliefs, background, research questions and aesthetic sense. What they expose is that snow indeed has an agency of its own – and that it has relations to the humans and other species with whom it shares space.

A NOTE ON ETHICS

Prior to, during and after my fieldwork in Ilulissat, it has been crucial for me to critically reflect on my own positionality in relation to the people and the place I was allowed to visit. There is a colonial history between Kalaallit Nunaat and Denmark, whose long-term effects are terrible and still influence the lives of the Inuit to this day. Since I am of Danish nationality, it has been necessary for me not only to approach this fieldwork with extreme care, but also to question whether it should be carried out at all.

In preparation for my fieldwork, I therefore turned to an Inuk friend with whom I was able to discuss how to best approach it in an ethical manner. It is important to highlight that, if my friend had not given me permission to go, I would not have carried out this project. I am aware that my friend is an individual and that they do not represent all people of Kalaallit Nunaat. But I also know that they have a deep knowledge of our countries' shared colonial history, as well as its current effects, so I chose to trust them on these matters.

Furthermore, I have been following the official guidelines of the Indigenous Circumpolar Counsel (ICC)[2] for ethical and equitable engagement with Indigenous Peoples. These guidelines include respecting and acting in accordance with Inuit values, respecting and avoiding misuse of Inuit knowledge, avoiding misconduct in Inuit communities, respecting Inuit methodologies for gathering information and validating knowledge, and always asking for informed consent.

2 Inuit Circumpolar Counsel, 2023.

Through several discussions with my friend, I realised that it deeply matters *how* we carry out ethnographic research and *what* we choose to study. The rights and safety of people are always more important than any research project, and it is important not to cause anyone harm or take space from someone else. It matters that we are kind to the people we meet, that we thoroughly research the places we visit before we go there, and it matters that we constantly are critical towards our own positionality and the actions we carry out – every single day.

For this particular research project, it felt valuable to carry it out as an 'outsider'. Most people I met during my fieldwork did not understand why I wanted to study snow – 'isn't it just something we have?' – or they were so used to dealing with snow on a daily basis that it was just another one of those boring, time consuming things that are part of everyday life. I, on the other hand, grew up without having to deal with heavy snowfall every winter. This resulted in me being the source of a great deal of laughter and pity as I tried to shovel snow for the first time. This happened before I arrived in Ilulissat, when I visited my friend in Nuuk, and we had to free their car from a heavy pile of snow in order to drive to the supermarket. In this sense, I had to learn a lot of things from scratch, and I often felt like a child – which I think makes the foundation for great anthropology.

REFERENCES

Bennett, Jane. 2010. *Vibrant Matter: A Political Ecology of Things*. Durham, NC: Duke University Press.

Bourdieu, Pierre. 1977. *Outline of a Theory of Practice* (trans. Richard Nice). Cambridge: Cambridge University Press.

Braun, Bruce. 2008. 'Environmental issues: Inventive life'. *Progress in Human Geography* **32** (5): 667–79.

Coole, Diana and Samantha Frost (eds). 2010. *New Materialisms: Ontology, Agency, and Politics.* Durham, NC: Duke University Press.

Deleuze, Gilles and Félix Guattari. 1987. *A Thousand Plateaus: Capitalism and Schizophrenia.* (trans. Brian Massumi). Minneapolis: University of Minnesota Press.

Haraway, Donna. 1991. 'A cyborg manifesto: Science, technology, and socialist-feminism in the late twentieth century'. In *Simians, Cyborgs and Women: The Reinvention of Nature*, pp. 149–81. New York: Routledge.

Haraway, Donna. 2008. *When Species Meet*. Minneapolis: University of Minnesota Press.

Ilulissat Icefjord Centre. Homepage. 13 December 2023: https://isfjordscentret.gl/en/ilulissat-icefjord-centre/

Ingold, Tim. 2000. *The Perception of the Environment: Essays on Livelihood, Dwelling and Skill.* New York: Routledge.

Ingold, Tim and Jo Lee Vergunst. 2008. *Ways of Walking: Ethnography and Practice on Foot*. New York: Routledge.

Inuit Circumpolar Council. 2023. 'Ethical and Equitable Engagement Synthesis Report: A collection of Inuit rules, guidelines, protocols, and values for the engagement of Inuit Communities and Indigenous Knowledge from Across Inuit Nunaat'. Synthesis Report. International.

Jackson, Michael. 1983. 'Knowledge of the body'. *Man*, New Series **18** (2): 327–45. London: Royal Anthropological Institute of Great Britain and Ireland.

Law, John. 2009. 'Actor Network Theory and material semiotics'. In Bryan S. Turner (ed.), *The New Blackwell Companion to Social Theory*. Oxford: Blackwell Publishing Ltd.

Pink, Sarah. 2015. *Doing Sensory Ethnography*. Second Edition. London, California, New Delhi, Singapore: SAGE Publications.

Sundberg, Juanita. 2011. 'Diabolic caminos in the desert and cat fights on the Río: A posthumanist political ecology of boundary enforcement in the United States-Mexico borderland'. *Annals of the Association of American Geographers* **101** (2): 318–36.

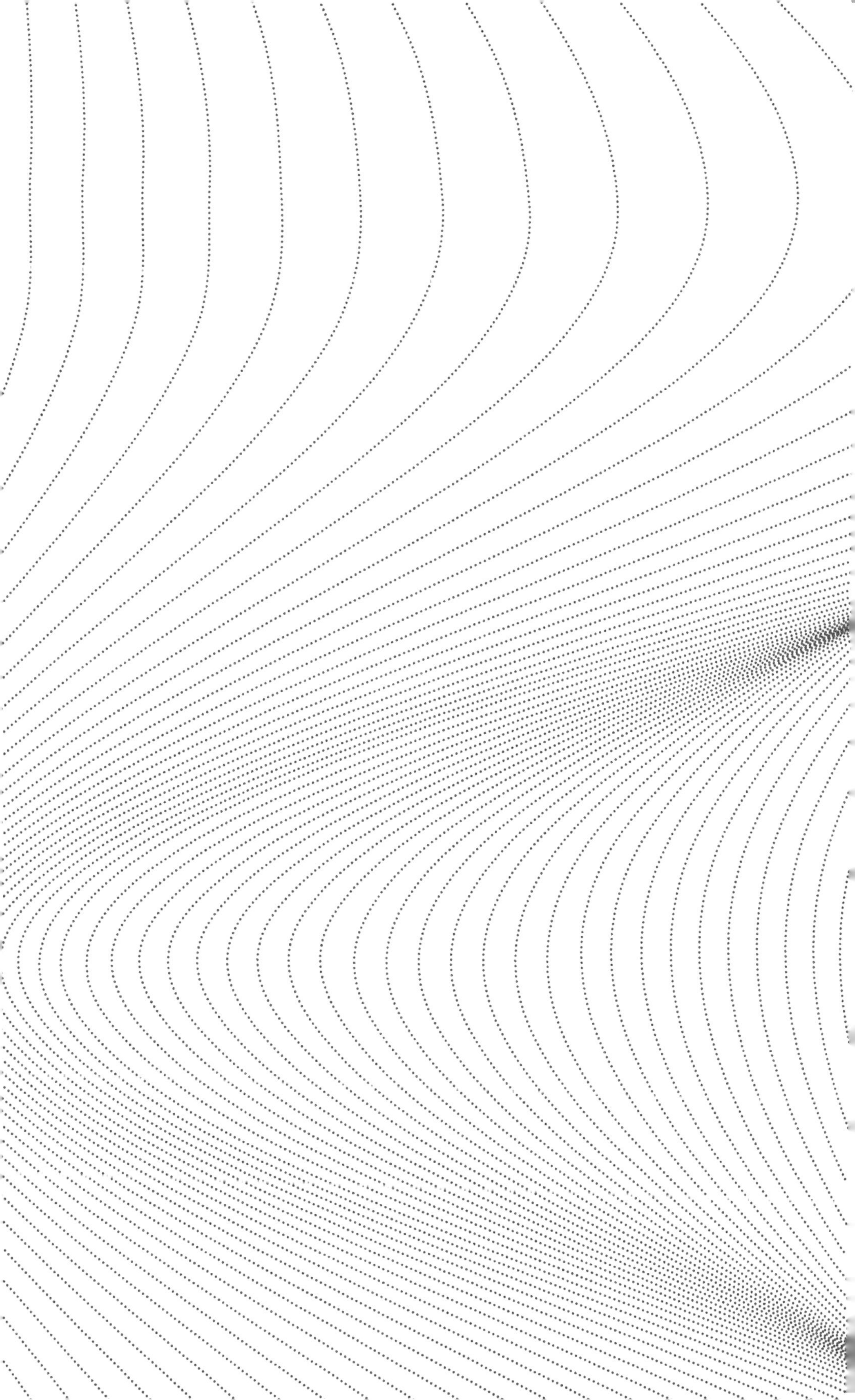

4. THE ENDURING PRESENCE OF THE EUCALYPTUS TREE: A PHOTO ESSAY.

Natasha Fijn

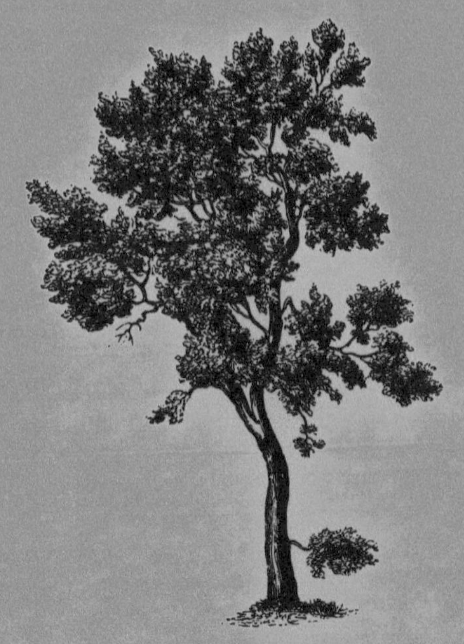

DOI: 10.63308/63878687083054.ch04

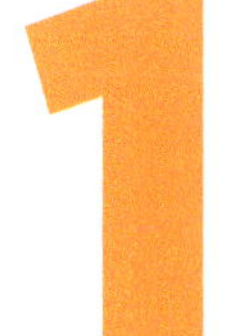

Belconnen Woodlands Corridor, Ngunnawal/Ngambri Country

Endangered Yellow-Box – Blakeley's Red Gum, Grassy Woodland Habitat, Canberra, ACT.

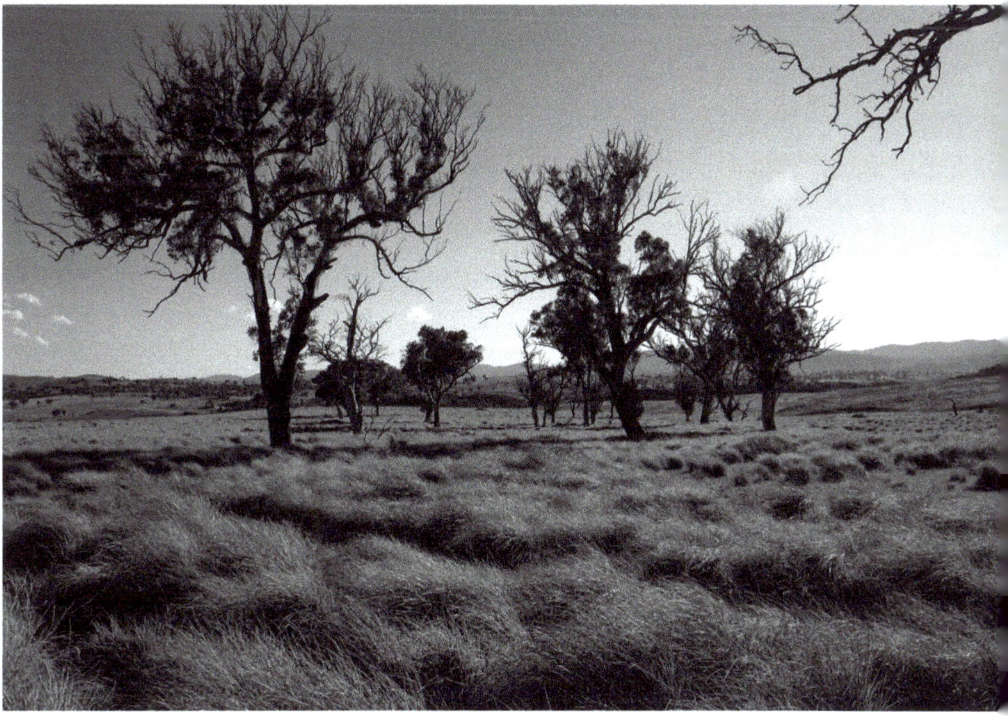

IMAGE 1

Paddock trees within grazed, open native grassland at the edge of the city of Canberra with the Brindabella Range beyond. The traditional First Nations custodians of the land, the Ngunnawal and Ngambri communities, would have conducted 'cool burns'. Cultural burning was a form of land management, which slowly burnt the grassland but did not reach the top of larger canopy trees, with the intention of encouraging hunting grounds for kangaroo, wallaroo and possums, once important food sources. Marsupials have now returned to these reserves, after largely being displaced by the grazing of cattle and sheep for over a century.

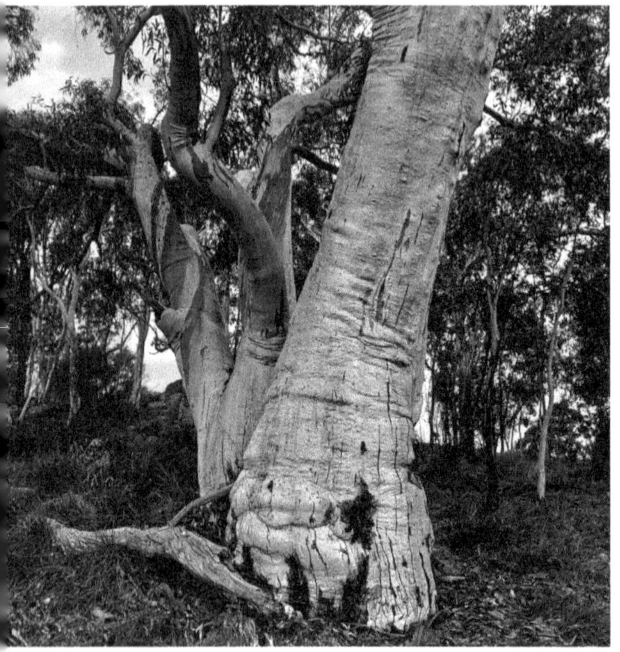

IMAGE 2

The eucalypt, or gum tree, is a means of connection with a deep past. When I see the large girth of a canopy tree, I think of the centuries it took to reach that size with separate trunks diverging to make up a unique individual being, patiently standing over many human generations, while engaging at an incremental pace with the surrounding soils, vegetation and foraging or nesting animals.

IMAGE 3

A Ngunnawal family group may have walked by these two leaning trees centuries earlier, perhaps utilising the bark of the tree for a canoe, or as a coolamon to hold a baby, or grain to make dough. The loop in the tree on the left could be a sacred 'ring' tree. An individual may have bent the young branches to form a loop, functioning to signal the direction of an important ochre site, or sacred place to passers-by.

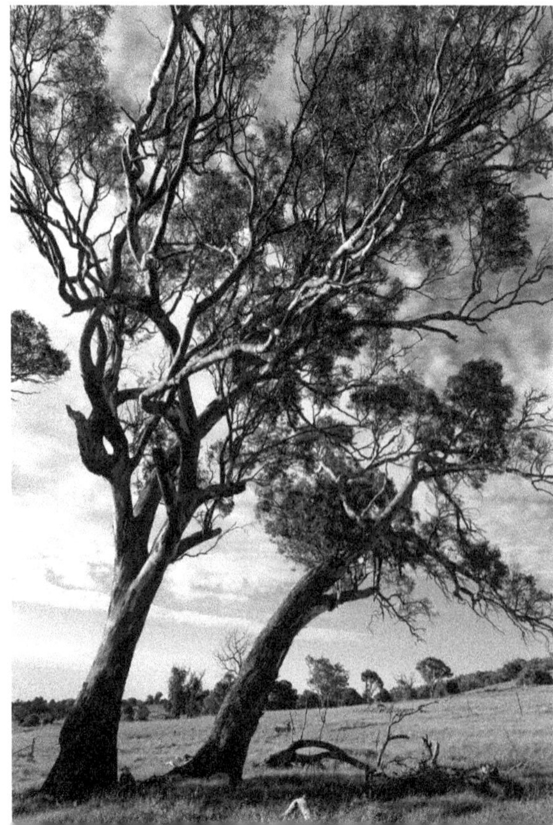

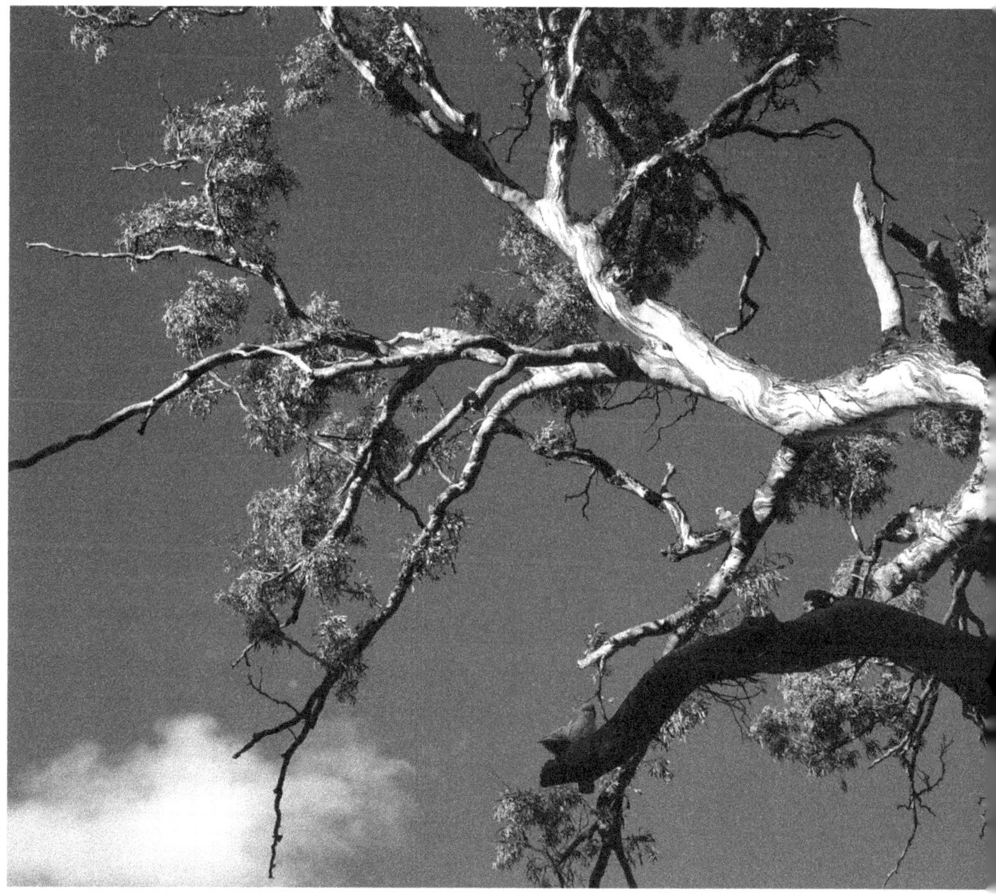

IMAGE 4

The Kama and Pinnacle Reserves were previously farmed, but they are now an important ecological corridor between the Lower Molonglo River and the Belconnen Woodlands, consisting of rare Yellow Box – Blakeley's Red Gum Grassy Woodland, forming key breeding habitat for local populations of rare gang gang, superb, swift and turquoise parrots. In this image two sulphur-crested cockatoos [lower-middle area of image] are guarding a hidden nest-hollow within a shaded branch of a Blakeley's red gum [*Eucalyptus blakelyi*].

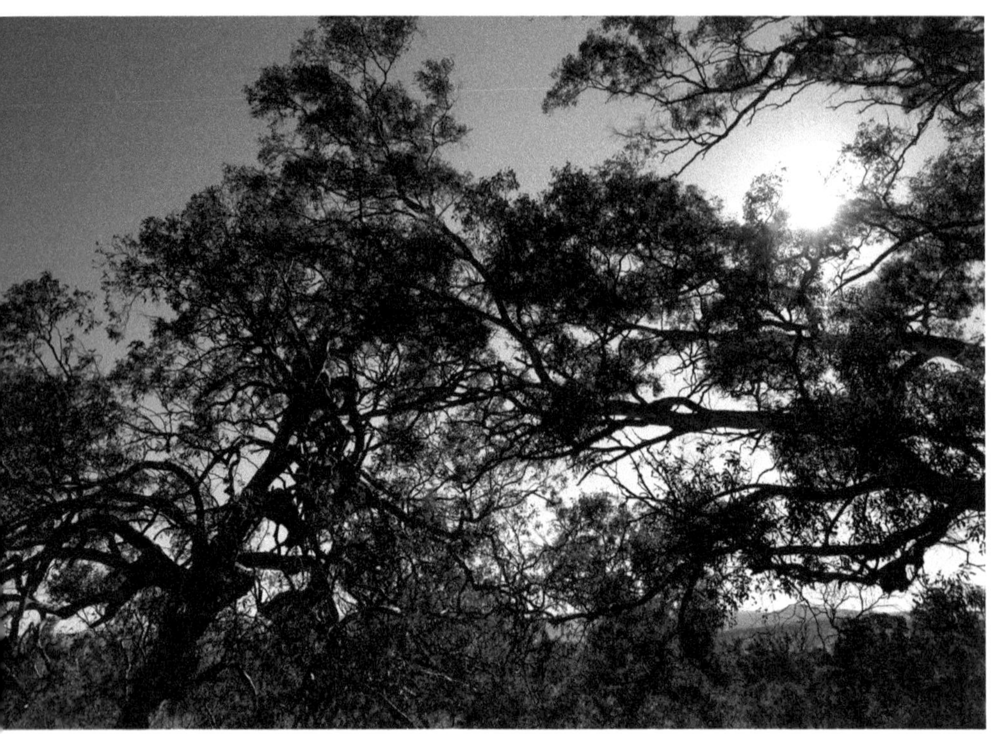

IMAGE 5

Two multi-limbed apple box [*Eucalyptus bridgesiana*] reach out and support one another. Large canopy trees communicate with one another, particularly through their root systems and fungal networks beneath the ground. One large tree may be the 'Mother Tree' to hundreds of surrounding saplings that spring up in areas that are not grazed too heavily by ungulates or marsupials.

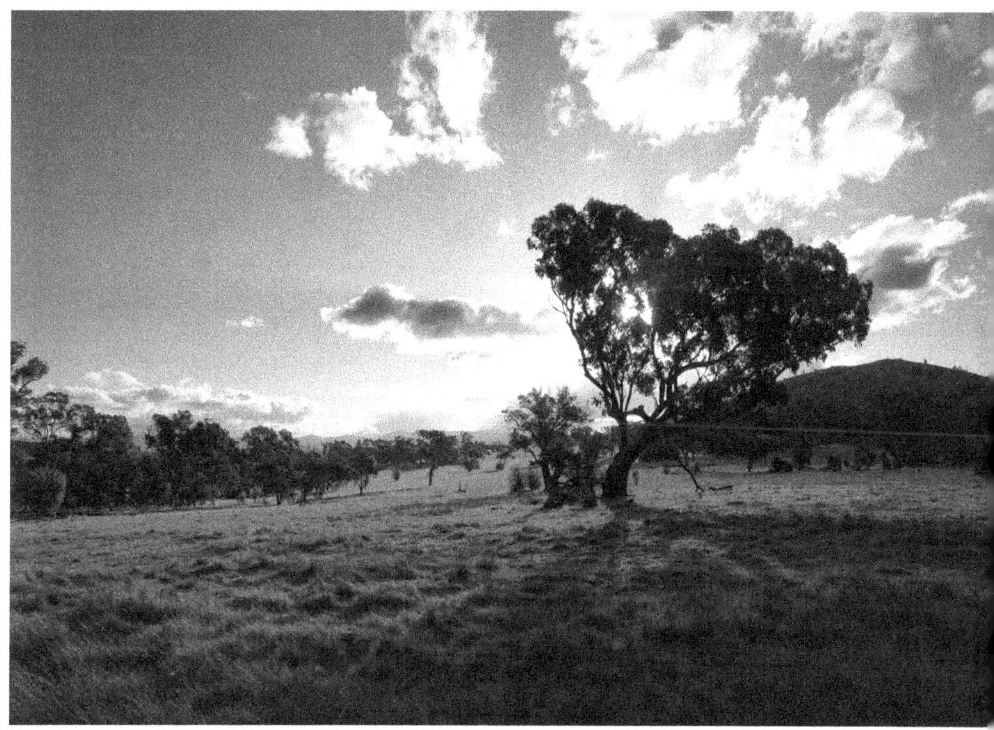

IMAGE 6

A lone canopy tree stands sentinel surrounded by grassy paddock with the Pinnacle Reserve beyond. Early settlers were drawn to open areas of grassland with just a few canopy trees. The select trees that have remained still standing are those that the farmer spared, perhaps as shade for stock, but often when the landscape was deemed too hilly, boggy or rocky to be productive as good grazing land.

2. Ginninderry Suburb Construction, 2021

Ngunnawal/Ngambri Country

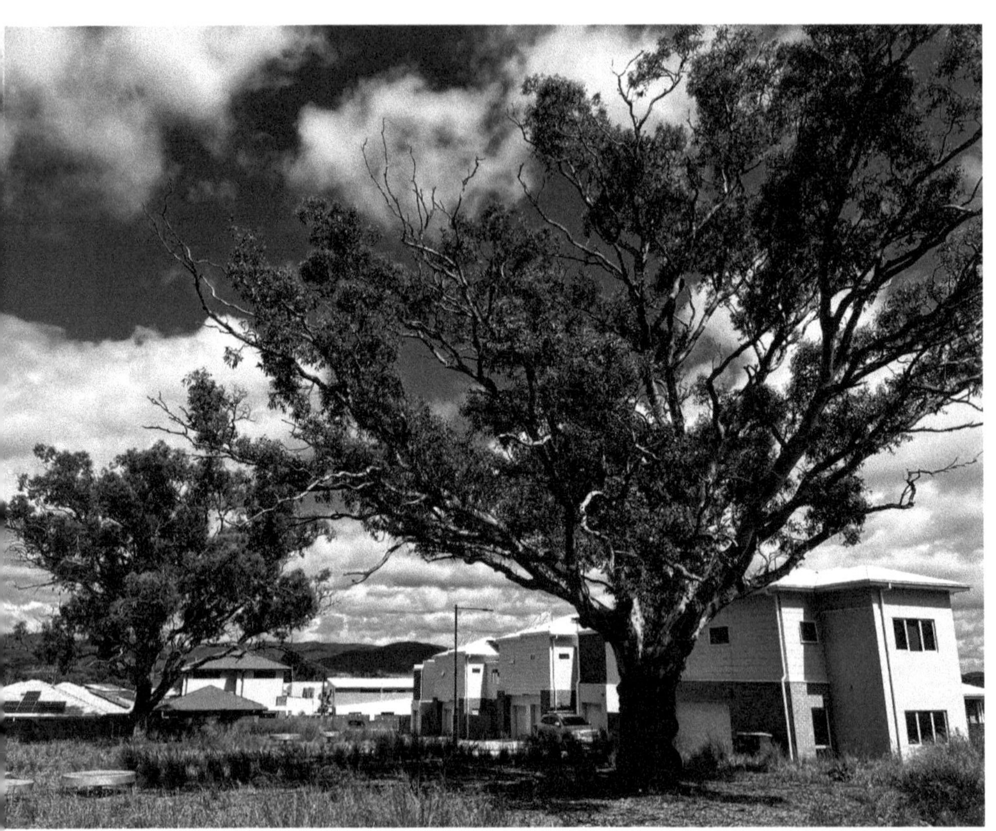

IMAGE 7

Brand new, tightly-packed, quick-build homes are a mere blip in the time-frame of the lives of these two enduring Eucalypts. On the edge of the fast-growing capital city of Canberra, Ginninderry suburb is in the process of being developed [a partial Aboriginal name with an English ending, named after a nearby creek].

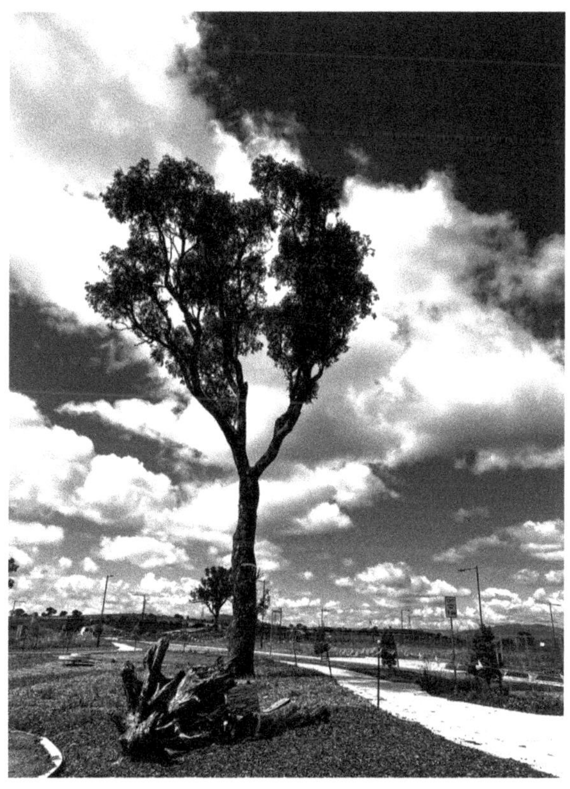

IMAGE 8.

Single paddock trees that would have not long ago been surrounded by grassland remain a stalwart presence, whilst relentless human settlement continues unabated, with newly formed concrete paths forming distinct lines and boundaries. One dead trunk has been left in place in an attempt to provide habitat for wildlife, yet the presence of this dead tree is also a reminder of the trees that have been felled in the name of progress.

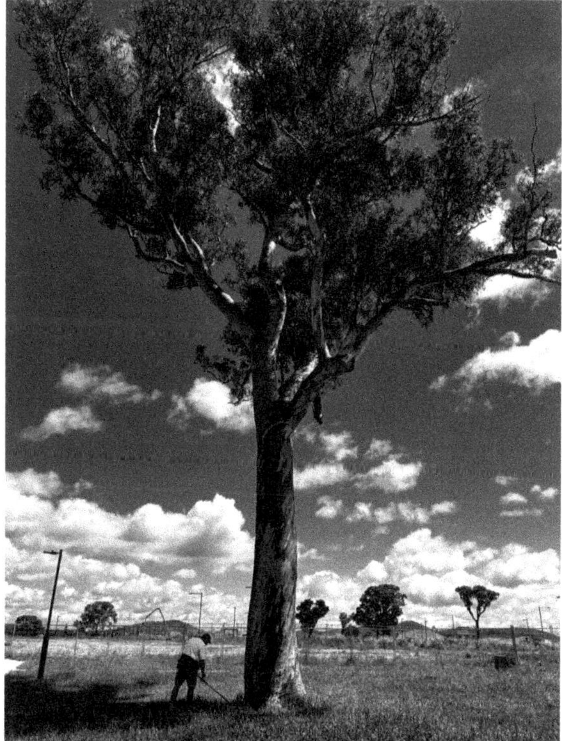

IMAGE 9.

A maintenance worker is maintaining the introduced grass with a whipper-snipper, effectively not allowing the canopy tree to produce saplings as offspring for future generations. These same trees will not be replaced naturally, but eventually substituted by human-propagated trees from elsewhere.

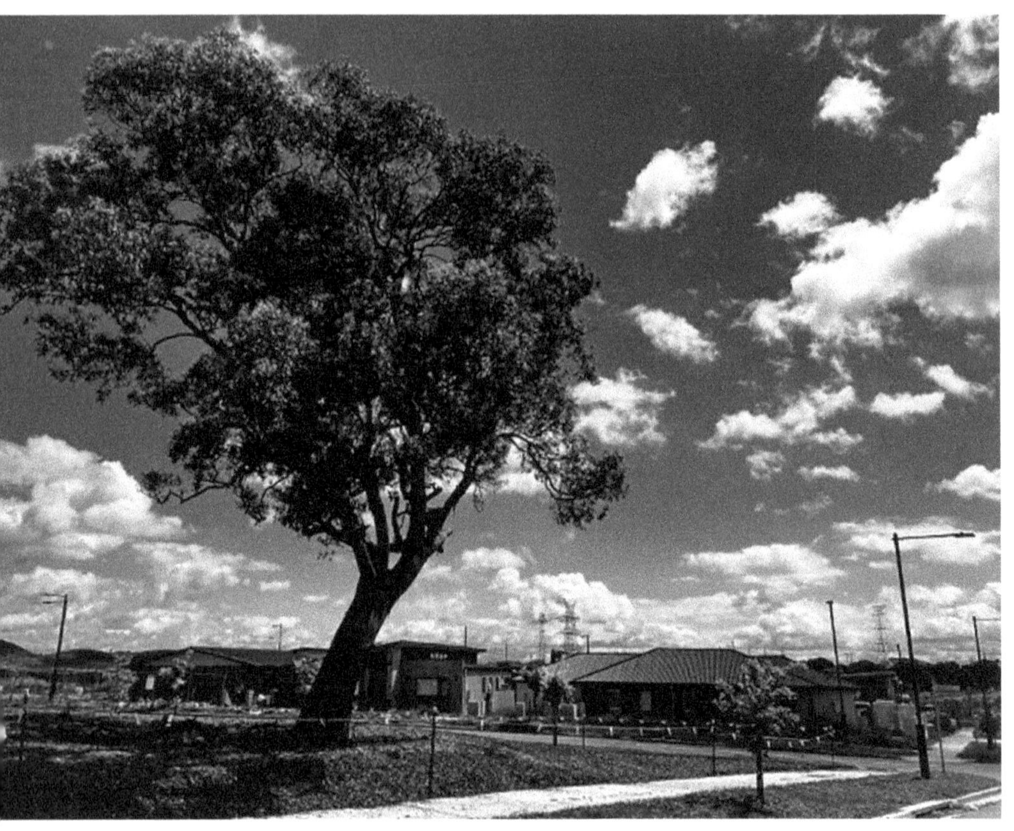

IMAGE 10

An individual Eucalypt leans at an angle, even though the neighbouring trees that it grew up amongst are no longer present. Now there is mulched up Eucalypt bark from other dead eucalypts spread across the ground to prevent any weeds from appearing, while the tree is being surrounded by new residential housing, lighting, electricity, concrete paths and roads.

The enduring presence of the eucalyptus tree

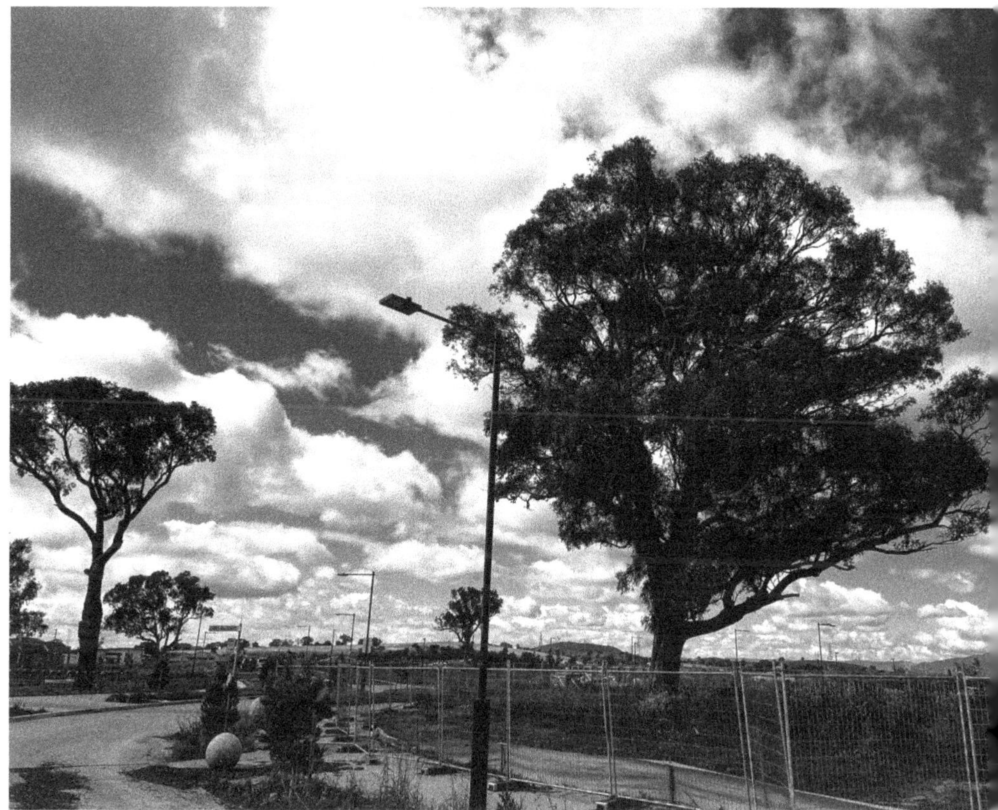

IMAGE 11

Makeshift fencing, as bounded safety for any human presence, with newly formed roads and edging are now surrounding the scattered canopy trees that have been allowed to remain in this rapidly changing, managed landscape.

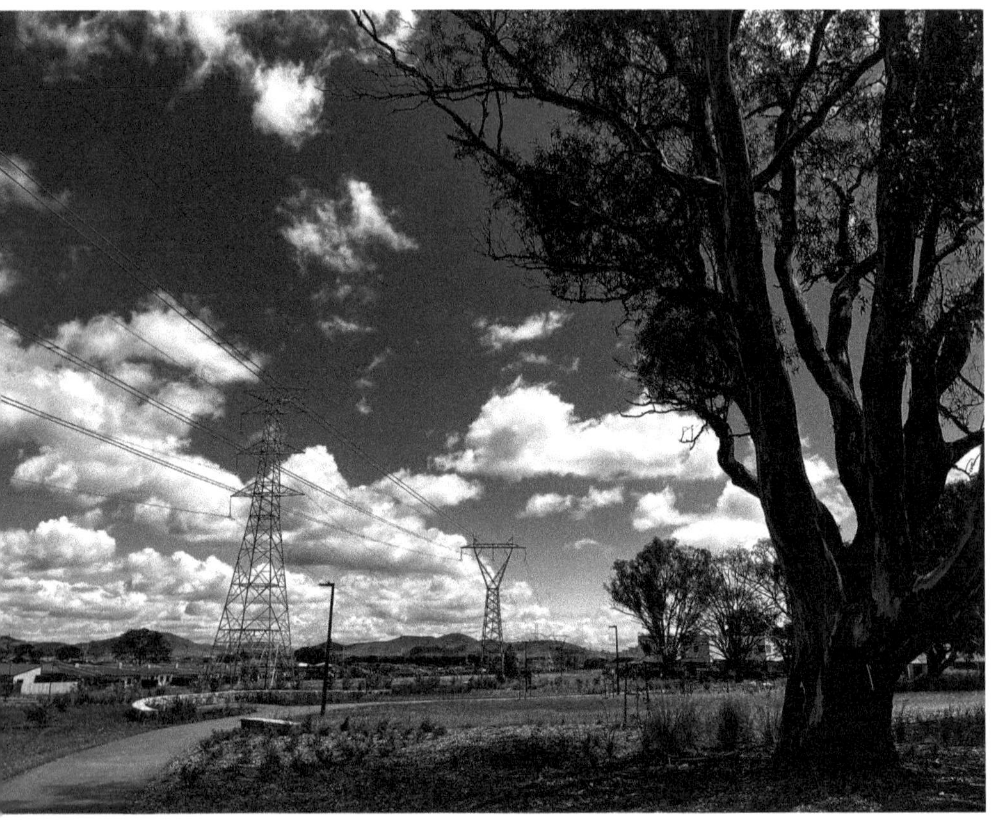

IMAGE 12.

High-voltage powerlines running right through the new suburb are the new prominent figures, dominating over the centuries-old paddock trees as sentinels in the landscape.

THE PRESENCE OF INDIVIDUAL EUCALYPTS

The photo essay comprises a series of images with accompanying text in the form of explanatory captions, the combination helping to build a multispecies story. Here, the intention is to highlight how the photo essay can be effective in allowing for more-than-human subjectivity and agency. All human cultures rely on language to communicate, but to engage beyond the human it is necessary to pay attention to cues beyond language and, therefore, not to rely on written text alone. The focus on individual eucalypt trees within this photo essay, is an extension of my connection with individual trees and is a part of my ongoing creative expression of sensorial and multispecies entanglements with significant others (see Fijn and Kavesh, 2023).

During the coronavirus pandemic, when the state government imposed a lockdown in September-October 2021, residents in the Australian Capital Territory (ACT) were allocated one hour of outdoor exercise per day. I used this time to walk in local reserves or explore new places through a form of *multisensorial auto-ethnography*. My photographic series featuring individual trees was partly inspired by an exhibition at the State Library of Australia that I had been to over a decade prior. The series by photographer Jon Rhodes, 'Cages of Ghosts' (2007), featured large-format images of scar trees bounded within cages (or as protection from vandalism).

During 2021 I was also a participant in the Bundian Way Arts Exchange programme, run by the School of Art and Design at the Australian National University. Members of the Canberra arts community signed up for the programme to learn from local Indigenous knowledge holders and arts practitioners in the region with the aim for the connections to contribute toward some form of individual artistic output. Usually the course is fieldbased, but, due to travel restrictions during the pandemic, we were limited to Zoom meetings alone. One of the speakers was Paul House, a proud Ngambri man. He talked about his family's intergenerational presence in the Canberra region, including during significant political moments in Australia's history. He continues the carving of Aboriginal designs on individual eucalypts as an important ceremonial act.[1]

The concept of one's homeland is perhaps universal to all mammals. In Aboriginal Australia one's clan land and the totemic beings that are part of this land are referred to as being on Country. In Mongolia, the term *nutag* is important on multiple scales, as the homeland that herding families and their herds migrate within, but also encompassing one's homeland on a national level. Having not been born on Australian soil, this time of travel restrictions was a means for me to explore Canberra as a place. Unable to travel to my own homeland of Aotearoa/New Zealand, or to travel into the field in Mongolia, it meant that connecting with these significant, large eucalyptus trees helped to deepen my connection to Australia as a place. I do not view where I live in

1 I observed Paul House continuing the tradition of carving trees through a ceremonial carving of a eucalypt outside the School of Culture, History and Language , The Australian National University: see https://www.anu.edu.au/news/all-news/tree-scarring-is-our-signature-in-the-land; also the video: https://www.youtube.com/watch?v=4udvkg14_r4 (accessed 16 Dec. 2023).

Canberra as my *homeland* or as my connection to Country, but it is my current home. I have developed a newfound respect for individual eucalypts where I live.

Although the eucalypt, or gum tree, is iconically Australian, many Australians do not revere these trees but instead have an overriding fear of them and prefer that they are planted nowhere near buildings. Eucalypts are prone to kill people by dropping large limbs and were thus referred to as 'widow makers' in the past. After a severe weather event, such as a storm, or if under stress during drought, their adaptive strategy is to drop a limb as a means of survival. I admire this trait in them, just as I do the skink's ability to leave a tail behind and regrow a new one. I am mindful of the threat of dropping limbs from above while camping, just as I have to be mindful to avoid standing on a venomous snake when walking through long grass in Australia. Eucalypts are remarkable at regrowing after being burnt by fire, as new stems and branches sprout up from what looks like an old, dead stump. Large Eucalypts can be around 300-400 years old, while mallees have been recorded as being up to 900 years old. When the top of the mallee tree is burnt, the old roots can produce new shoots.[2]

Historian Bill Gammage and writer Bruce Pascoe have successfully made the wider Australian public aware that before settlement the land was carefully managed by Aboriginal peoples across the Australian continent, including through the method of seasonal cultural burning (Gammage and Pascoe, 2021). Before settlement there were already large tracts of grassland that First Australians would walk through unimpeded, with scattered prominent eucalypts.

Prospectors searching for land came to the Canberra region only around 200 years ago, whereas communities of Aboriginal people, the Ngunnuwal (or Ngambri), had been living in the area continuously for more than 20,000 years. In 1817 Oxley described the following scene: '[T]he country was broken in irregular low hills thinly studded with small timber, and covered with grass: the whole landscape within the compass of our view was clear and open, resembling diversified pleasure grounds irregularly laid out and planted…' (Oxley, 1817, cited in Gammage, 2011: 44). When surveyor Robert Hoddle later travelled to the broad Monaro Plains in 1832, he witnessed open grassland and fine trees of Blakeley's Red Gum, Ribbon Gum, Apple Box, and Yellow Box trees on lighter soils with native kangaroo grass beneath (Gammage, 2011). Ngunnawal, therefore, had been actively promoting the scattered stands of large eucalypt trees. Some of the reserves that I walked through in 2021 still resembled these descriptions. To me, large 'paddock trees' are a sign of a lasting presence: they

2 https://blog.csiro.au/national-eucalyptus-day-five-things-you-might-not-know-about-these-flowering-giants/ (accessed 16 Dec. 2023).

were already there when Ngunnuwal were walking past, utilising their bark to make into various objects and to perform ceremonies, forming what are now known as 'scar trees'.

Anthropologist Francesca Merlan writes how the Manggarrayi of the Roper River Region in the Northern Territory linked specific individual trees to people, or ancestors: 'it is meaningful for a member of the [Mangarrayi] society to talk about links between trees and persons, even to the extent of saying that a certain tree "is" a certain person'… 'Only certain trees of any species represent people; these are inevitably older ones that have not grown visibly during a human lifetime' (Merlan, 1982: 162).

The cultural attitude toward eucalypts by settler Australians, however, was and still is quite different. Large tracts of land were cleared of vegetation to make way for introduced grasses and allow for the grazing of sheep and cattle, replacing whole grassy-woodland ecosystems. The easiest way for farmers to get rid of trees when clearing the land was to ringbark them, which involved cutting a deep wound right around the trunk, resulting in the tree slowly dying while still standing; while forests of eucalypts were sawed down as timber for building the nation's capital. With very few grassy-woodlands with yellow and apple box eucalypts left across the wheat-belt of eastern Australia, farmers are now realising the importance of conserving the last remaining paddock trees, as important shade for livestock during the heat of summer, but also as important nest habitat for native birds and marsupials (Fijn et al., 2019).

The series of images forming the photo essay above are in black-and-white as a means of tapping into this window on the past. The intention of the contrast is also to draw out the silhouette and unique structure of each individual tree. When walking through the Belconnen Woodlands Corridor, one can envisage the presence of the First Australians who may have walked past these same trees, living a different way of life by hunting and gathering on the land; followed by farmers with the introduction of strange new species and the grazing of sheep; to now, where these same trees are now being conserved as rare stands within reserves, or have been spared as the few remaining sentinels surrounded by rapidly encroaching residential development to accommodate a burgeoning human population in the nation's capital. The two sections within the photo essay are not meant to be in opposition to one another, as both are interconnected through being a part of Ngunnuwal/Ngambri Country. There is a need to recognise that reserves and encroaching urban development were originally part of the same grassy-woodland ecosystem.

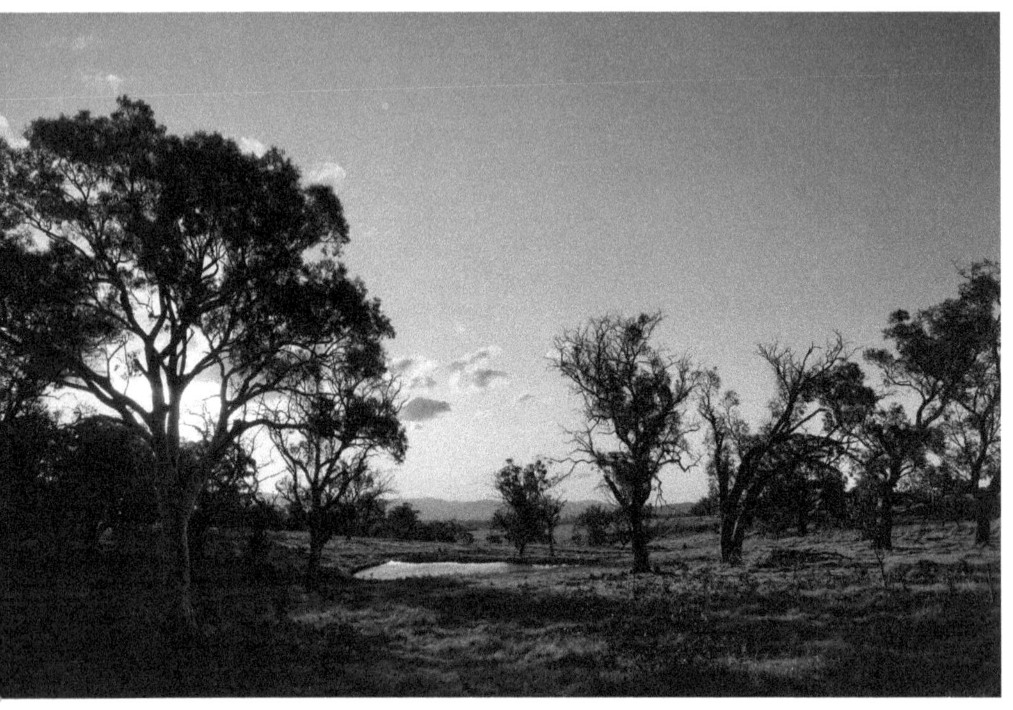

FIGURE 1.

Eucalypts as ancient sentinels on the edge of a Canberra suburb. Individual image in black-and-white. Photo by the author, 2021.

ARTNOGRAPHIC STATEMENT

My fieldwork has predominantly been based in both Australia and Mongolia, while an ongoing focus has been on cross-cultural perceptions and biosocial connections with significant animals. An integral part of my research involves the communication of academic output through visual material, integrated with accompanying text. The recording of 'data' in the field has often been through an observational form of filmmaking, inspired by mentors based in Australia, particularly David MacDougall's (2006) and Ian Dunlop's approaches to filmmaking (see Fijn, 2019).

As I mainly engage with multispecies contexts, this has required a different style from more human-oriented filmmaking, employing what I have referred to as etho-ethnographic filmmaking: a combination of natural history with ethnographic filmmaking techniques (Fijn, 2012). In keeping with a broader observational filmmaking style, I edit images down from a large number of images, but the shots I take in situ are representative of what my eye sees.

I have also been interested in exploring creatively with photo essays in a multispecies-ecological context. Within a multimodal volume on the theme of fluids and medicine, my individual contribution stemmed from field research focusing on the transfer of knowledge surrounding Mongolian medicine. Through three ethnographic vignettes, employing text, images and video, I focused on herders' use of Mongolian bloodletting techniques on horses as a means of building immunity and preventing illness (Fijn, 2020).

In relation to Australia, for many years I have drawn inspiration from the philosophical writings of Val Plumwood. I published a photo essay, 'A Shadow Place: Plumwood Mountain' (Fijn, 2016) where, through just five images, I tried to convey the feeling of encountering the driveway up to Plumwood Mountain, as a means of exploring Val Plumwood's (2008) concept of a 'shadow place'.[3] Plumwood would refer to plumwood trees (*Eucryphia moorei*) as individuals with distinctive, often human like, characteristics, such as the trunk taking on the form of a person with long limbs.

I photographed the Plumwood Mountain forest and the regeneration of the canopy trees after fire swept through the property on 19 December 2019, forming a juxtaposing narrative between my experience of the very real effects of climate change and a similar observational form of documentation by my Grandfather, through the photographs he took 75 years earlier at the end of World War II in Maastricht, the Netherlands. The exhibition was held at PhotoAccess in Canberra in February 2022, entitled 'Between Hope and Despair'. In this dialogue between my grandfather and myself, I experimented with black-and-white as an artistic form of output in this context too, as it enabled me to extend across generations and across time.[4]

In the present photo essay, the viewer can gain an immediate explanation in the form of individual captions, but can choose whether to read each accompanying caption or not. In that sense, the integration with text is similar to an exhibition in an art gallery or museum space, where the viewer may engage only with the images or can read the accompanying text for more details, but at their own pace. In contrast, with films or video installation, the maker decides upon the depth and speed at which the audience engages with the work (Figure 1).

3 In another photo essay, I focused on the deaths of animals on the road and how few stop to consider the loss of life, in a piece entitled 'Impact on the Kings Highway': see https://plumwoodmountain.com/multimedia-gallery/photo-essay-by-natasha-fijn/ (accessed 16 Dec. 2023).

4 See: https://www.gallery.photoaccess.org.au/between-hope-and-despair (accessed 16 Dec. 2023).

REFERENCES

Fijn, Natasha. 2020. 'Bloodletting in Mongolia. Three visual narratives'. In N. Köhle and S. Kuriyama (eds). *Fluid Matter(s). Flow and Transformation in the History of the Body*. Asian Studies Monograph 14. Canberra: ANU Press. https://press-files.anu.edu.au/downloads/press/n7034/html/05-bloodletting-in-mongolia/index.html

Fijn, Natasha. 2019. 'The multiple being: multispecies ethnographic filmmaking in Arnhem Land, Australia'. *Visual Anthropology* **32** (5): 383–403.

Fijn, Natasha. 2016. 'A shadow place: Plumwood Mountain'. *Landscapes: The Journal of the International Centre for Landscape and Language* **7** (1). Retrieved from https://ro.ecu.edu.au/landscapes/vol7/iss1/12

Fijn, Natasha. 2012. 'A multispecies etho-ethnographic approach to filmmaking'. *Humanities Research* **18** (1): 71–88.

Fijn, Natasha and Muhammad A. Kavesh. 2023. 'Towards a multisensorial engagement with animals'. In Phillip Vannini (ed.) *The Routledge International Handbook of Sensory Ethnography*. London: Routledge.

Fijn, Natasha, Michelle Young and David Lindenmayer (eds.) 2019. *Learning from Experience: Conversations with Family Farmers from the Woodlands of Southeastern Australia* Canberra: Sustainable Farms, ANU.

Gammage, Bill. 2012. *The Biggest Estate on Earth: How Aborigines made Australia*. Australia: Allen and Unwin.

Gammage, Bill and Bruce Pascoe. 2021. *Country: Future Fire, Future Farming* Australia: Thames and Hudson.

Köhle, Natalie and Shigehisa Kuriyama (eds). 2020. *Fluid Matter(s): Flow and Transformation in the History of the Body*. Asian Studies Monograph 14. Canberra: ANU Press.

MacDougall, David. 2006. *The Corporeal Image: Film, Ethnography and the Senses*. Princeton: Princeton University Press.

Merlan, Francesca. 1982. 'A Manggarrayi representational system: environment and cultural symbolization in northern Australia'. *American Ethnologist* **9** (1): 145–66.

Plumwood, Val. 2008. 'Shadow places and the politics of dwelling'. *Ecological Humanities* 44. http://australianhumanitiesreview.org/2008/03/01/shadow-places-and-the-politics-of-dwelling/

Rhodes, Jon. 2007. Exhibition. 'Cage of Ghosts'. Canberra: National Library of Australia.

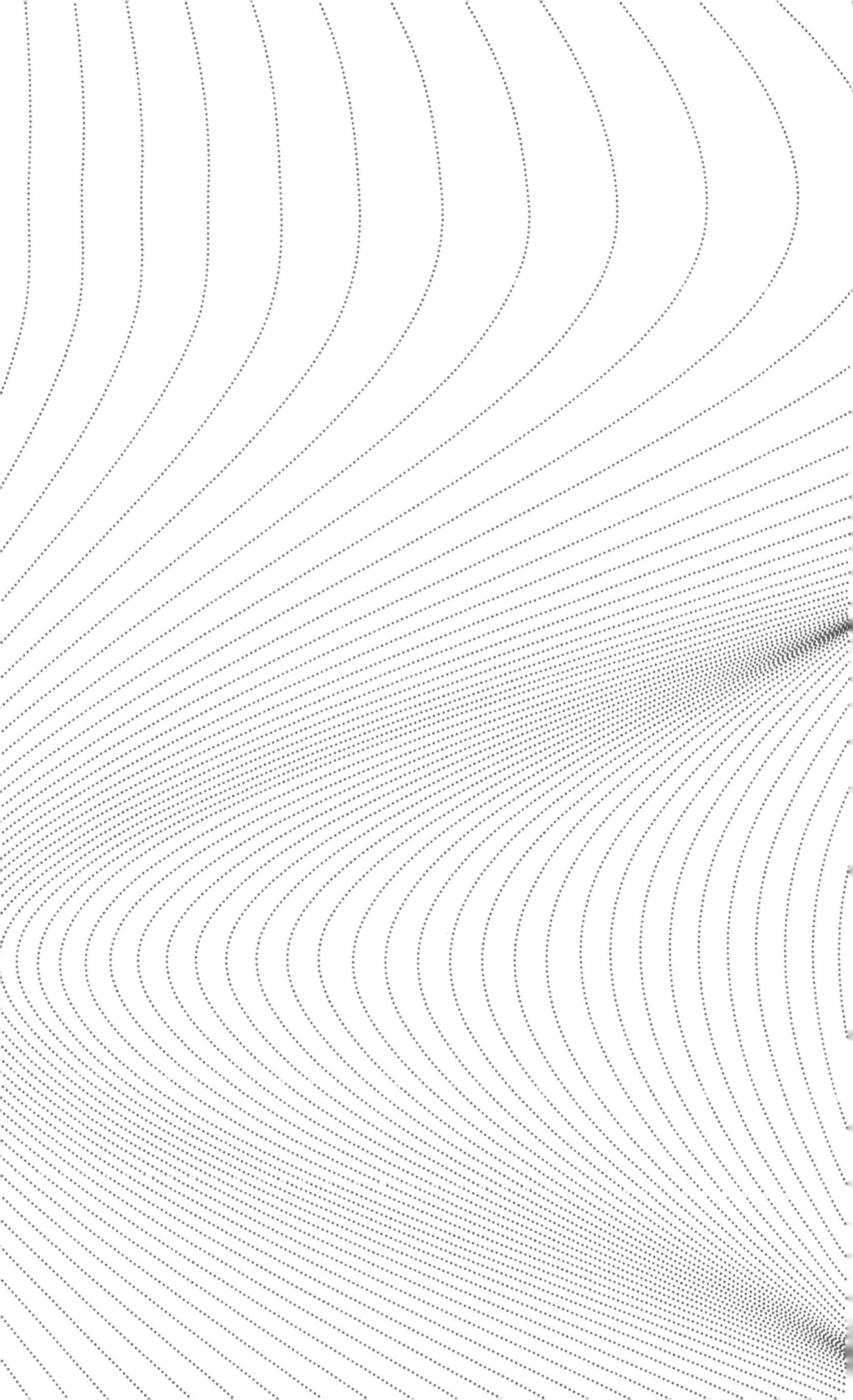

5. ARTISTIC CO-DISCOVERY IN MULTISPECIES COLLABORATION.

Bartram
+
Deigaard

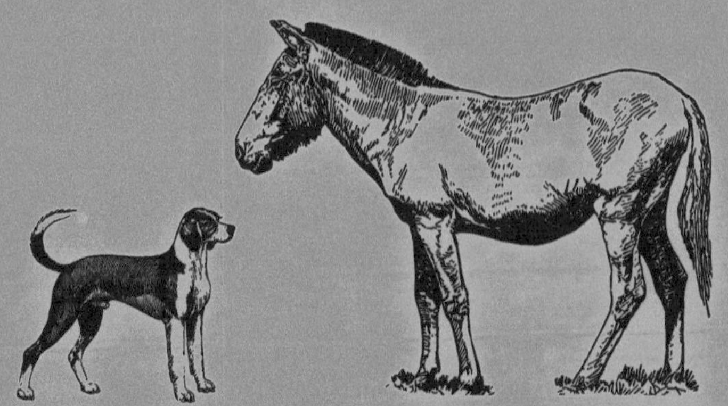

DOI: 10.63308/63878687083054.ch05

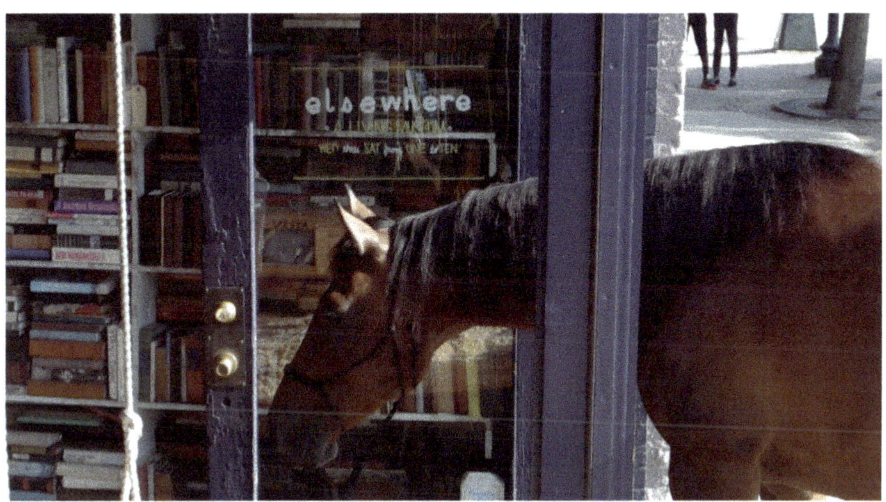

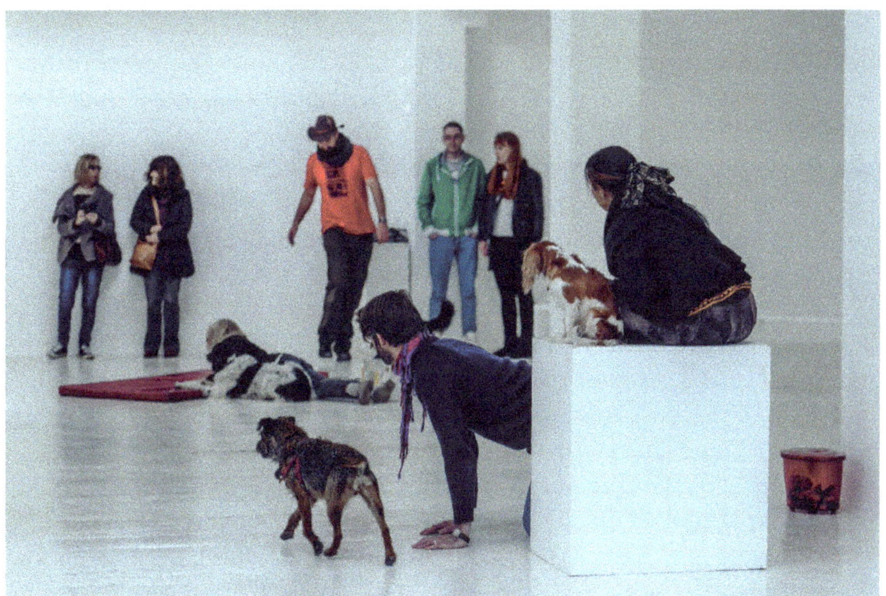

COMPOSITE 1.

Deuce stands at the threshold of Elsewhere Museum considering whether to enter. From *Horses at the Museum: Gus and Deuce Go Elsewhere*, Lee Deigaard, Elsewhere Museum, Greensboro, North Carolina, USA, 2014, *Be Your Dog*, Angela Bartram, KARST Gallery, Plymouth, UK, 2016 in which dogs with their human companions enter a gallery space as artists. Instructions to humans are to do as their dogs do, to follow their dog's lead.

ETHOD: TO INVITE, AND BE INVITED BY, ANIMAL COLLABORATORS INTO A NON-HIERARCHICAL, NON-DETERMINISTIC CREATIVE PROCESS

Bartram+Deigaard are artists working in sympathetic praxis and creative research within an ethos of multispecies parity. Our collaborative and solo projects invite animal collaborators into non-hierarchical, non-deterministic creative processes which invert hypothesis-driven methodologies. This is often through an invitation into human privileged cultural sites, to give the animal full access and to disrupt conventional organisational politics of which bodies belong where and in what context. We recognise that animal sites are significant, but for the context of this work it is important that the invitation sees the animal cross thresholds into and within the conventional governing principles of museum and gallery interiors where they can be considered artists by virtue of their active presence. Our approach seeks opportunities for convergent consciousness among non-human and human investigators; hypotheses, learning and insights occur not only through collaborative improvisation but also through retroactive review of documentation, development of work for exhibitions and writing accompanying text and essays. Collaborations proceed according to principles of mutual respect and autonomous engagement and are shaped by revelatory moments of co-discovery.

In our solo practices and collaborations as the duo Bartram+Deigaard, we have identified a 'shared brain' sensibility embedded within ethical commitments and considerations in working with other animals, identifying ourselves within that category. Despite considering ourselves as animal, we will henceforth refer to the non-human with this term for clarity of bodies/species derivation in the discussion. For the purposes of this text and abbreviated reference, we refer to our shared methodology, developed through our animal partnerships and with their full credit, as the B+D method, with the keen declaration that so much arises from the '+' representing animal connectivity and inter-relating to our immense benefits. This relates to inviting animals to enter the creative space, in site and process, and of the acceptance of their reciprocal invitations into acts of animal-led creativity.

Key characteristics of the B+D method:

Porous, *improvisational, intuitive; non-prescriptive, non-proscriptive, non-preconceived; open to the unexpected, embracing surprising results; iterative, aggregative*

Artistic research has only relatively recently considered our kind of creative fieldwork as possibly predating much of the literature on the subject. This shift sees it eligible for scholastic merit, in addition to that of the existing contribution of literature. We have been working beyond the literature in practices informing critical references, presenting exhibitions and events, and delivering presentations at multidisciplinary international animal conferences since the inception of animal studies as a discipline. The B+D method favours the improvisational over the prescriptive, and does not enter projects with preconceptions about what will emerge materially or conceptually. This approach is designed to remain open to the unexpected, the tangential, the reflexive and the aggregative. It makes room for the embrace of surprise and the ways in which outputs can pivot on the action or reaction of a single participant – non-human or human. When all available energy and attention are focused on the play of intuition among co-investigators, useful and meaningful experiences are bound to result, some of which can be documented and named. It is assumed that the participants will arrive, on paths impossible to predict, at 'wholes' which are greater than the sum of their parts. The goal is understood to be a set of working conditions and a commitment towards becoming or being animal, rather than any kind of product or conclusion.

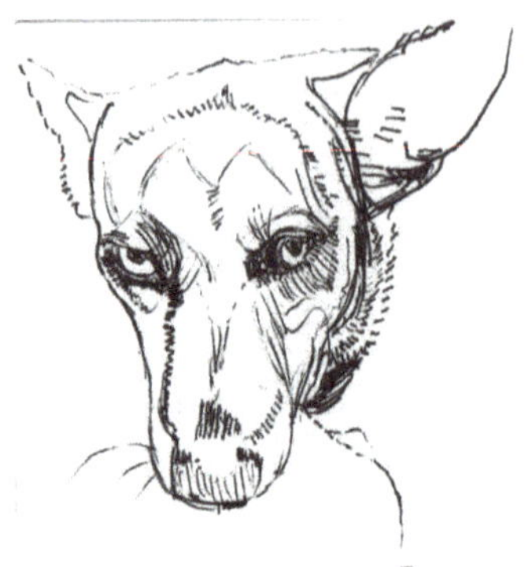

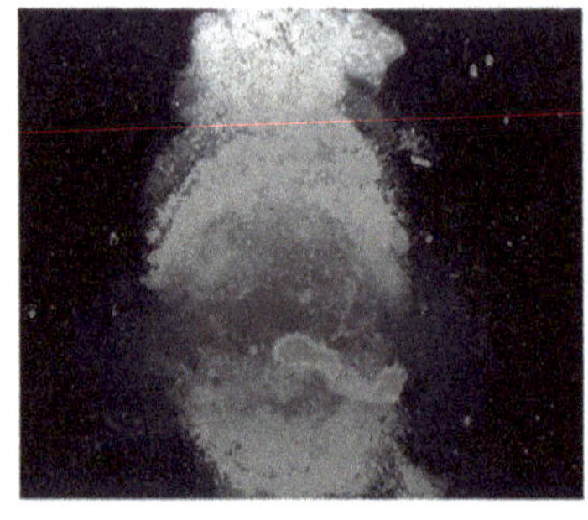

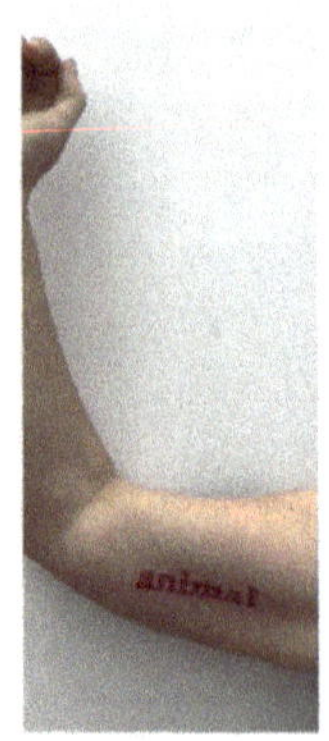

draw | breath | animal

Recent and new collaborative works in drawing, printmaking, photography, and video by

ANGELA BARTRAM & LEE DEIGAARD

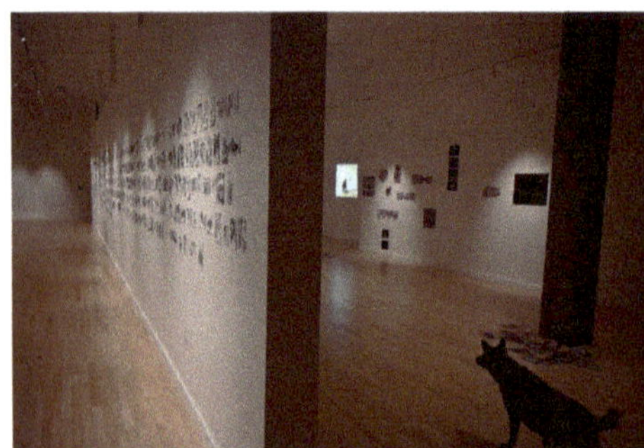

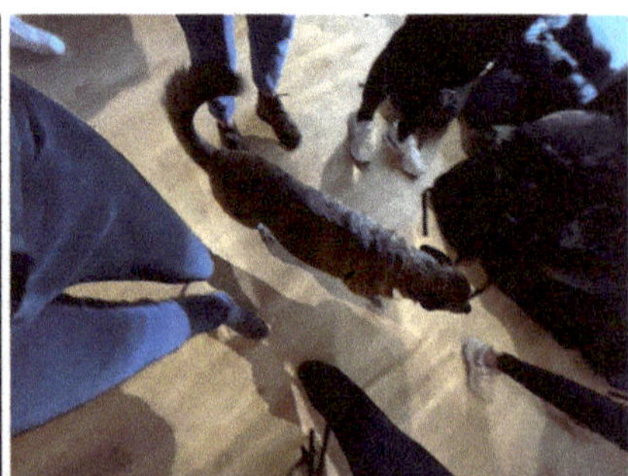

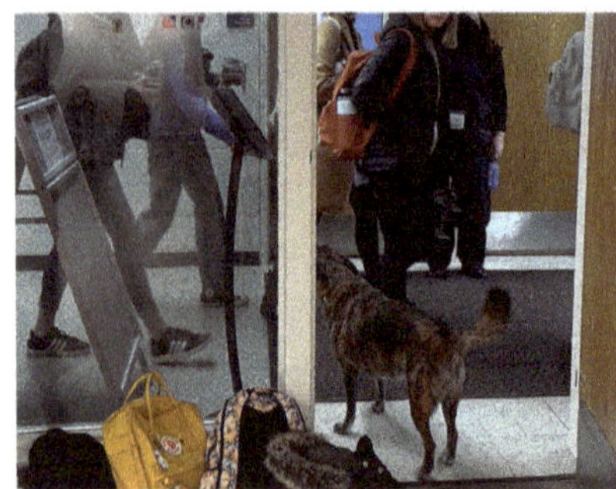

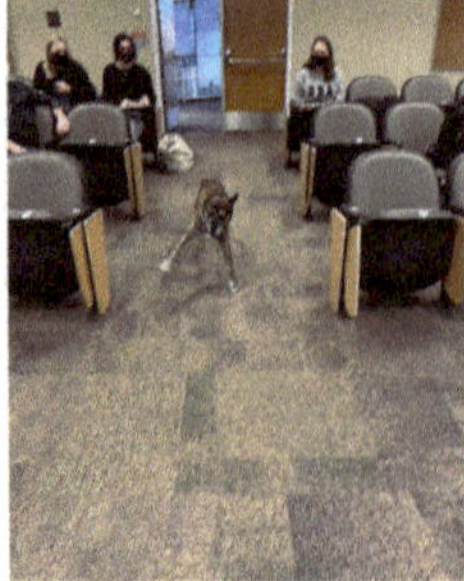

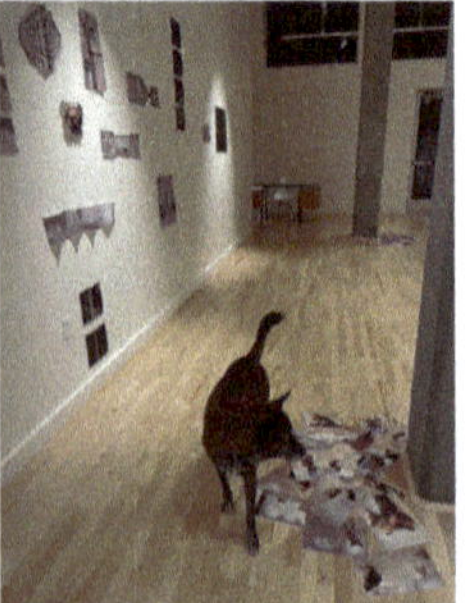

COMPOSITE 2.

Bartram+Deigaard, **draw | breath | animal**, exhibition of collaborative and sympathetic solo projects, Tippets and Eccles Galleries, Logan, Nov. 2021; Elvira, Deigaard's companion dog, was written into the visiting artist contract as a collaborator and artist. Bartram+Deigaard ensured that, as an artist, contractually she was never leashed in the gallery (although she had to be beyond its walls) and was therefore free to interact and assign herself roles during installation of work and artist lectures; documentation of her responsive and curious interactions yielded new, on-site work conceived from her choices, presence and participation.

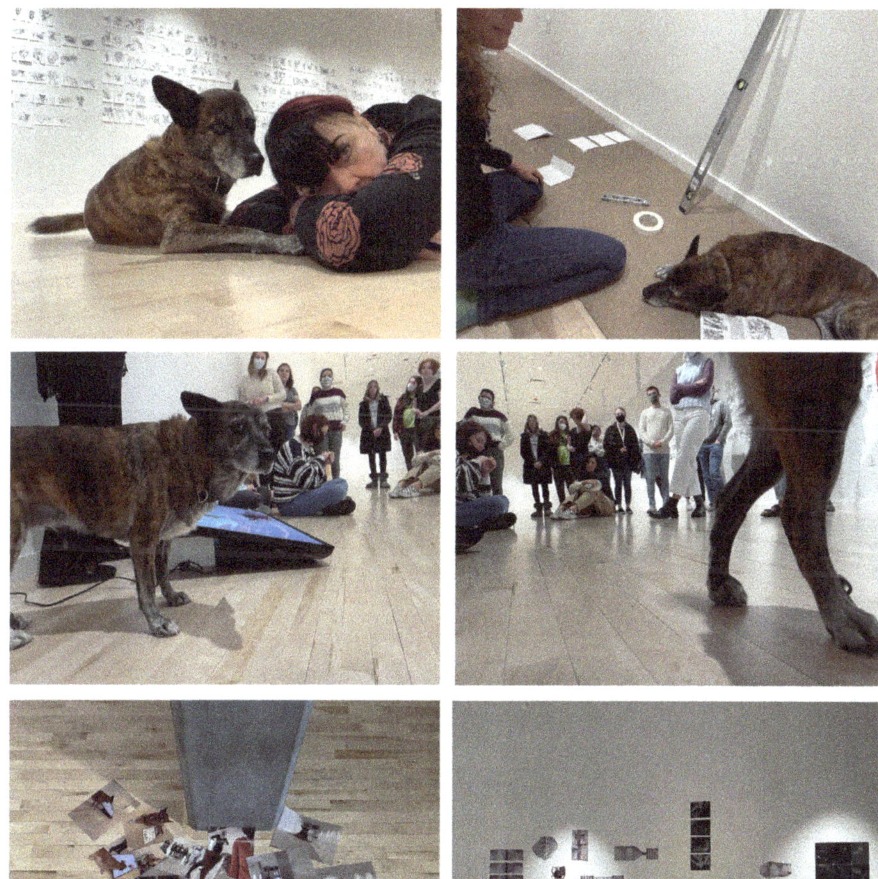

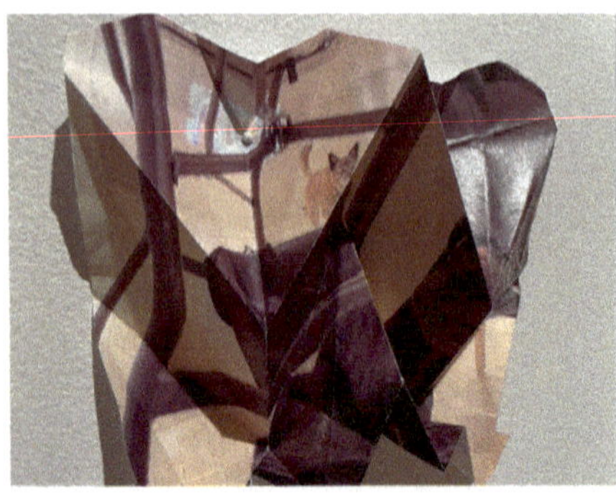

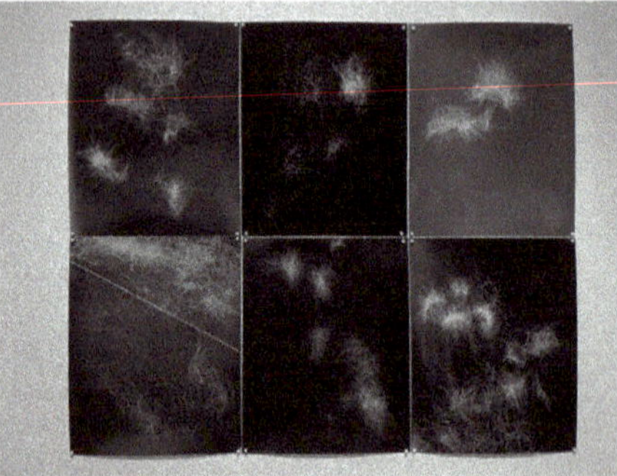

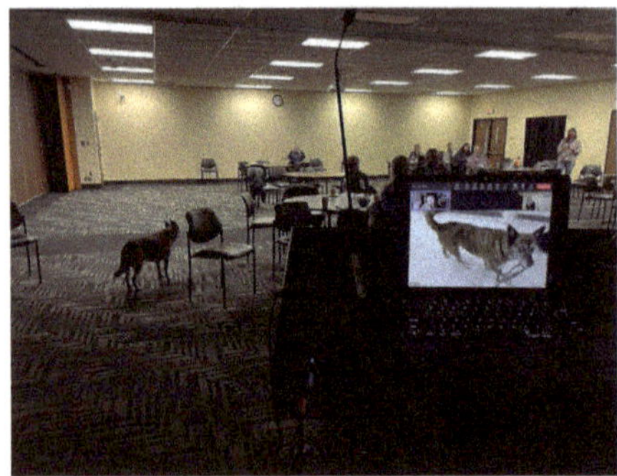

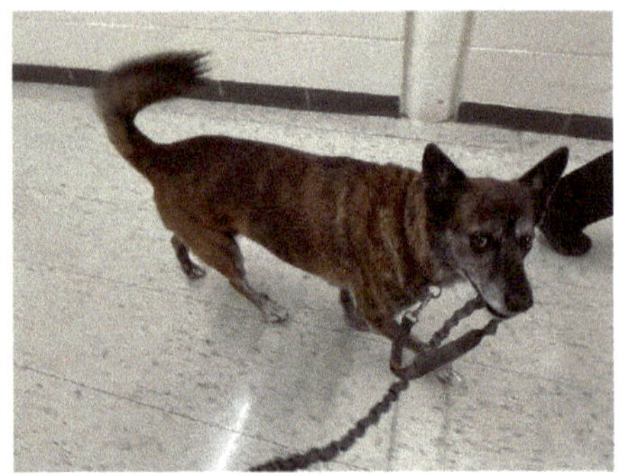

COMPOSITE 3.

For Elvira and her contractually permitted presence, this included her being in the darkroom for the making of new photograms using hair [hers and Bartram+Deigaard's] swept from the gallery floor. Prints of her investigations within the gallery and its adjacent spaces [creative and transitional, such as art studios and hallways] were positioned and exhibited on the gallery floor to mirror the placing of the video monitor for *Be Your Dog*. Accordion and pleated book dummies drawing from her presence are examples of iterative and aggregative processes in co-creative spaces as documentation and opportunities enabling further engagement that were created on-site and exhibited within the gallery. *Be Your Dog* and *Gus and Deuce Go Elsewhere* were part of this exhibition. Elvira was also present in the lecture hall at the subsequent *Living with Animals* conference in 2023, Eastern Kentucky University, where Bartram + Deigaard presented findings from their Tippets and Eccles Galleries residency. In the final image above, also visible on the presentation screen to its left, Elvira takes charge of the required leash in the hallway of the building. That she acted freely and to her own purposes and alliances in spaces normally closed to animals [but where animals were being discussed] is both provocation and establishment of creative equality.

Co-learning, *co-investigation; shared leadership, shared initiative, shared curiosity; shared agency, shared access, free movement; diverse forms of hearing | listening | understanding; not oriented to human sensibility, desire, expectation*

The B+D method invites all participants into a process of co-investigation, and assumes that each can take a share of leadership and initiative as events unfold. This approach is grounded in a learned awareness that all forms of consciousness feel and express curiosity, though their vocabularies and means of communication may differ. We have designed projects and situations in which agency – and any decision making around content and meaning – is shared without ranking or priority among participants. This necessitates shared access to project resources, including space for free movement and for mechanisms which allow all co-investigators to be seen and heard as they explore. For success, this method requires the cultivation of diverse forms of hearing, listening and understanding which are not oriented exclusively – or, perhaps, at all – to human sensibilities, desires and expectations. The way we approach our collaborative work asks human participants to interrogate these habits and presuppositions to pool multi-species creative abilities in more dynamic ways. This acknowledges that the animal may also be doing this themselves but, to avoid coercive or intrusive measures, we use intuition, observation and sensing only, and not externally determinable and quantifiable systems and measures. In the sense of artistic research, ours is a thinking-through process via methodological enquiry within a given context, whereby there is a placing of the research question into the interspecies debate within a cultural site and articulation of practice with respect and trust in all bodies. That is ethnographic as a working-through of trajectories of unbounded becoming. The exploring of creative synergies is mapped and detailed within cartographies of method and process to be reflective and observational of concomitant effects on those involved.

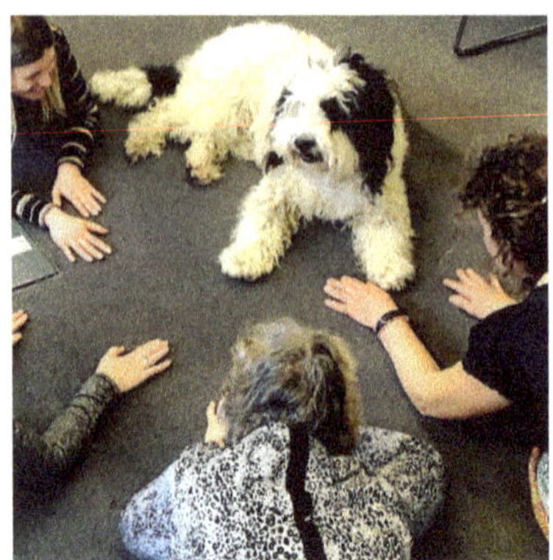

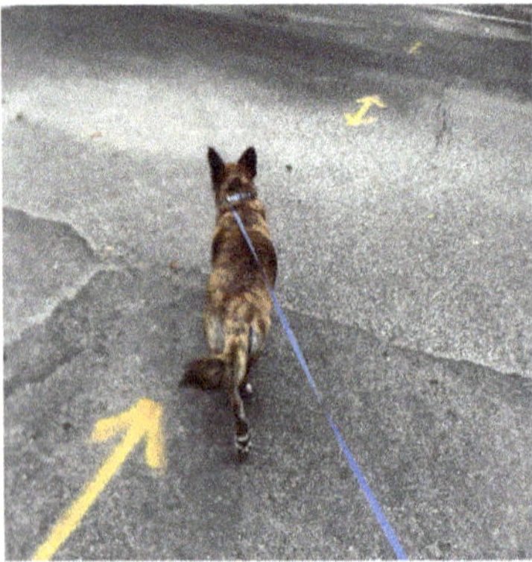

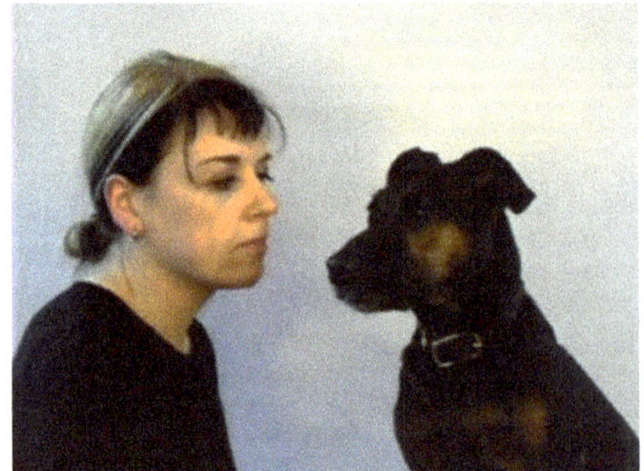

COMPOSITE 4.

Be Your Dog, Angela Bartram, workshop, Feminist Canine Ethnography Conference participants, Amsterdam, January 2020; Detail from *Vixen.Vector*, Lee Deigaard, 2016–17, a photographic installation depicting a former street dog who defies cartesian dualism and explores cartesian geometry in bodily expressive and deliberate alignments fluidly responsive to her changing environment. *Vixen.Vector* is drawn from the shared experiences of daily dog walks in which American leash laws require their use. It depicts Elvira's clever conversion of her tether into a hypotenuse or connecting vector; *Licking Dogs*, Angela Bartram, *2008*, a four-screen video installation shown across floor-based monitors, which aims to confront the role of danger and asks to which species does this display belong.

Choice, *trust, clear exit options; recognise all forms of implicit coercion or even benign expectation [try to minimise]; mutual legibility; working without harness or leashes*

The B+D method is predicated on the assumption that all participants will exercise choice with parity throughout the discovery and exchange process, irrespective of species derivation and any markers of difference. The method aims to not allow difference – in species, body and mind ability, class, gender, or race – to obstruct engagement. This implies, as with most social situations, a high degree of mutual trust. Both Deigaard and Bartram have benefited for decades from long-term relationships with animal teachers and companions. They often work with animals whom they know and are known by well. The choice to participate is open, and no coercion or regulation is enforced; if the animal is not interested then their lack of interest constitutes the manner of the collaboration. They enter and leave as they wish. The non-human participants, beginning generally at a disadvantage in their interactions with human projects, must be provided with ample agency and the option to quit the process at any point, just as humans would expect. Much of this operates in the background of purposeful explorations; it is an ongoing effort to recognise and address all forms of implicit coercion imposed (consciously and subconsciously) by humans onto non-humans. This approach strives towards conditions which foster mutual legibility, and it stems from a sense of mutual respect and embracing animality and full ranges of self-expression among animal collaborators. One way to externalise these intangibles is to adopt inclusive pronouns like 'we' and 'us' (which assert parity among co-investigators rather than division by species) and 'she/he' (which recognises individual agency within collective play). Central questions to ask include: does the animal want to be there? Do they feel trust and security? Do they have the freedom to leave and to decide the duration? How can processes and experiments build on precedent and iteration, which are implicit to growing familiarity and improvisation? By engaging with empathy and shared cognisance with animal collaborators, and in being sensitive to their needs and preferences, we are better able to instrumentally gauge their interest and comfort. We offer a way out by opening a literal and metaphorical door and, if this is wanted and accepted, then the moment of engagement ends. How to read (and respond to) animals' reactions is necessarily a subjective process, and this is where the artists' training by diverse animal companions, their extensive direct observation for many years and their related research into the sensory and emotional worlds of animals comes into play.

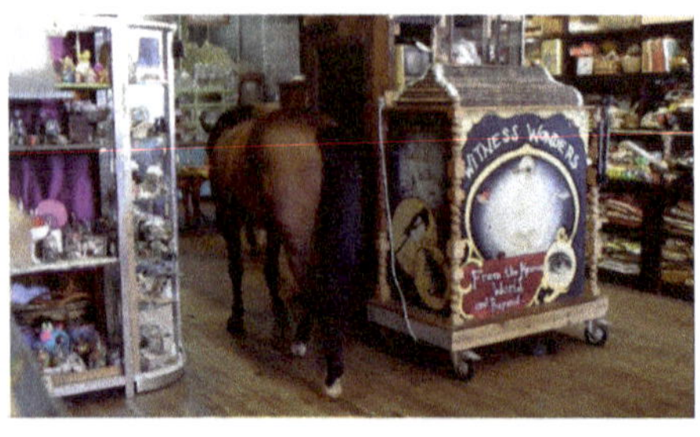

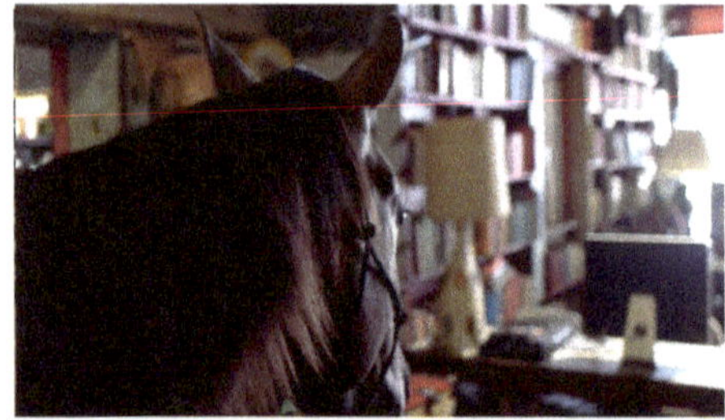

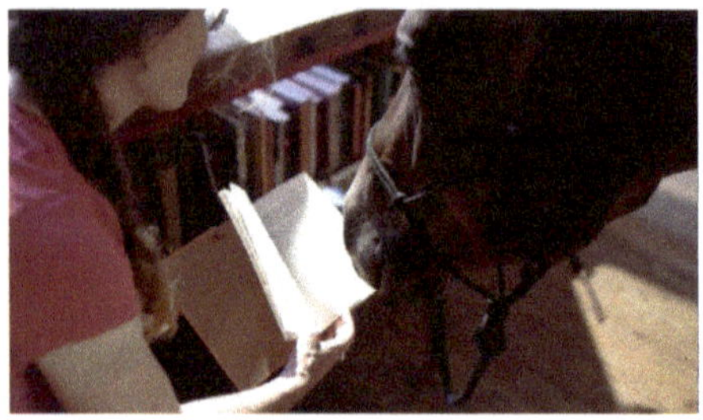

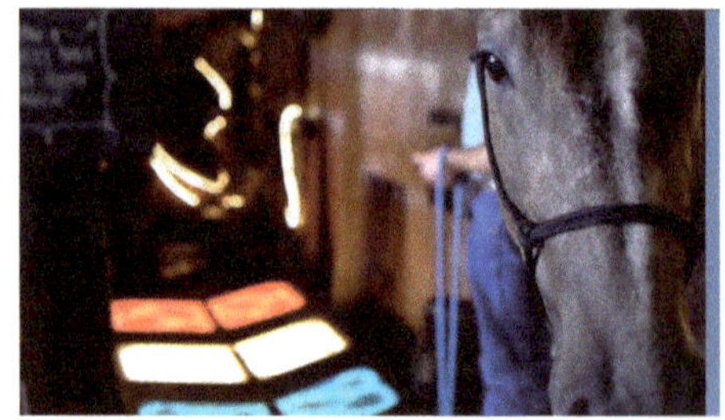

COMPOSITE 5.

Horses at the Museum: Gus and Deuce Go Elsewhere, Lee Deigaard, Greensboro, NC, Elsewhere Museum, 2014, composite [clockwise]: 'Witness Wonders', Deuce heads to the kitchen; Deuce in the library; Deuce and Deigaard among the books; Gus returns the camera's gaze after shooting pinball with human companion.

Key benefits of the B+D method:

Expansions *of experiential and creative bandwidth; builds connectivity and 'group genius';*[1] *learning new ways of hearing, seeing, inhabiting, new durations while abiding in states of possibility not previously envisioned; openness and receptivity to the sensory world and differing sensitivities of perception, leading with the body, not mind, for processes of exploration and cognition; to 'embody' research*

Our methodology is not formulaic, and therefore calls for a lot of improvisation on the part of participants at every stage of implementation. It is, at the same time, by nature flexible, scalable and idiosyncratic. The benefits it generates are not determined in terms of tangible outputs or static findings. Rather, they are felt directly by participants in the form of heightened and shared experience. Experiential and creative bandwidth expands as proprioceptive connections multiply and the scope of connectivity grows between co-investigators. In this regard, we learn often from non-human collaborators a heightened openness to our shared sensory environment, becoming observant and staying present and within the moment, being receptive and porous and patient. How to lead with the body when conducting research and letting the mind follow is a kind of embodied exploration linking cognition directly to the somatic processes involved with gathering information. When interaction among project participants becomes part of this gathering process, there can emerge a kind of 'group genius'.[2] This is a kind of creative space-making – understanding space to be physical, emotional and psychological – which precedes the undertaking of any investigation. In this way, our method is part of a lengthy artistic legacy of foregrounding the positive potential of nonconforming behaviours; creative investigation is a pathway to domains of convergent imagination in which non-human and human participants are invited to describe what is and what could be. This in turn promotes equity, and the cycle continues. Our approach seeks to assert conditions allowing co-investigators to abide in states of possibility not previously envisioned, and for all to emerge with broadened powers of perception.

1 '*Genius*' from Greek was internal, congenital 'tutelary spirit'.

2 K. Sawyer, *Group Genius: The Creative Power of Collaboration* (New York: Basic Books, 2007).

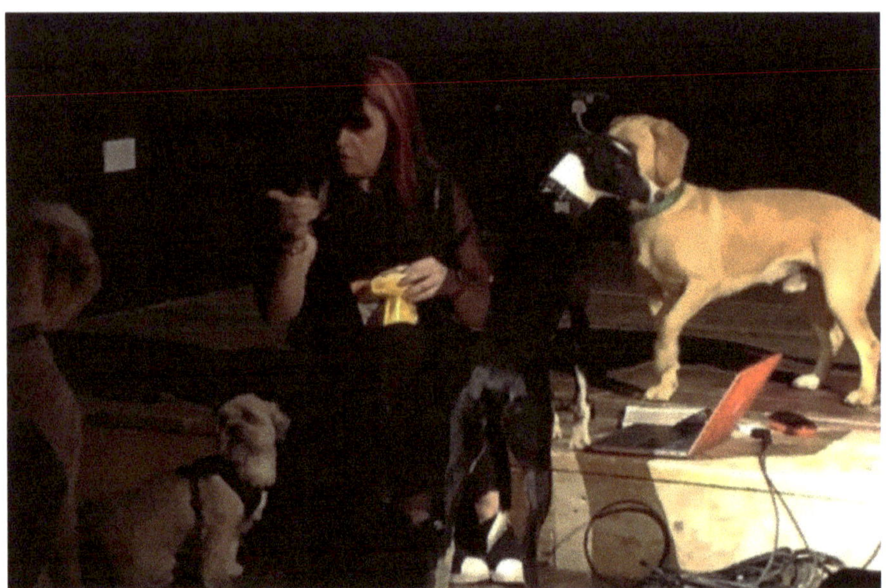

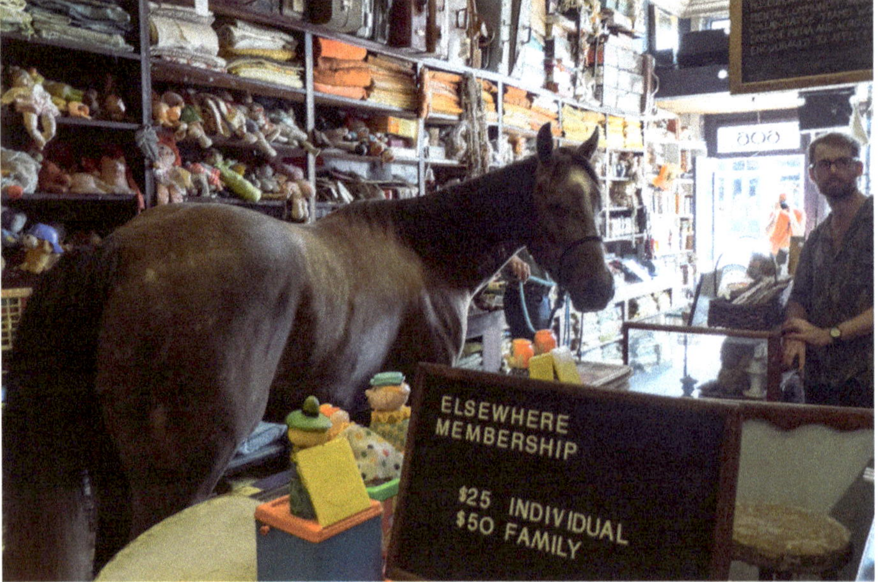

COMPOSITE 6.

Teaching an Old Dog New Tricks, Angela Bartram, Tempting Failure Festival, Croydon, UK, 2018; *Gus and Deuce Go Elsewhere*, Lee Deigaard, 2014, Gus departs the museum after lengthy exploration with his partner Deuce.

Co-discovery,[3] *reciprocal caretaking, checking, monitoring, protecting, ruminating within shared meditative space*

The risks and uncertainties that are bound up with the B+D method strongly suggest the need for a lot of trust and shared security. In the process of improvisational co-discovery, we find it useful to recall that the root of that word relates to notions of protection, defence, inclusion and a comprehending embrace. These are precisely the characteristics of the creative 'enclosure' which our method fosters. Within this exploratory space, there can be reciprocal caretaking, monitoring and constant adjustments (micro- and macro-) as circumstances evolve and co-investigators shift to meet them. It is especially important for non-human participants to feel safe and at ease, since many situations in which the work takes place (including barns and pastures but certainly within cultural spaces like museums and galleries) will be heavily imprinted by the shapes of assumptions of human primacy. Once a space of trust and inclusion is established, then the core work of simultaneous rumination and pooling of impressions may proceed within a shared, mutually-reinforcing meditative environment that is safe and comfortable. We ensure this process by being sensitive to the animals' needs and wants, noticing how and where they are comfortable and involved. We invite them to enter (if they choose), enjoy breaks (led by them), moments to disengage (led by them), and opportunities to leave (called for by them). What is learned or generated by that type of environment, after it is established, emerges non-deterministically according to the nature of the event. Hospitality and being welcoming is part of a shared etiquette within groups, herds and packs. From mutual respect arises freedom and a sense of comfort and play.

3 To *cover* being from Old French *covrir* 'to protect or defend from harm' also 'to include, embrace, comprehend' also 'enclose'... inherently ruminative, from *rumen* (genitive *ruminis*) 'gullet' and of course all animals who chew the cud: learning to THINK animals can teach how to think.

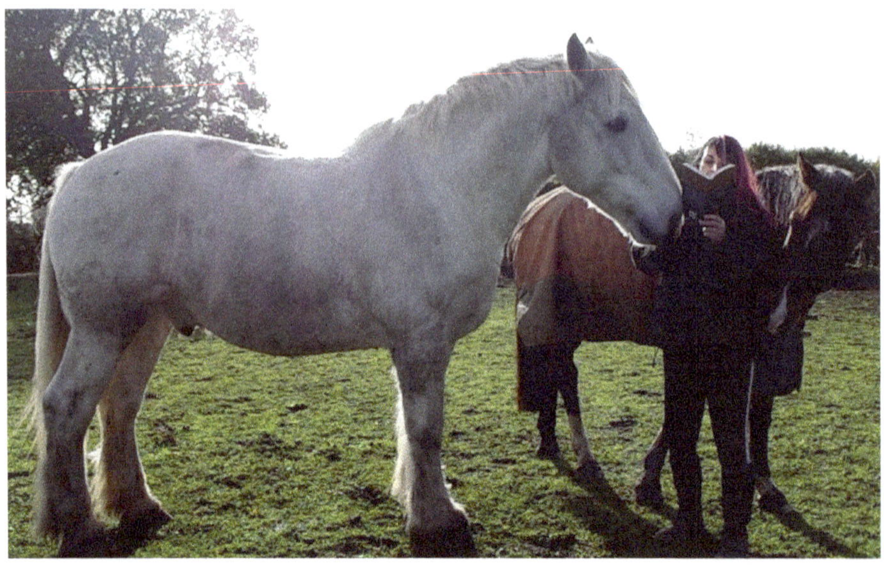

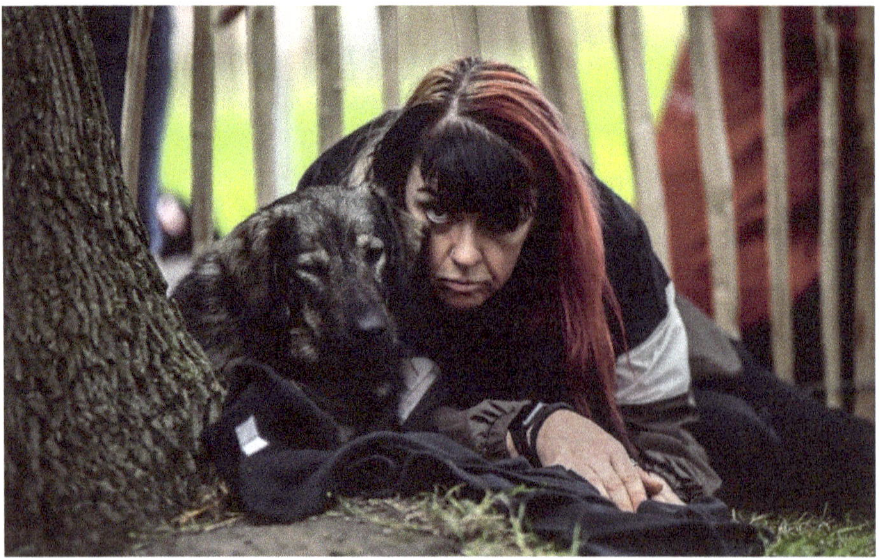

COMPOSITE 7.

Reading Animal Theory to the Animals – Horse, Angela Bartram, 2017–ongoing; Angela Bartram, *Human School [Be Your Dog]*, *Manchester International Festival, 2019.*

Erodes hierarchies *of knowledge, experience, vantage, sense, consciousness, sensibility, access, sequence, etc.; presents tangible, constructive critique of human privilege; breaking up the determinism of standard human cognition*

A central benefit of the B+D method is the systematic erosion of conventional hierarchies of knowledge, experience and sensibility. So durable and familiar is the anthropocentric approach to creative work, that while ethnographers have traditionally presumed that every human culture can and will pursue – under any conditions of climate, social structure, or material affluence – artistic activities which are intentional, they often formerly, and formally, did not recognise the overwhelmingly obvious and ubiquitous creative activities of non-human species, which, drawing from vastly diverse *umwelts* and life experiences, priorities and preoccupations, can only enrich our own. Our method overturns this pattern by assigning to all participants fully developed and rendered creative consciousnesses, forged by the experiences, insights, impressions and emotional associations unique to each of us. This approach allows the project to achieve internal parity while asserting a tangible, constructive critique of human privilege and the automatic preferencing of standard human cognition. These privileges have asphyxiated creative work long enough; this method presents an alternative that greatly multiplies both inputs and outputs in relation to a shared creative project. The B+D method considers which animals might enjoy novelty and an experimental experience. This means considering animal personality in posing the invitation and being responsive to their counter-offers and the questions they pose in turn. Bartram + Deigaard approach projects with ethical and mutual enrichment recognising that (not all but many) animals enjoy exploration, invention, sensory novelty and play with other animals, often including human animals.

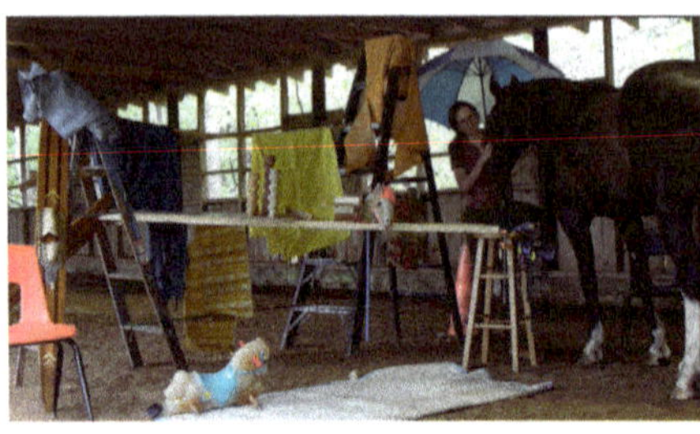
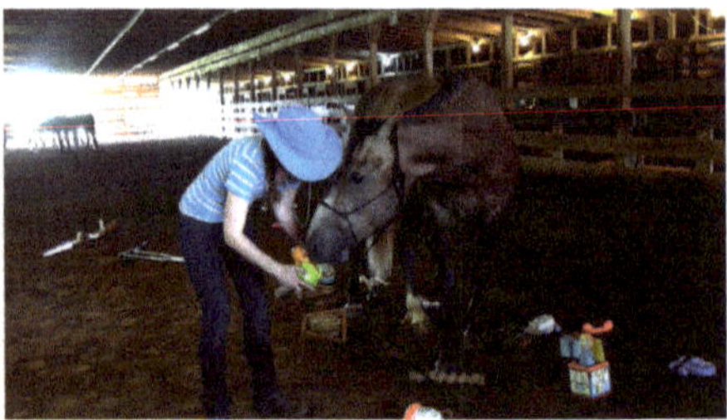

COMPOSITE 8.

Horses at the Museum: Field Trips, Lee Deigaard, Mason and Gus investigate items from the permanent collection in arenas where they are free to engage or withdraw according to their curiosity, North Carolina, 2014.

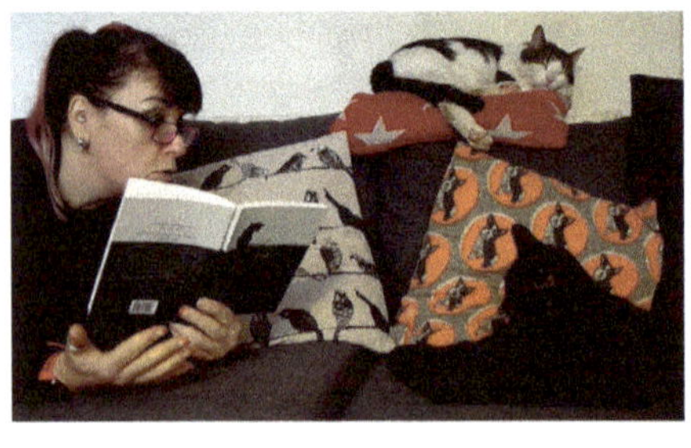
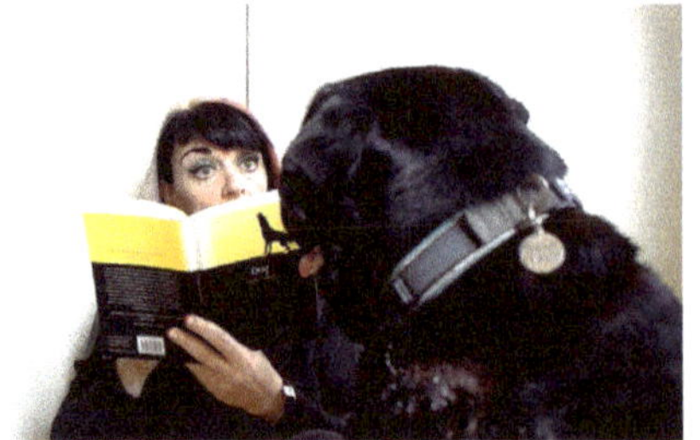

COMPOSITE 9.

Reading Animal Theory to the Animals – Cat and Dog, Angela Bartram 2017–ongoing. Bartram noted the absence of animals at conferences discussing animals and conceived of bringing animal studies to animals where they live. Like Deigaard's *Field Trips*, Bartram's reading (all animals free to engage or leave in both projects) draws animal curiosity and cultivates creative co-bonds derived from mutually enriching shared experiences. The engagement for the dog is sensed through their willingness to listen and passages are read or stopped in response to their perceived interest.

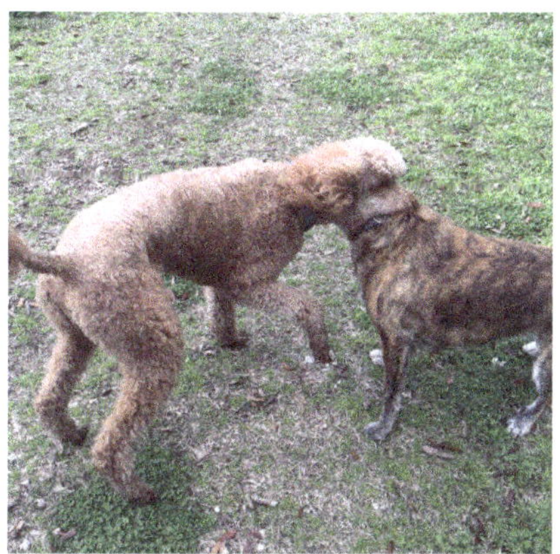

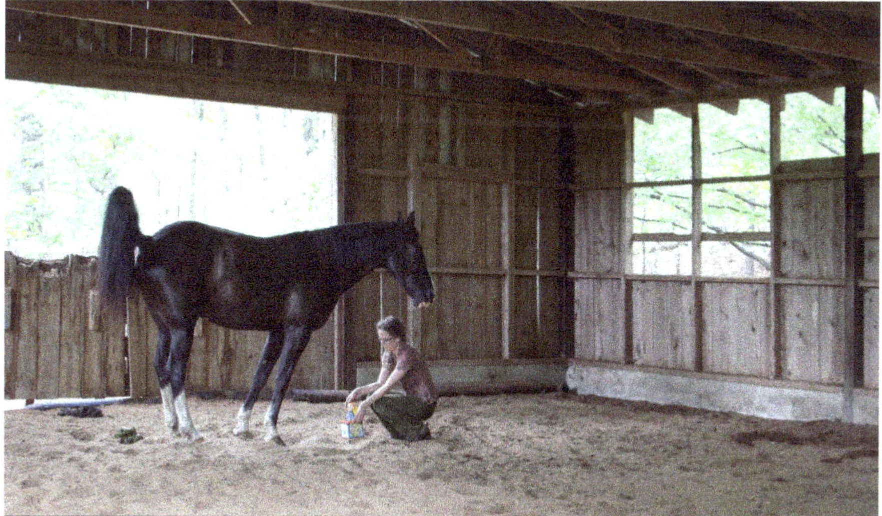

COMPOSITE 10.

Vixen.Vector, Lee Deigaard, 2013–17, example of inventive improvisation by canine play partners in a revelatory (and characteristic to their qualities of play) optical illusion; *Horses at the Museum: Field Trips*, Lee Deigaard, 2014. Bartram+Deigaard foreground the animal being freely themselves in all collaborative spaces. Sometimes, project imagery may suggest to a human viewer a humorous reading of an animal's action as a specific referendum on a project or novel object. All proximity to animals is inherently creative and generative and recognised by the artists as immense pleasure and an abiding privilege.

ARTNOGRAPHIC STATEMENT

As artistic creative researchers, we act responsively and idiosyncratically according to our animal (non-human predominantly and very occasionally human) collaborators' wants and preferences, both in siting (and citing) our work and its adaptive structure and reason for existence. The result is never preordained, as individual agency is embedded as a reason and means by which improvisation becomes situated as collaborative. An intersection of species and bodies that is co-created encourages optimal interest and engagement.

Non-human animals pose hypotheses and theorems just as the humans do and occupy, too, the position of artist. Our artwork arises from long-term relationships with non-human animals we have each conducted intimately and domestically for over thirty years, benefiting from our companions' teaching and reciprocal care of us and, most specifically, their demonstrated curiosity within environments and relationships in which they feel secure. These histories are part of our inter- and multispecies ethnographic journey leading to the collaboration that is Bartram+Deigaard. Our methods, whereby we are responsive to the daily and the durational, to animal knowledge and sensitivities far surpassing ours, were developed cooperatively with non-humans we know and who know us, who engage with us and we with them. Artistic creative research has only relatively recently considered our kind of fieldwork (predating much of any literature on the subject). We are often working (and have been working) beyond the literature in practices informing critical references, presenting exhibitions and events. We have also been delivering presentations at multidisciplinary international animal studies conferences since its inception as a discipline. As artistic research, ours is a thinking-through via methodological enquiry within a given context – placing the research question into the interspecies debate within cultural sites and articulations of practice. That is ethnographic as a working-through of trajectories of unbounded becoming. The exploring of creative synergies is mapped and detailed within cartographies of method and process to be reflective and observational of concomitant effects on those involved.

How we include non-human animals in cultural spaces, as artists, features in the explorations we discuss here. Some animals are curious about where we go when we enter doors otherwise closed to them; others choose to observe while still others run freely, marking the interiority of the cultural site or place counter to expectation. Through the interspecies intersection, its participating bodies, the space and the encounter become fertile. Working improvisationally and responsively means being alert to interest demonstrated through voluntary participation. Their meaningful ways to contribute (and preemptively hijack, we hope) any latent ideas of design or hoped-for outcome informs the mechanics of the collaboration. We propose the value of practice to challenge normative rules of engagement and process from critical references informing research to what and who goes into a gallery. We embrace classical views of failure as successful outcomes through our commitment to reciprocal and non-hierarchical values.

6. ATTENDING TO FIREBUGS: ARTISTIC INVESTIGATIONS FOR RESPECTFUL CORRESPONDENCES

Charlotte Dorn

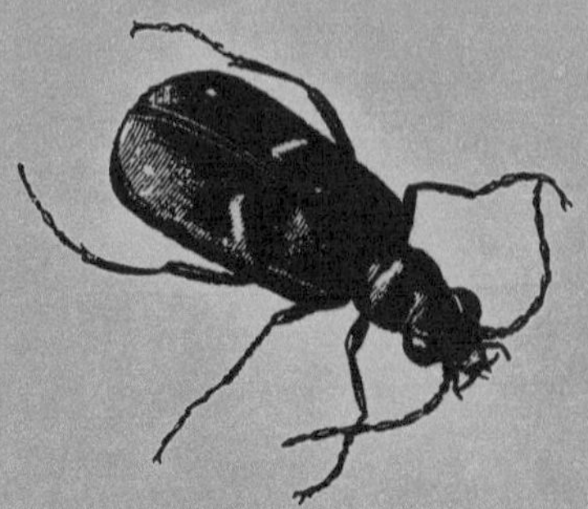

DOI: 10.63308/63878687083054.ch06

PHOTO ESSAY

It is a warm, sunny August day in the countryside of West Germany. Firebugs enjoy sunbathing and gather in warm spots with food in the form of nuts or fruits, so I am tracking down the insects by walking around potential meeting spots around the village (Wels, 2020; Morizot, 2020). Soon, a colony of firebugs that live around a lime tree outside of the village of Wittersheim in Saarland is discovered. This group will be observed and registered in the following weeks, so, carefully placing my steps to avoid crushing one of these tiny beings, I find an observation point in the grass near the lime tree.

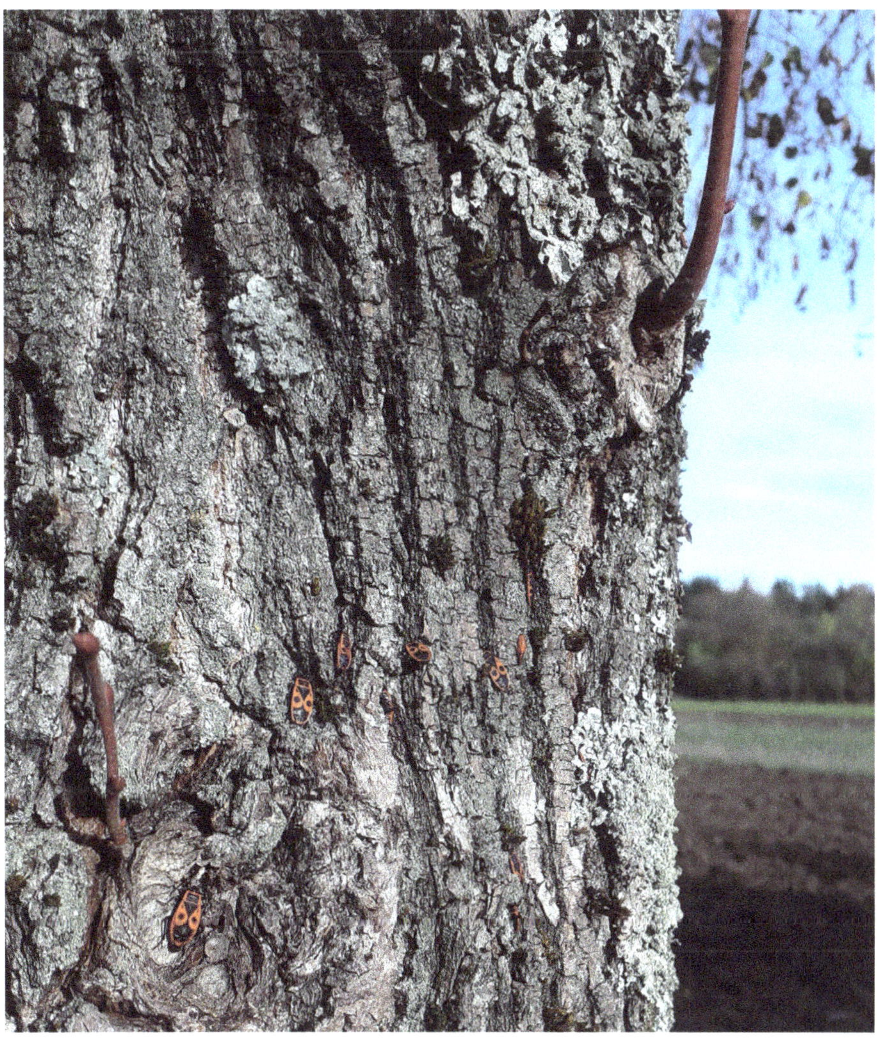

When engaging in fieldwork, firstly there needs to be focused attention on the observed, to perceive the atmosphere; then an aim for the day can be fixed and method of engagement chosen. Observing firebugs during the first days, the eyes were not habituated to focus on such tiny forms and it was hard to grasp these beings because of their small size and fast, sudden movements. The aim was to get to know their bodies and the possibility to enlarge photographs and film movement sequences suited this objective. After having gathered more information about the firebug's body shape and getting used to their behaviour, life drawing, drawing from pictures and also sound recordings were used to diversify and intensify the relation with these beings.

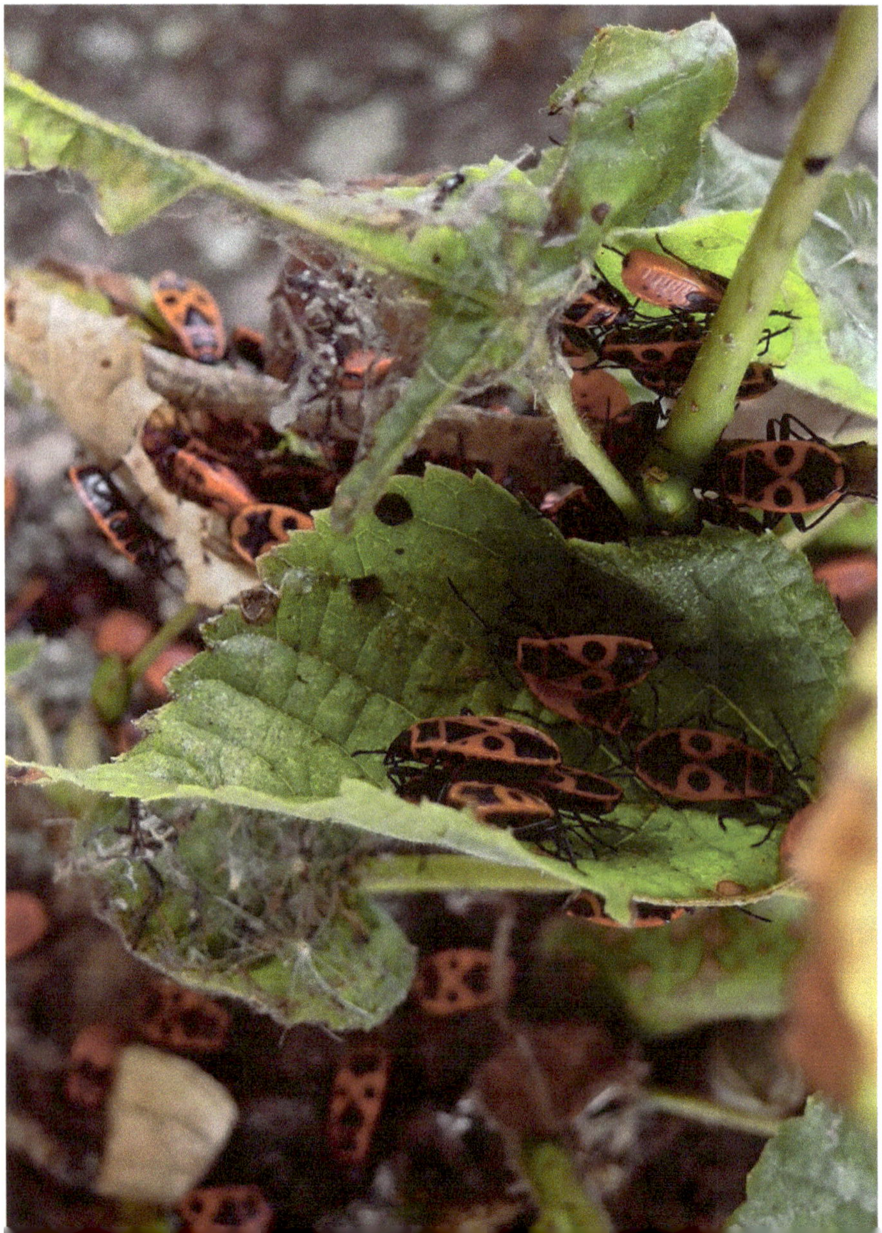

Attending to firebugs

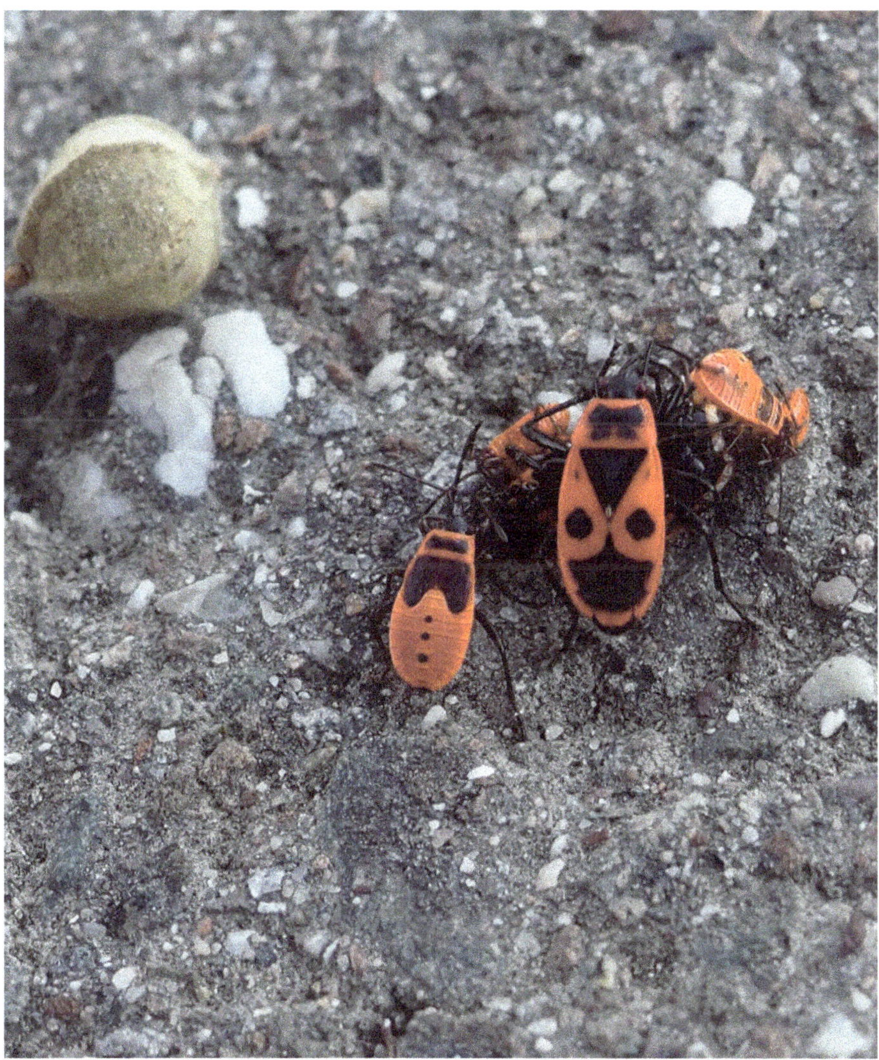

The reason for using situation-specific, varying artistic methods is to have a multi-layered view on the observed animal. Believing in a relational existence (Barad, 2007; Bennett, 2009) and the importance of trying to listen to the research subject, the method is chosen once in contact with the firebug. To have a more rigid protocol would make it impossible to engage with these beings with the greatest possible openness. This trust in intuition when choosing a medium of registration has developed through a shifting research subject from sheep to firebug. The first year of my Ph.D. was dedicated to observing three sheep in an animal sanctuary in Saarbrücken, Germany. Shifting the focus from a farmed animal and mammal to a wild insect, I realised the importance of being sensitive to the specificities of species, beings and their environment when in the field, and to adapt.

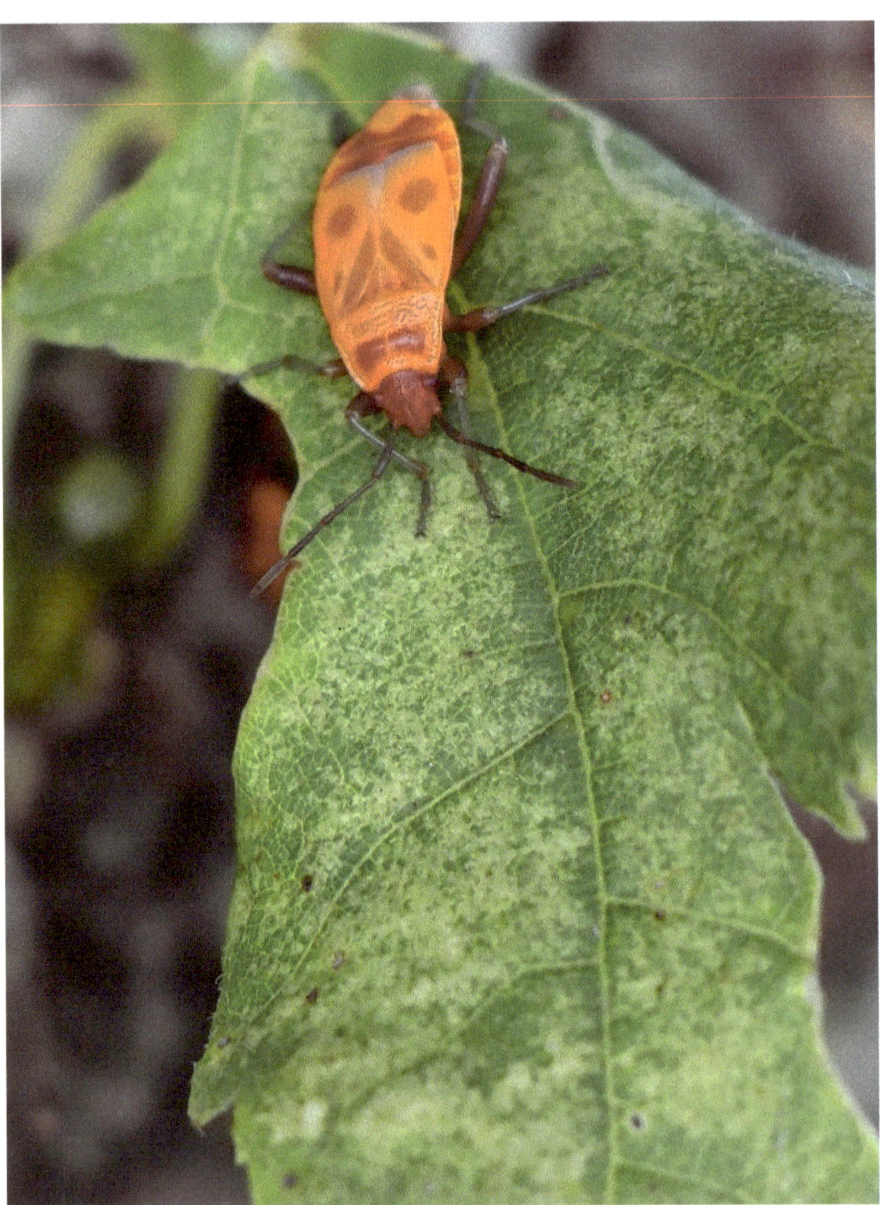

When photographing, the aim is to capture the firebug's body and take a closer look by zooming in the picture, to register firebug activities, such as eating or moulting and to capture the animal within its living environment. The purpose of filming is gathering information about the firebugs' way of moving and sound recordings register sounds made by the animals and their environment.

Attending to firebugs

Drawing requires longer attention spans in which the form of the firebug must be grasped and reproduced, implying the risk that lines and shapes may be interrupted by the firebug's movements. It shows the artist's dependence on the subject and the agency of other-than-human life, combining to 'reconceive reality as a "subject-subject continuum" instead of a "subject-object dualism"' (Freya Mathews, cited by Donovan, 2016: 79). The physical effort and concentration required to perceive and reproduce create intense moments of engagement and intimacy with the other, referring to Willa Cather's aesthetics of care, where the artist 'must thus be personally and emotionally immersed in a conversation with the world she transcribes' (Donovan, 2016: 56).

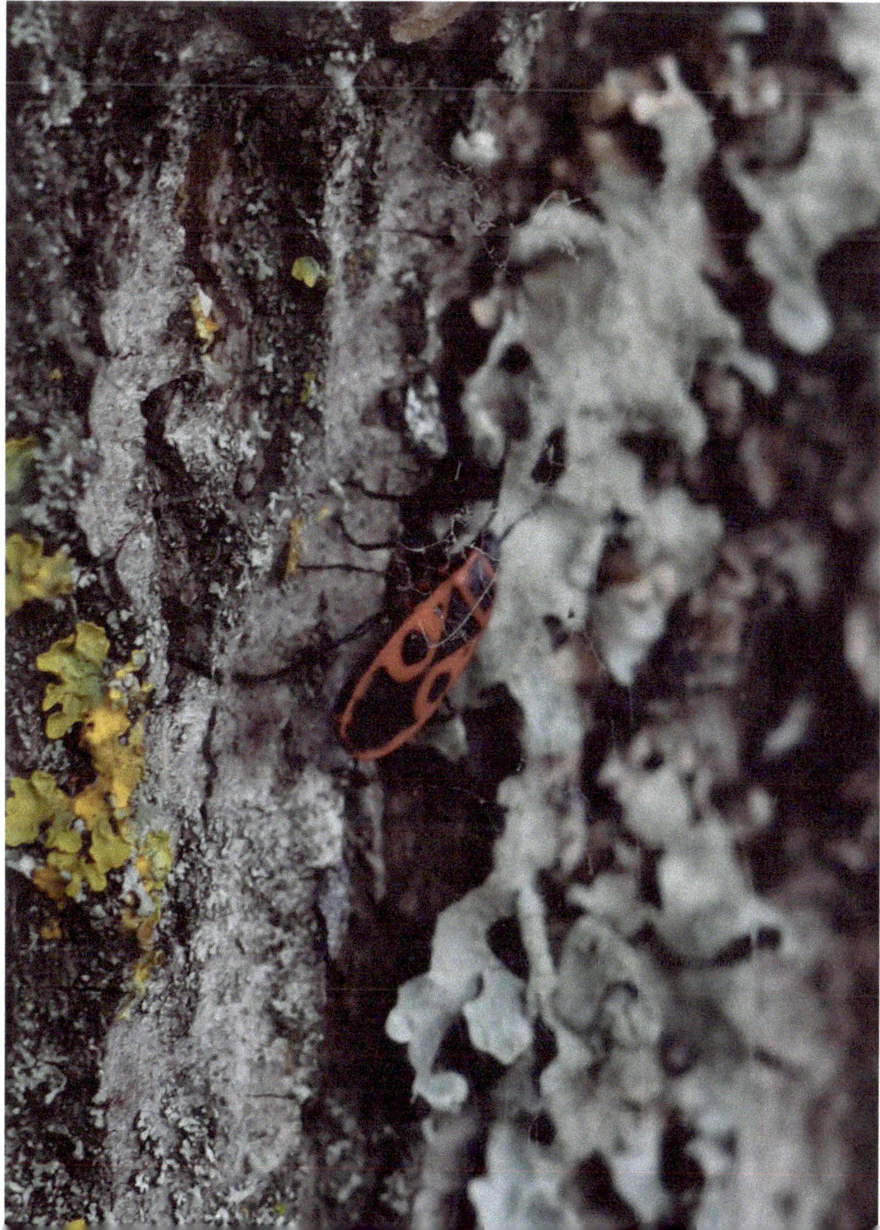

Throughout the summer months, firebugs can be observed in wide areas of Europe, whereas during the colder periods of the year they hibernate in the earth or tree cracks. Throughout their one-year growth process, the animals moult five times. Shortly after the moulting, their body is coloured in orange and red tones which then transform in the black and red pattern. In September, the firebugs slowly start to disappear for hibernation and I as well withdraw into the atelier to process the information gathered during fieldwork. The choice to work on the firebug in the first place is explained by wanting to engage with a species that is mostly overlooked or encountered with discomfort and disgust, little overlaid by symbolic meanings, trackable without technical instruments and sharing spaces with humans, without being domesticated.

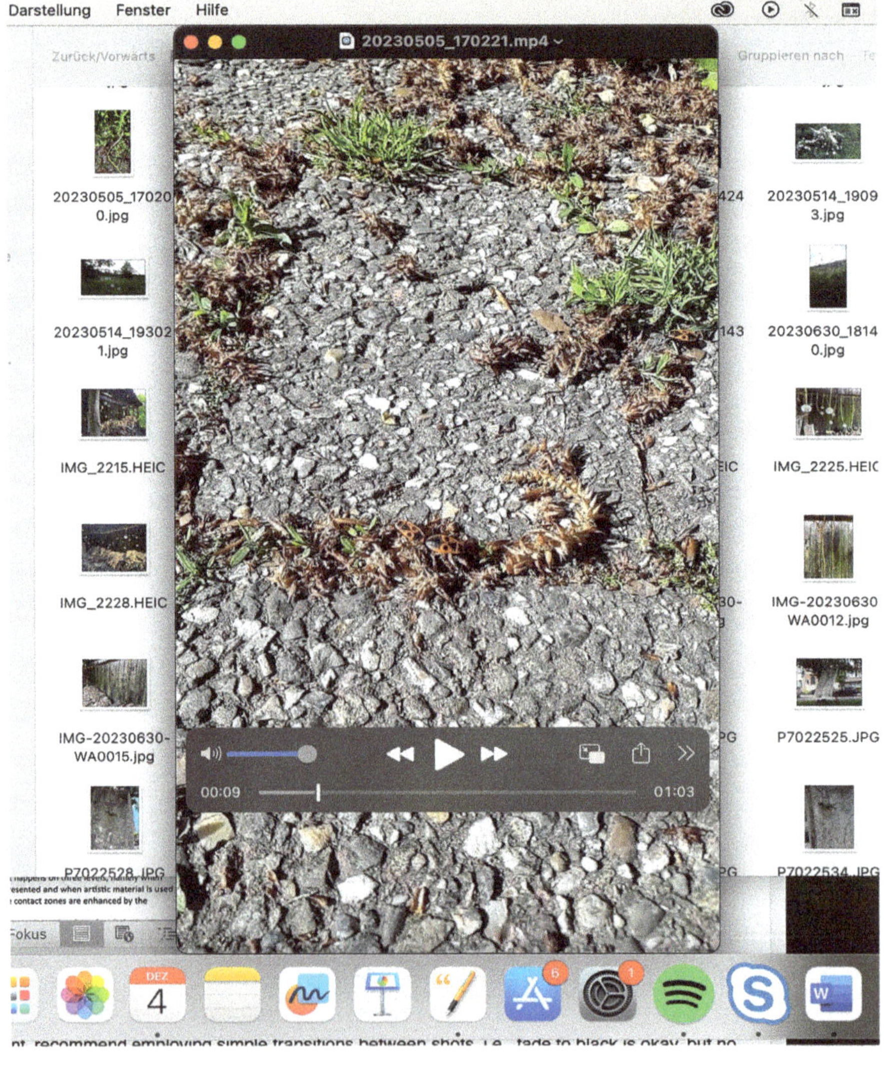

Attending to firebugs

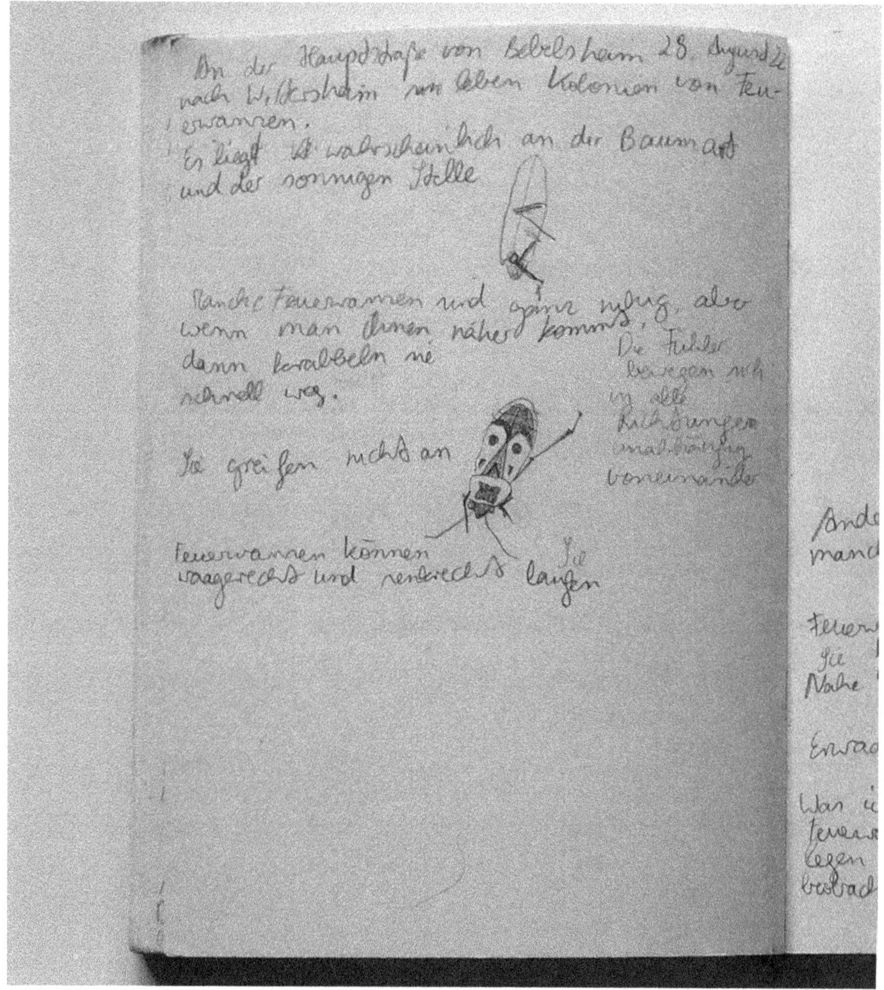

Compassion is a concept that frames the engagement with firebugs as well as the creative process. In *Cognitive Based Compassion Training* [*CBCT*] it is defined as a warm-hearted concern that unfolds when we witness the suffering of others and feel motivated to relieve it [Tenzin Negi, 2021: 18]. It distracts from self-centredness and puts the focus on the other who is valued and respected [Karen Armstrong, Charter of Compassion]. Compassion training is relevant to the research because it formulates a way to learn to be more sensitive and attentive to one's surroundings. This skill is interesting as a more sensitive handling of artistic material can lead to better artworks. Also, when critiquing existing power relations, a compassionate handling of artistic material is important so as to not reproduce criticised power-relations within the creative process.

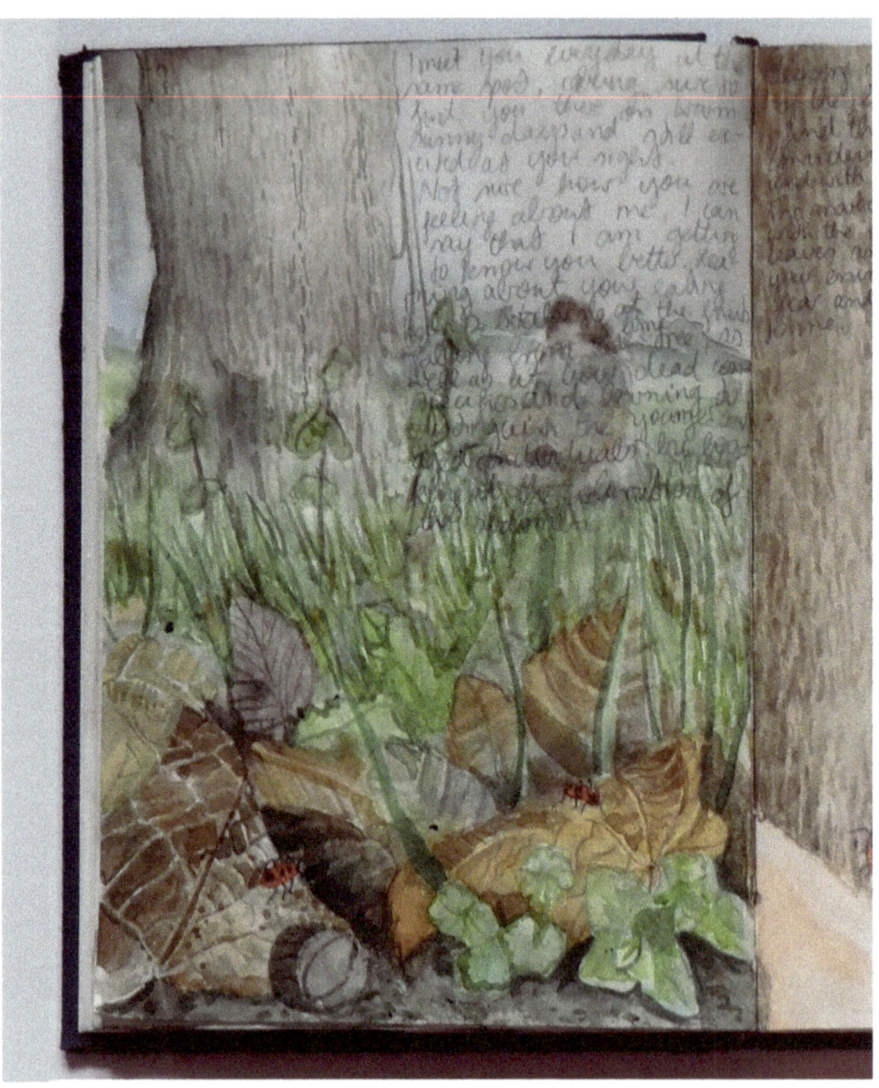

As the project investigates the human-animal relationship in art and aims for greater animal welfare, the contact with other-than-human animals should be analysed. This happens on three levels, namely when animals are observed during fieldwork, when animals are represented and when artistic material is used in whose creation process a variety of beings are involved. These contact zones are enhanced by the integration of compassion training. An important aspect of *CBCT* is that, in order to strengthen compassion, a number of underlying mental stages should be cultivated. These include being able to create and maintain a sense of safety and security within oneself; the awareness of one's own thoughts and feelings; and critical self-reflection.

Attending to firebugs

There are parallels between a mental stage necessary to become creative and foundational elements of compassion training. In moments of calmness, ideas emerge. It should be said, though, that there are many engines of creative work that do not necessarily require inner peace, but also arise from emotional or other turmoil. In moments of calm before the creative work, however, I make more conscious decisions towards the material and the depicted than when becoming creative out of an inner unrest. Therefore, in order to be able to shift towards a more concerned artistic practice, I exercise to be in a more calm and aware state of mind.

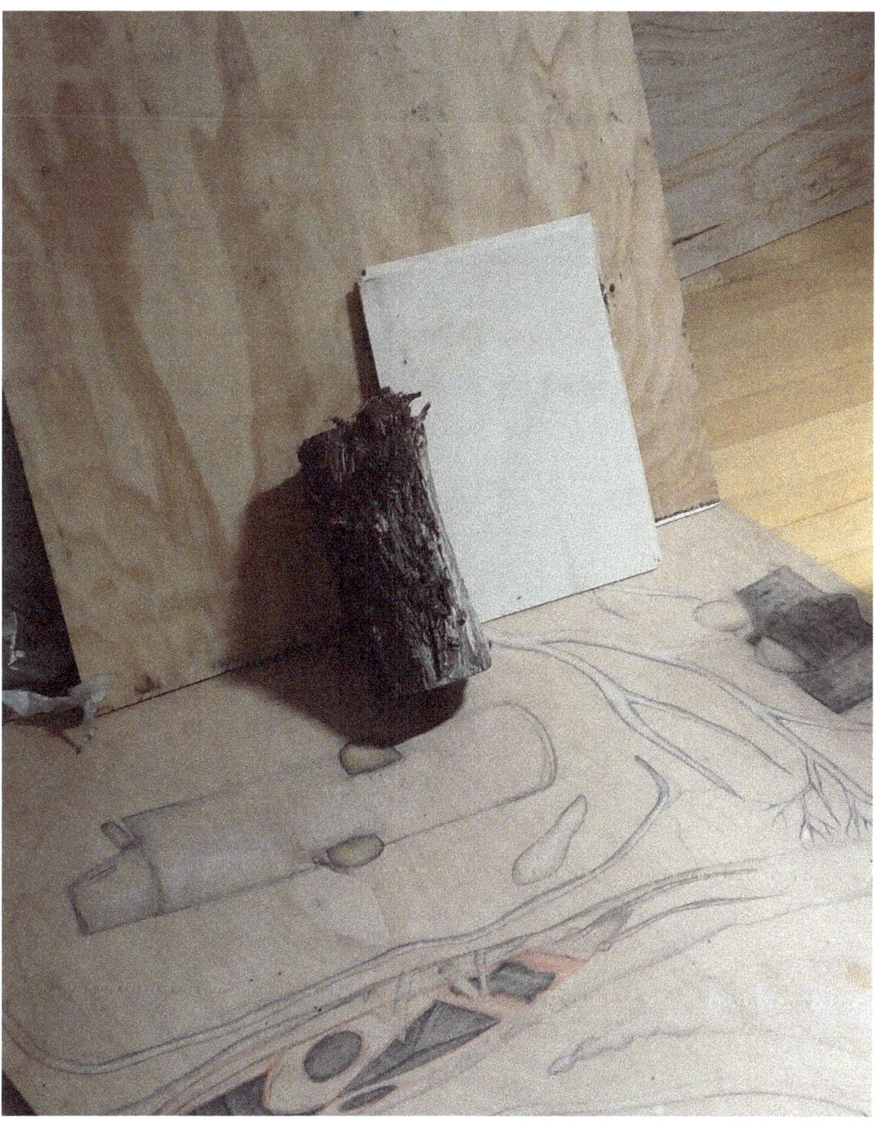

The fieldwork observations are further processed by speculating (Despret, 2016; Haraway, 2016) about what the animals might be doing. When considering how a particular situation comes into being, one must take into account the consequences as well as the underlying elements. This connection between thought and empirical limits constitutes speculative thinking, as in a speculation something given is observed and also questioned. It is a method of inquiring what a situation is composed of, how its different elements relate and matter and where the situation might lead. (Hendrickx, 2017) Donna Haraway describes `speculative fabulation´ (Haraway, 2016: 2) as a method of tracking lived experiences and getting involved with others to see a situation from a perspective that leads to greater multispecies justice. The research implements the concept of speculation to create images of firebugs.

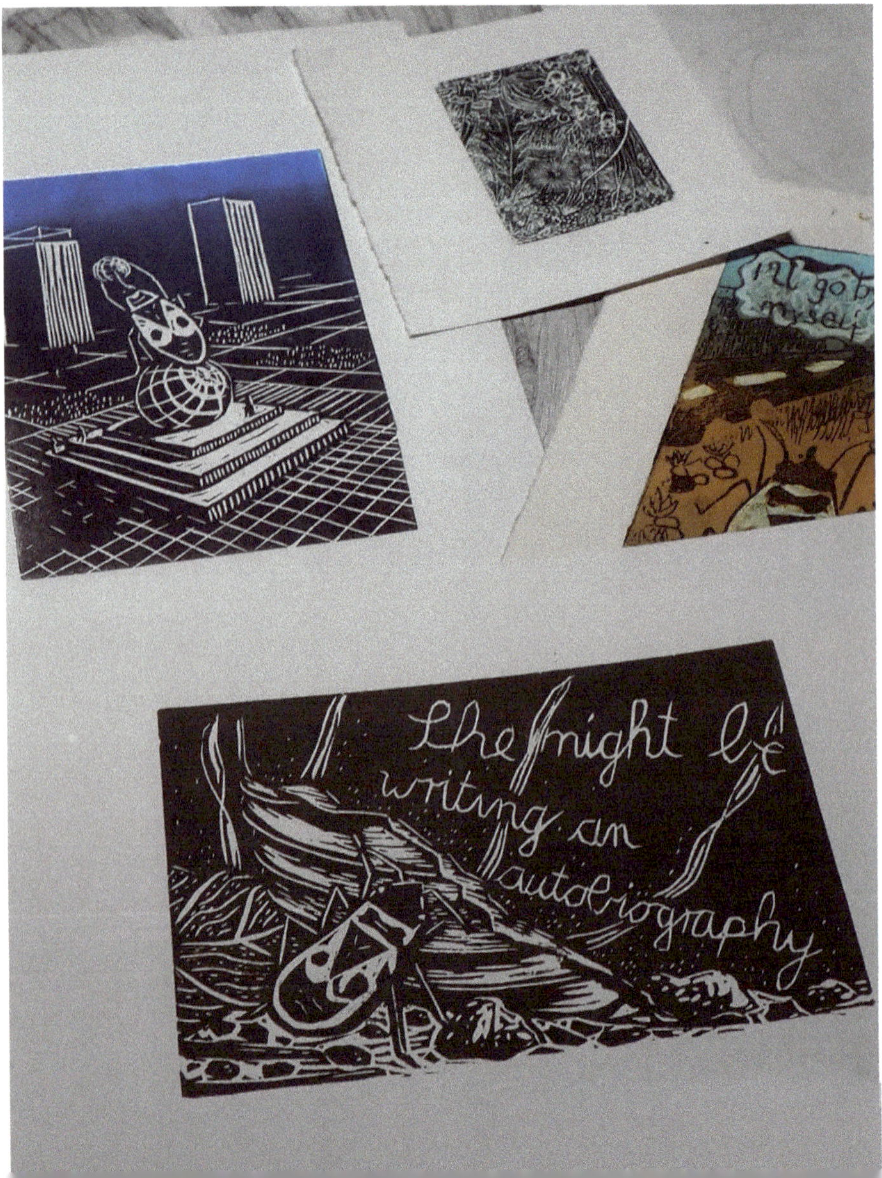

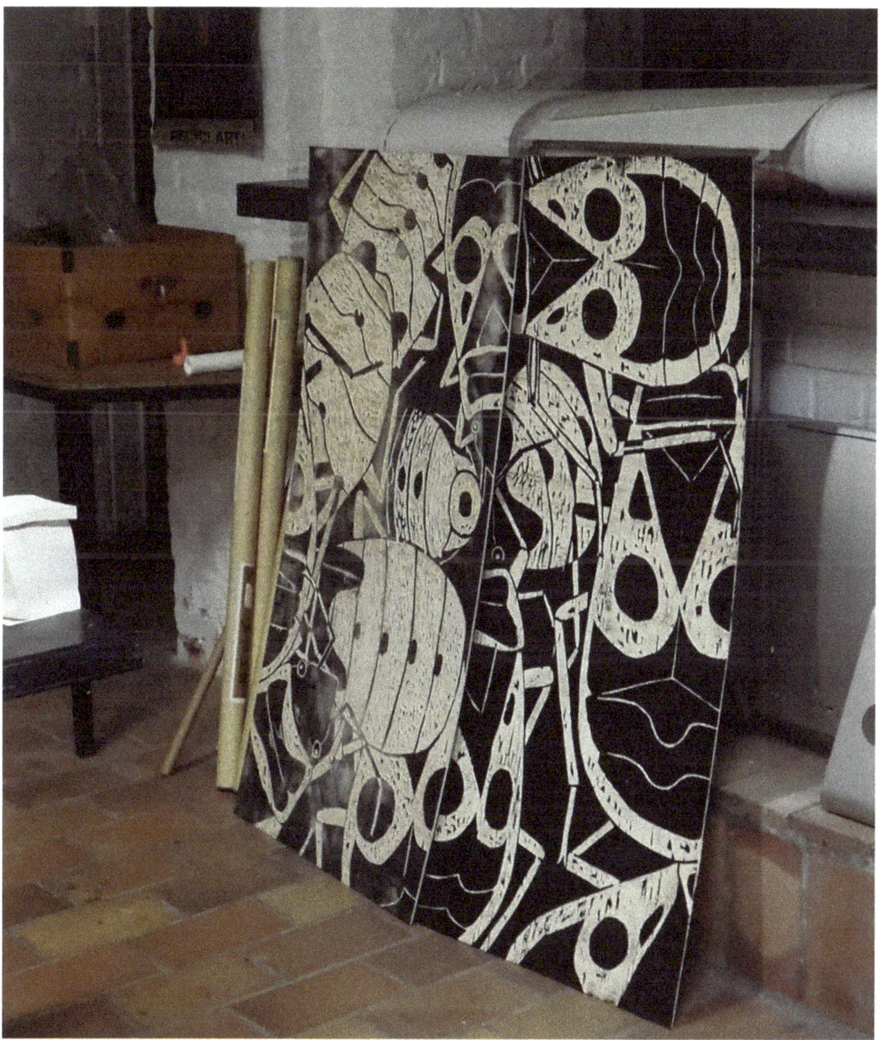

The ideas on firebugs and multispecies worlds are further developed and rendered tangible through drawing as well as wood- and linocut. This intense relationship between a human and something non-human in the printing process creates tacit knowledge (Polanyi, 1966) on human-other-than-human relationships and trains to trust the senses when engaging with something that doesn't speak human language. Furthermore, the wood is a way to connect with the more-than-human world. Its grain tells stories that are brought to paper and disseminated. Tracing how the original tree is processed into wooden boards and paper that is used for the printing process helps being aware of the interrelatedness of existence. The process of printmaking goes from a printing ground to diverse prints and symbolises the concept of a common ground from where diversity arises.

The slowness of the creative process gives space to let the fieldwork experience with firebugs sink in and to come back to it over and over again. The physicality of the printing process further serves as a connecting point between my body, the artistic material and the research subjects. Also, woodcut is a non-toxic printing technique and appropriate for bigger formats. From a viewer's standpoint, artworks touch various sensorial stimuli and provide multi-layered, sensitive connections with the art piece, which in itself is something other-than-human, but also other non-human existences.

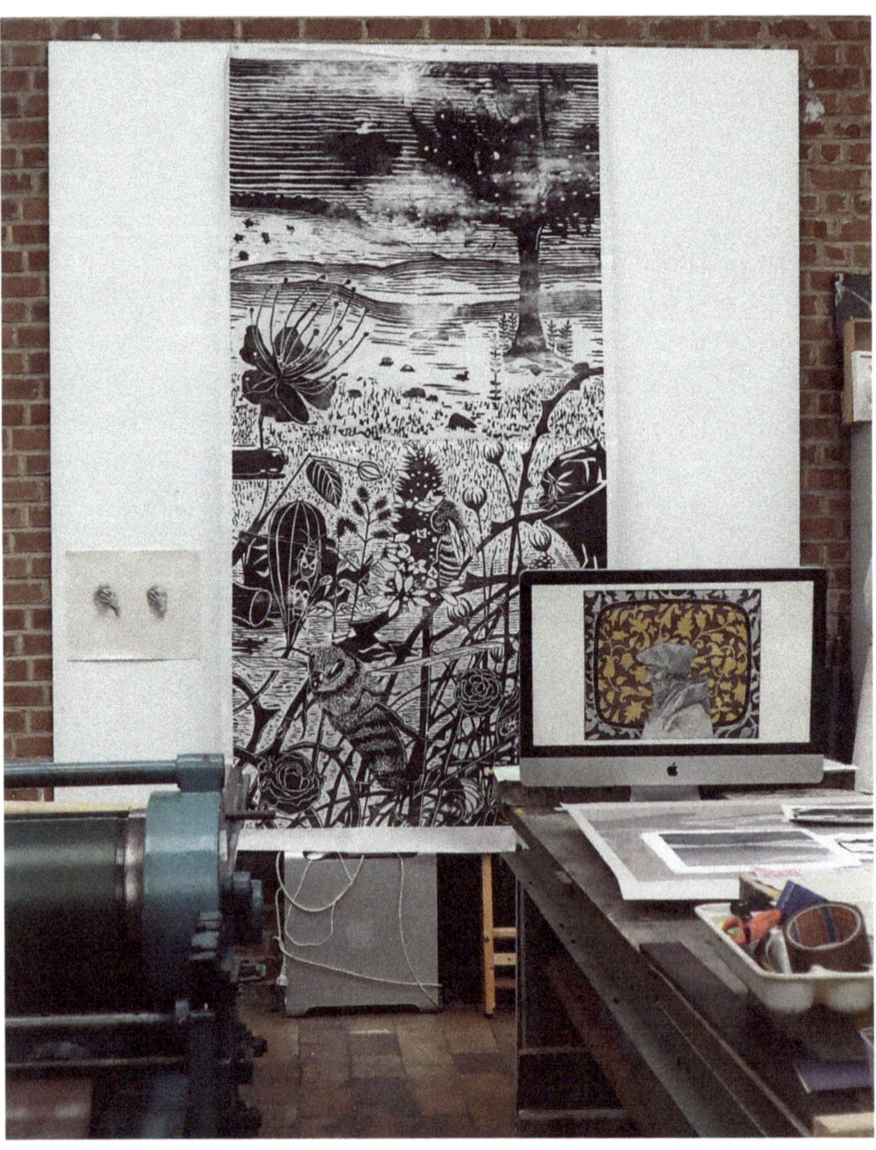

ARTNOGRAPHIC STATEMENT

When engaging in Multispecies Ethnography the question arises of how to understand and translate the animal's perspectives. According to anthropologist Harry Wels, 'developing fieldwork methodologies in multi-species ethnographic research confronts researchers with the explicit need for and training in multi-sensory methods and interpretations' (Wels, 2020: 343) and find 'methodologies without words'. (348) Wels proposes the art of tracking, whereby the tracker 'must project themselves in the position of the animal in order to create a hypothetical explanation of what the animal was doing' (2020: 345). He talks about three aspects within this method, which are, firstly, observing for longer periods of time; secondly, imagining what the observed animals might be up to; and, thirdly, getting physically habituated to the field in which one is working (353–56). When researching multispecies environments, there is agreement on the need for multisensorial methods, knowledge about the environment, patient observation and speculations (Despret, 2016; Haraway, 2016). Sheep and firebugs, two species encountered throughout the research, live in a familiar environment, namely the countryside of Saarland, Germany. This common habitat already creates a connection and understanding of these animals. Artistic methodologies are then used to observe, register and speculate about their lives.

The style of attention that is cultivated when observing other-than-human animals does not aim to create knowledge for knowledge's sake, but to learn how to inhabit this world differently. It refers to the vision of naturalist Arabella Buckley, who in her work *Life and her Children* (1882) says:

> And now, since we live in the world with all these numerous companions, which lead, many of them, such curious lives, trying ourselves to make the best of their short time here, is it not worthwhile to learn something about them? May we not gain some useful hints by watching their contrivances, sympathizing with their difficulties, and studying their history? And above all, shall we not have something more to love and to care for when we have made acquaintance with some of life's other children besides ourselves? (Buckley, 1882: 8; see also Mengual, 2021: 64).

This kind of 'loving attention' (Weil, 1947: 137) towards the natural world is the basis for an ethical aesthetic, developed throughout the research.

> The poet produces the beautiful by an attention fixed to the real. Similarly, the act of love. To know that man who is hungry and thirsty really exists as much as I exist-that is enough, the rest follows automatically. Authentic and pure values of truth, beauty, and goodness in the activity of a human being are produced by one sole and the same act, a certain application to the object of complete and full attention (Weil, 1947: 137; translated and cited by Donavan, 2016: 7).

This focused, caring attention reveals presences that remain uncovered through objectivation and abstraction. Through loving attention, the moral, qualitative and emotional significance becomes visible, that remains hidden in an unfeeling gaze. It also englobes empathising with the other, recognising it as a subject with its own reality (Donavan, 2016: 8). This valorisation of the observed as a subject with agency with its own point of view demands a respect and ethical reasoning regarding the wellbeing of the research subject that is absent in depersonalised methodologies.

Loving attention is cultivated through artistic methodologies. They represent a form of knowledge that connects instead of objectifies. Knowledge that functions by objectivation and by cutting off the affective dimension towards the research object creates distance and reduces the actual engagement with the other. Inversely, a holistic approach to experiences with animals gives space to cognitive, physical, sensorial and affective aspects of the encounter (Mengual, 2021: 98–102). The sponginess of artistic modes of perception lead to individual and multi-layered perspectives on animality. It also suggests that much of the non-human animal is not yet understood and remains mysterious.

Also, Art is a tool for critical reflection on ethnography and its operational exclusions. Arnaud Gerspacher maintains that

> The positivist killjoys will have to loosen up and realize that the entities and modalities that evade the scientism of their disciplinary nets are not therefore mere pseudo-object fit for the dustbins of New Age speculation. For their turn, aesthetic practices will have to remain vigilant of jejuneness, of the trivial instrumentally interesting and of its institutional contraints (Gerspacher, 2022: xii).

By integrating artistic methodologies in ethnographic research, artists can be critical about its 'reductive assumptions and operational constrains' (Gerspacher, 2022:14).

Moreover, animals, because of their complexity, consistently find ways to elude disciplinary limitations. Artistic processes may provide a constructive position free from ethnographic constraints, from which creaturely modes of existence can be speculated on (Gerspacher, 2022: 13).

The preceding photo essay elaborates on the concrete artistic methodologies used during fieldwork on firebugs. The photos consist in a selection of fieldwork registrations and their further artistic processing.

REFERENCES

Barad, K. 2007. *Meeting the Universe Halfway. Quantum Physics and the Entanglement of Matter and Meaning.* Durham, London: Duke University Press.

Bennet, J. 2010. *Vibrant Matter. A Political Ecology of Things.* London and Durham: Duke University Press.

Buckley, A. 1882. *Life and her Children: Glimpses of Animal Life from the Amoeba to the Insects.* London: E. Stanford.

De Bloois, J., S. De Cauwer and A. Masschelein. 2017. *50 Key Terms in Contemporary Cultural Theory.* Kalmthout: Pelckman.

Despret, V. 2016. *What Would Animals Say If We Asked the Right Questions?* Minneapolis: University of Minnesota Press.

Donovan, J. 2016. *The Aesthetics of Care. On the Literary Treatment of Animals.* New York: Bloomsbury Academic.

Gerspacher, A. 2022. *The Owls Are Not What They Seem: Artist as Ethologist.* Chicago: University of Minnesota Press.

Haraway, D. 2016. *Staying with the Trouble. Making Kin in the Chthulucene.* Durham and London: Duke University Press.

Hendrickx, K. 2017. 'Speculation'. In De Bloois, De Cauwer and Masschelein (eds). *50 Key Terms in Contemporary Cultural Theory.*

Morizot, B. 2020. *Manières d'être vivant. Enquêtes sur la vie à travers nous.* Arles: Actes Sud.

Polanyi, M. 1966. *The Tacit Dimension.* Chicago, London: The University of Chicago

Tenzin Negi, L. 2021. *The CBCT Guide.* Atlanta: Emory University.

Weil, S. 1988. *La Pesanteur et la Grâce*, Paris: Librairie Plon. POCKET.

Wels, H. 2020. 'Multi-species ethnography: methodological training in the field in South Africa'. *Journal of Organizational Ethnography* **9** (3): 343–63.

Zhong Mengual, E. 2021. *Apprendre à voir. Le point de vue du vivant.* Arles: Actes Sud, Mondes Sauvages.

7. FARMING COWS AND WORMS

Simone de Boer
Hanna Charlotta Wernersson

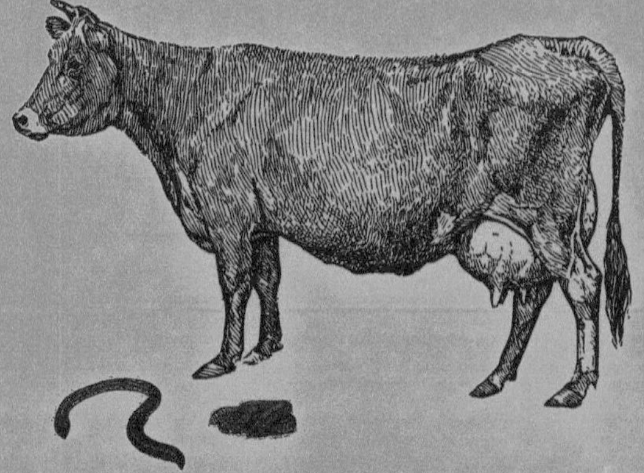

DOI: 10.63308/63878687083054.ch07

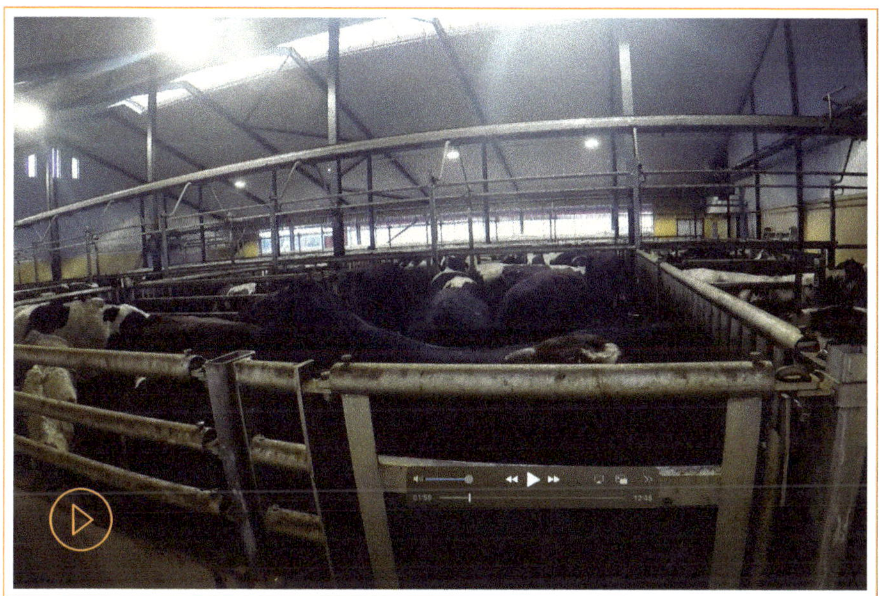

LINK TO SCREEN FILM

www.meamresearch.com/farming-cows-and-worms

ONTAGE COMPANION

Farming Cows and Worms brings together some of the collective ponderings inspired by our individual Ph.D. research on farming. Hanna studies human-animal relationships in regenerative cattle farming in Sweden, trying to understand the agricultural shapeshifting that is suggested by this alternative model of farming. Specifically, she focuses on what environmental knowledges and ethical relations are produced, and how. Simone studies the development and meaning of smallholder organic farming and permaculture in Kyrgyzstan, focusing on the creation of 'good farmer' identities in relation to changing perspectives and practices of more-than-human engagement.

In 2022, we attended a winter school on 'Digital Visual Engagements in Anthropological Research' at Leiden University, the Netherlands. This became the starting point for our artful research collaboration. We think of our joint research process as 'cross ethnography': we share our more or less raw research materials – consisting of different media – with each other and interpret and respond to them in both written and (audio)visual formats. It is an iterative mode

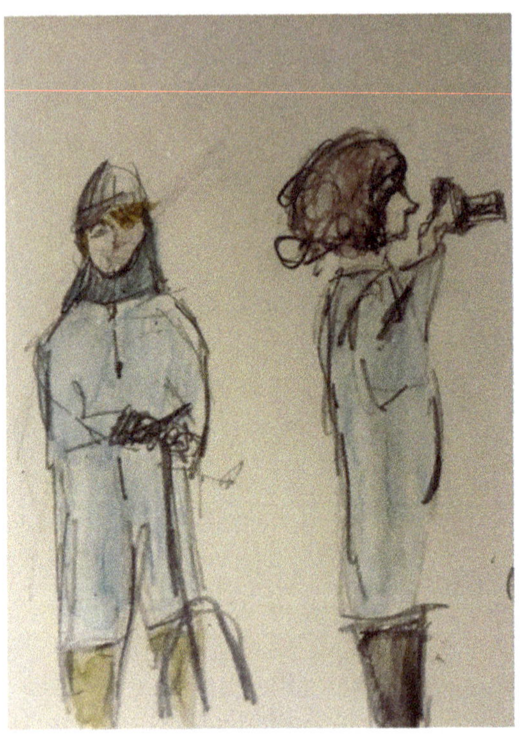

of working where we create cross interpretations of materials from our individual fieldwork. Through these 'creative respondings' (Thorpe et al., 2023), the research *process* is emphasised (see also Matsutake Worlds Research Group, 2009).

This montage is the product of the creative forces of cross ethnography: it is a multimedia exploration of how we can make sense of the more-than-human relationships we encountered on Swedish farmyards and around Kyrgyz compost heaps. Being spaces of agricultural production, these sites host multispecies relationships that are characterised by human use and, oftentimes, killing. However, as Donna Haraway points out, '[t]o be in a relation of use to each other is not the definition of unfreedom and violation' (2008:74). We should allow for relationships of use to, potentially, be good ones. So, we wonder: how can we make sense of 'good' relationships of use? What do they look, feel, sound, taste, smell like? In this work, we are guided by the notion that both the 'good' and the 'bad' make more-than-human entanglements (Govindrajan, 2018; Bear and Holloway, 2019), and that 'good' and 'bad' are not always distinguishable. In 'agrarian worlds' (Galvin, 2018), love and mutuality are not opposite to violence and hierarchy. As we show in this montage, they can even go together in one act.

This is emphasised by the chapter titles in which terms that are often thought of as juxtapositions are joined by 'and' or a comma, instead of 'or': *Producing and Nurturing; Controlling and Supporting; Caring Enough, Caring Too Much; Keeping Alive, Ending A Life.*

Open-endedness and continuous curiosity

Our method of cross ethnography and, subsequently, this montage, fit our understanding of ethnography as an open-ended way of working where the goal is to introduce the audience to lifeworlds in a way that sparks curiosity and encourages explorations (Ingold, 2011; Laplante, et al. 2020; Pink, 2015). This means we do not aim to serve up definite conclusions of what 'is', but to take the audience along in the process of experiencing, reflecting, and asking the critical questions. It is a move from representing to presenting (Ingold, 2002; Pitt, 2015).

The goal of ethnographic research is not to capture 'a' reality, but to come to understand and share temporally and socially situated versions of reality (Pink 2011, 2015; Ingold 2011). Artful methodologies accentuate this understanding of research. For instance, the soundscapes of this montage are not 'sonic realities' but rather 'partial truths' that aim to create new experiences while being indexically connected to our experiences in the field (Littlejohn, 2021:43). In our work, we are guided by Favero's (2017) notion of 'thin description': the process wherein we experience, sense and feel, and where observations and perceptions have not been finally subjugated to description, interpretation and explanation.

In our collaboration, sharing our multiple-media materials through cross ethnography nurtures an ongoing dialogue between us that helps keep our minds open. By enabling us to re-view, and therefore re-engage, with our fieldwork contexts, artful materials invite us to come to understand our field experiences anew and thus appreciate multiple perspectives (Pink and Morgan, 2013; Freidenberg, 1998).

Multispecies and multisensorial

Our work is part of a contemporary movement in ethnography that explores how 'ways of knowing are shaped by the affective and sensorial' (Culhane, 2017: 11). This mode of ethnography goes beyond that what is written or said and understands knowing as a multisensory phenomenon.

This is key when researching multispecies socialities, because while we do not share language with nonhuman animals, we do share 'contact zones' (Haraway, 2008). Using artful methods, we explore how to account for embodiment, feelings, and creativity in these zones of contact (Culhane, 2017). Our work is premised on the notion that farmyards are formative meeting spaces shaped by and shaping multispecies entanglements (Galvin, 2018). To make sense of the agrarian worlds of this montage, we have ventured 'beyond the human' (Kohn, 2013: 7) and explicitly broadened the study scope to include nonhuman farm dwellers as co-responding ethnographic subjects. We have been doing 'ethnographic hang-around' (Pink, 2015) with human farmers, compost worms and cattle. In this research process, creative methods allow us to 'make sense' (Howes, 2019) differently and more intently.

Throughout the piece, we intentionally work with combinations of media to engage multisensory experiences. We use silences and blank screens to 'pace' the piece, creating a narrational rhythm to accentuate affective sensations and offer micro pauses for reflection.

We also explicitly use artful methods to foreground the nonhumans of this montage. Through photography, film and soundscapes we offer them space to 'speak for themselves' (Bear et al., 2017). While we cannot take ourselves out completely, these methods leave the doings and dwellings of nonhumans open for further interpretation. Drawings, on the other hand, act as visual explorations of the human imagination and experience – both our interlocutors' and our own.

Creative writing is an important tool for us to process the multisensorial experiences we have in the field and to constructively explore the limitations that apply to knowing nonhuman perspectives and experiences. It allows space for emotional, affective and sensorial dimensions of interactions and nurtures a capacity to empathically *imagine* what the perspective of the other might be (Ingridsdotter and Sillow Kallenberg, 2018; Elliott, 2017; Richardson, 2000). Put differently, creative writing helps us approach the nonhumans while staying, humbly, on the human side of things.

Some challenges, to close

As likely is becoming clear, we find artful and collaborative methods to be powerful companions in multispecies research fields. Through cross ethnography, they also immensely enrich our Ph.D. journeys – journeys that are often described as lonely and tough. We would, however, like to end by offering a number of challenges for consideration with this methodology.

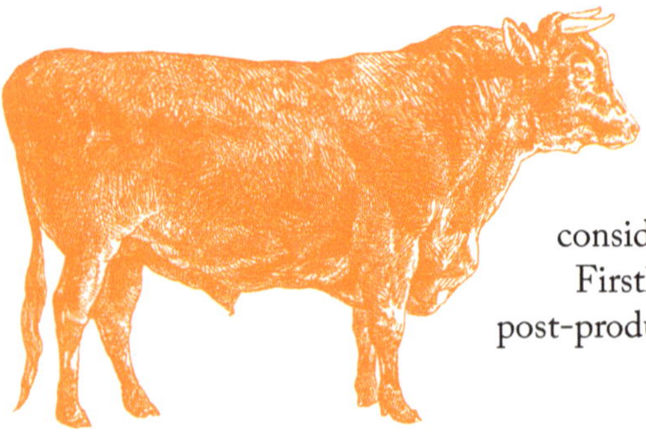

Firstly, (black) magic can be done during post-production. There is a tendency for audiovisual works to gravitate towards the aesthetically pleasing (Grasseni, 2009; Wernersson and De Boer, 2022). This risks creating blind spots, if what is not easily/prettily captured on camera/recording is left out. This means that the critical questions may not be asked. We find collaboration to be an effective tool to uncover aesthetic preferences that may push the material in a potentially less truthful direction. Yet, limitations apply. As a collaborative pair we too develop shared aesthetic and ethical standards, and our joint objectives may cloud our judgements. And while we use 'we' throughout this work, we are two different individuals holding different opinions and viewpoints (see also Gordon et al., 2006; Matsutake Worlds Research Group, 2009). The ethical question at play here evolves around how to create awareness and raise reflection around the mediation itself (De Musso, 2021).

MONTAGE GUIDE

How do we make sense of 'good' relationships of use?

Part I: Producing and nurturing

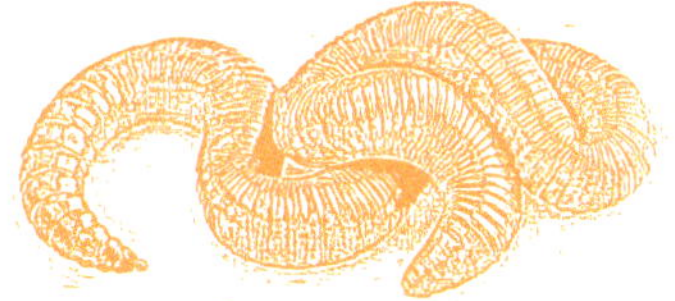

Bull Life, Industrial Bull Farm, Sweden
Worm Life, Organic Farming Site, Kyrgyzstan

Ultimately, farming is humans doing things to nonhumans for productive purposes, deciding on the frames of nonhuman lives. What kind of lives do farming humans create, protect and grant in these processes of productive care (Harbers, 2010)? And how much space is there for co-creation?

In *Bull Life*, video gives us a feeling of 'meeting' the bulls. We are in the barn together with the bulls, yet not with them on their side of the fence. We are looking *at* them, not *with* them. Video and poem invite us to reflect on the multispecies relationship of this space: a living environment given and guaranteed by human hands. Yet, while space is human built, what the bulls do in and with that space is of their own making. The bulls are standing, walking, stopping, laying down, standing again; using all space that is given on their side of the fence.

Worm Life is a reaction to *Bull Life* in both style and content. When put into dialogue with one another, these poems enable a comparative pondering of different species lives.

While initially built by human hands, most of what goes on inside compost heaps is invisible to human eyes. It is a living environment that allows freedom of movement and agency to compost worms to rework it (Bennett 2010: 97).

While the food is provided by humans, there is a logic of choice. The visuals in *Worm Life* represent the worms' environment as experienced and understood by humans. The black screen invites us to imagine what happens beyond our sensory reach.

Part II: Controlling and supporting

Sweeping Care, Industrial Bull Farm, Sweden
Layering Labour, Organic Farming Site, Kyrgyzstan

Living spaces both shape and are shaped by multispecies care. In the high-tech industrial bull stable, caring is monitoring growth and keeping a safe distance. In low-tech Kyrgyz worm farming, caring is feeding, building and maintaining a safe environment.

As is evident in *Sweeping Care*, technology and built environments may tear species apart, but farm dwellers are not without a say and can resist these forces. In this piece, text and sound complement and contrast one another to get at a sensorial experience of the ambiguities that make farming (Wernersson and Boonstra, 2024; Wilkie, 2017). The written story introduces us to human emotions and feelings of attachment to animals, while the audible story introduces us to the nakedness and noisiness – or the rawness – of this human-built, industrialised, farm setting.

Layering Labour is an instructive compost building poem based on ethnographic material that draws attention to the materiality and sensorial dimensions of compost heaps and care practices with the aim to explore the connection and labour between worms and humans. By layering the compost heap, humans create an environment for worms in which the two species become simultaneously invisible and connected to each other. Worms and humans cannot see or (fully) comprehend the work the other does, but they can engage with the result of the other's labour. Labour is the intersubjective connector across species lines (Porcher, 2017, 2020; Govindrajan, 2018; Jones, 2019).

Part III: Caring enough, caring too much

Exposing Care, Organic Farming Site, Kyrgyzstan
Mommy, Family Farm, Sweden

What is good for the nonhuman animal, what is good for the human, and is it possible to achieve what is good for both?

Exposing Care explores the way humans interact with worms, care for them and produce knowledge about them. Because worm lives are largely invisible, humans must draw on other senses and their imagination to come to know and manage worms. Sometimes, however, the boundary between visibility/light and invisibility/darkness must be transgressed. The process of becoming attuned to worms (Abrahamsson and Bertoni, 2014) thus involves possibly harming them.

Mommy tells us about a hierarchy of relationships at play. Farmer and cow are to have a good relationship to make business smooth running. Cows too, are to have good relationships and care for one another, but not to the extent that they threaten the human-cow relationship. It is humans that decide when there is enough, or too much, care (Emel et al., 2017).

Part IV: Keeping alive, ending a life

Warm Worms, Organic Farming Site, Kyrgyzstan
Rugged Friendships, Family Farm, Sweden

Having others care for your life can be both reassuring and perturbing (Govindrajan, 2018). Caring and nurturing do not preclude hurting and killing and, in farming, keeping alive and ending a life are not opposites. In *Warm Worms* and *Rugged Friendships*, drawings and narration address closeness and distance, love and death, and questions of power inherent to farming.

Warm Worms explores the dynamics between selfcare and human care. Worms can take their fate into their own hands when human care falls short but, in response, compost caretakers may change their practices and redirect the worms' course. It is enacting both love and control (cf. Abrahamsson and Bertoni, 2014).

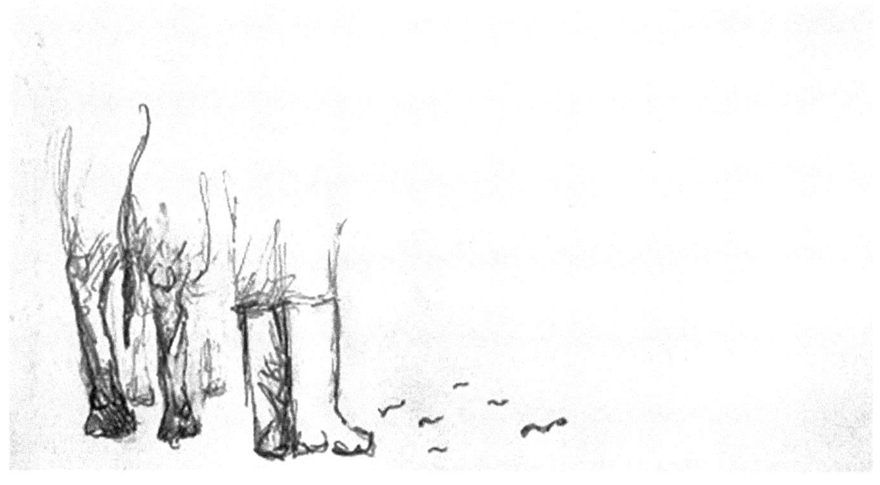

Rugged Friendships suggests that, rather than treating animals 'as objects so that we can kill them' (Bernadina, 1991:35 in Buller, 2013), to know the other well may be a prerequisite for eating, wearing or using the other as a rug. Through death, a closeness is created that is unattainable through life alone.

ARTNOGRAPHIC STATEMENT

This multimedia montage explores multispecies relationships in three different farming contexts: human-worm relationships in Kyrgyz compost heaps, and human-cow relationships on two Swedish cattle farms, one family farm and one industrial farm.

Using photography, video, drawing, creative writing, and collaboration with artists, we explore the nature and rhythm of the shared lives of human and non-human farm dwellers. The artful materials making this montage have been created both during our individual fieldwork (Hanna in Sweden in 2019[1] and Simone in Kyrgyzstan in 2022) and through 'cross ethnography'. In cross ethnography, we craft multi-layered interpretations and multilinear narrations by engaging with, and interpreting, parts of each other's individual data through artful research practices.

Artful methods help us and our interlocutors explore and express sensorial ways of being, knowing, and learning – for instance the look/feel/sound/taste/smell of a 'good' relationship – as well as (re)presenting the invisible, desirable, or yet unknown. Through these practices, we invite our human interlocutors to actively participate in our research in ways that make sensorial sense to them. Going beyond the linguistic, artful methods are crucial as they allow us both to engage with non-human interlocutors and to think through what engagement means in different sites and with different nonhumans.

For instance, filming everyday life on Swedish cattle farms encouraged Hanna to think through animal spaces: what they are, how animals use them and how they shape multispecies encounters. The enclosed space of the industrialised bull stable enables, if not enforces, intimate interaction. On the family farm, interactions instead have to be initiated by the free roaming cows. For Simone, hanging around compost heaps and audiovisually capturing them, alerted her to the materiality and aliveness of the heaps. She was, moreover, encouraged to pay attention to what – and who – is (in)visible in compost building, and how the largely invisible lives of worms are imagined by human compost caretakers.

1 See Wernersson and Boonstra (2024) for a more elaborate discussion of this fieldwork and the moral sustainability of cattle farming.

Our artful and collaborative methods furthermore encourage us to continuously re-engage with the material and the contexts of their production. As we edit and shape the material to fit specific forms of presentation, new questions emerge. Through collaboration in 'cross ethnography', we question and add to each other's interpretations, (tunnel)visions and edits to reveal and prevent blind spots and to question what we show and do not show. It is a circular way of working that emphasises research and knowledge production as *process;* an open-ended way of arriving at the research task of interpretation, analysis, explanation and, ultimately, asking the critical questions.

ACKNOWLEDGEMENTS

We are grateful to the human and nonhuman farm dwellers who let us think, learn and work with them.

We want to thank Claes Wernerson, the artist that interpreted cattle farm fieldnotes in oil paintings. One of these paintings features in *Rugged Friendships*.

We would also like to express our gratitude for the helpful feedback we received from the MEAM editorial team and an anonymous peer reviewer, as well as colleagues and friends.

We thank the 'Food Citizens?' project team at Leiden University for a stimulating Winter School on 'Digital Visual Engagements in Anthropological Research' which inspired us to creatively collaborate.

Fieldwork in Kyrgyzstan was made possible by funding from Gabrielle van den Berg's NWO Vici/Aspasia project 'Turks, Texts and Territories: Imperial Ideology and Cultural Production in Central Eurasia' (Leiden University), as well as a travel scholarship from the University of Gothenburg Donation Board.

We want to acknowledge that the fieldwork on the two Swedish farms was part of Hanna's master's thesis work at Stockholm University, 2020.

REFERENCES

Abrahamsson, S. and F. Bertoni. 2014. 'Compost politics: Experimenting with togetherness in vermicomposting' *Environmental Humanities* **4**: 125–48.

Bear, C. and L. Holloway. 2019. 'Beyond resistance: Geographies of divergent more-than-human conduct in robotic milking'. *Geoforum* **104**: 212–21.

Bear, C., K. Wilkinson and L. Holloway. 2017. 'Visualizing human-animal-technology relations'. *Society & Animals* **25** (3): 225–56.

Bennett, J. 2010. *Vibrant Matter. A Political Ecology of Things*. Durham/London: Duke University Press.

Bernardina, D.S. 1991. 'Une Personne pas tout à fait comme les autres. L'animal et son statut'. *L'Homme* **31** (120): 33–50.

Buller, H. 2013. 'Individuation, the mass and farm animals'. *Theory, Culture & Society.* **30** (7–8): 155–75.

Culhane, D. 2017. 'Imagining: An introduction'. In Elliott and Culhane (eds). *A Different Kind of Ethnography*, pp. 1–22.

De Musso, F. 2021. 'Interactive documentaries'. In C. Grasseni, B.A. Barendregt, E. de Maaker, F. De Musso F., A.L. Littlejohn, M.E. Maeckelbergh, M.A. Postma and M.R. Westmoreland (eds). *Audiovisual and Digital Ethnography: A Practical and Theoretical Guide*, pp. 143–67. London: Routledge.

Elliott, D. 2017. 'Writing'. In Elliott and Culhane (eds). *A Different Kind of Ethnography*, pp. 23–44.

D. Elliott and D. Culhane (eds). *A Different Kind of Ethnography: Imaginative Practices and Creative Methodologies.* Toronto: University of Toronto Press.

Emel, J., C.L. Johnston and E. Stoddard. 2015. 'Livelier livelihoods: Animal and human collaboration on the farm'. In Gillespie and Collard (eds). *Critical Animal Geographies: Politics, Intersections, and Hierarchies in a Multispecies World*, pp. 164–83. London: Routledge.

Favero, P. 2017. 'In Defence of the 'thin:' Reflections on the intersections between interactive documentaries and ethnography'. In E.G. Cruz, S. Sumartojo and S. Pink (eds). *Refiguring Techniques in Digital Visual Research*, pp. 51–65. London: Palgrave Macmillan.

Freidenberg, J. 1998. 'The social construction and reconstruction of the Other: Fieldwork in El Barrio'. *Anthropological Quarterly* **71** (4): 169–85.

Galvin, S.S. 2018. 'Interspecies relations and agrarian worlds'. *Annual Review of Anthropology* **47**: 233–49.

Gordon T., P. Hynninen, E. Lahelma, T. Metso, T. Palmu and T. Tolonen. 2006. 'Collective ethnography, joint experiences and individual pathways'. *Nordisk Pedagogik* **26**: 3–15.

Govindrajan, R. 2018. *Animal Intimacies: Interspecies Relatedness in India's Central Himalayas.* Chicago: University of Chicago Press.

Grasseni, C. 2009. *Developing Skill, Developing Vision: Practices of Locality at the Foot of the Alps*, European anthropology in translation. New York: Berghahn Books.

Grasseni, C., B.A. Barendregt, E. de Maaker, F. De Musso F., A.L. Littlejohn, M.E. Maeckelbergh, M.A. Postma and M.R. Westmoreland (eds). *Audiovisual and Digital Ethnography: A Practical and Theoretical Guide.* London: Routledge.

Haraway, D.J. 2008. *When Species Meet.* Minneapolis: University of Minnesota Press.

Harbers, H. 2010. 'Animal Farm love stories: About care and economy'. In A. Mol, I. Moser and J. Pols (eds). *Care in Practice: On Tinkering in Clinics, Homes and Farms*, pp. 141–70. Bielefeld: transcript Verlag.

Howes, D. 2019. 'Multisensory anthropology'. *Annual Review of Anthropology* **48**: 17–28.

Ingold, T. 2002. *The Perception of the Environment: Essays on Livelihood, Dwelling and Skill.* London/New York: Routledge.

Ingold, T. 2011. *Being Alive: Essays on Movement, Knowledge and Description.* London/New York: Routledge.

Ingridsdotter, J. and K. Silow Kallenberg. 2018. 'Ethnography and the arts: Examining social complexities through ethnographic fiction'. *Etnofoor* **30** (1): 57–76.

Jones, B.M. 2019. '(Com)Post-Capitalism: Cultivating a more-than-human economy in the Appalachian Anthropocene'. *Environmental Humanities* **11** (1): 3–26.

Kohn, E. 2013. *How Forests Think: Toward and Anthropology Beyond the Human*. Berkeley/Los Angeles: University Of California Press.

Laplante J., W. Scobie and A. Gandsman. 2020. 'Introduction: Lines of flight'. In. J. Laplante, S. Willow and A. Gandsman (eds). *Search After Method: Sensing, Moving, and Imagining in Anthropological Fieldwork*, pp. 1–17. New York/Oxford: Berghahn Books.

Littlejohn, A.L. 2021. 'Sonic ethnography'. In Grasseni et al. (eds). *Audiovisual and Digital Ethnography*, pp. 35–60.

Matsutake Worlds Research Group. 2009. 'A new form of collaboration in cultural anthropology: Matsutake worlds'. *American Ethnologist* **36** (2): 380–403.

Pink, S. 2011. 'Multimodality, multisensoriality and ethnographic knowing: Social semiotics and the phenomenology of perception'. *Qualitative Research* **11** (3): 261–76.

Pink, S. 2015. *Doing Sensory Ethnography*. London: Sage.

Pink, S. and J. Morgan. 2013. 'Short-term ethnography: Intense routes to knowing'. *Symbolic Interaction* **36**: 351–61.

Pitt, H. 2015. 'On showing and being shown plants - a guide to methods for more-than-human geography: On showing and being shown plants'. *Area* **47**: 48–55.

Porcher, P. 2017. *The Ethics of Animal Labor: A Collaborative Utopia*. London: Palgrave Macmillan.

Porcher, P. and J. Estebanez (eds). 2020. *Animal Labor: A New Perspective on Human-Animal Relations*. Bielefeld: transcript Verlag.

Richardson, L. 2000. 'Writing: A method of inquiry'. In N. Denzin and Y. Lincoln (eds). *The SAGE Handbook of Qualitative Research*. London: Sage.

Thorpe, H., J. Newman, S. Zarabadi, A. Pavlidis, S. Fullagar, J. Rosiek, E. Nichols, P. Markula, A. Bayley and M. Adkins-Cartee. 2023. 'Diffractive respondings and cutting together-apart: Toward more-than-human academic community'. *Cultural Studies ↔ Critical Methodologies* **23** (2): 181–92.

Wilkie, R. 2017. 'Animals as sentient commodities'. In Linda Kalof (ed.) *The Oxford Handbook of Animal Studies*. Oxford: Oxford University Press.

Wernersson, H. and S. de Boer. 2022. '"Lights, camera, action!": PhD reflections on doing audiovisual ethnography in Pairs'. *Blogal Studies*: https://www.blogalstudies.com/post/lights-camera-action-phd-reflections-on-doing-audiovisual-ethnography-in-pairs.

Wernersson, H.C. and W.J. Boonstra. 2024. 'Making meat moral: A comparison of cattle farming practices in Sweden'. *Sociologia Ruralis* **64**: 254–79.

8. TO TOUCH LIGHTLY IN PASSING

Merlijn Huntjens
Nina Willems
Leonie Cornips

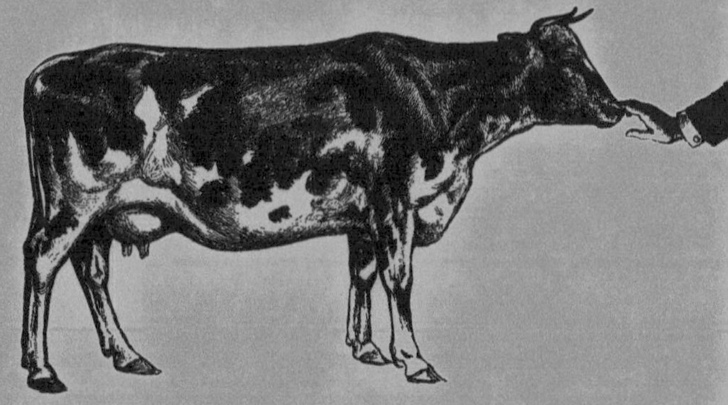

DOI: 10.63308/63878687083054.ch08

the herd

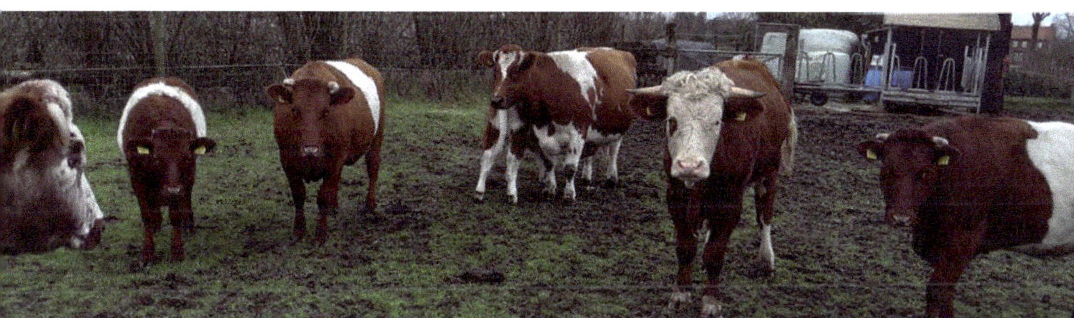

Here is the herd
they introduce themselves by positioning in
a half-circle
Surrounding
Equal distanced between the adults

Looking, watching, eye-gazing
Connecting
Relating
Earthing
Blowing time through their noses

From left to right

Cato looks at Piet.
shows a white vertical stripe on her back, a white belly and brown spots on her head, Cato is a Witrik
Cato is infertile, she adopted Piet immediately
when they arrived as a small calf

[nosing, touching, licking, standing close, mooing to Piet, watching over Piet].

Saar and then her mother Noor,
are dusky red Lakenfelders
they show a white belted colour pattern
holding heads lower than their backs
Friendly attitude

Janneke – the leader of the herd – with her calf Sandy,
directs always her calf close nearby

Piet, definitely looking into the camera
Piet is a Fleckvieh, intersex. They has a dark brownish-reddish [brandrood] body with white socks, white tip of the tail, white face but a dark spot on their right eye, long white eye-lashes, pink nose...

holds head a bit higher than their back
ears wide
attentive attitude

and then Roos
Noor's daughter and Saar's older half-sister

Janneke and Cato are sisters,
Janneke, her calf Sandy and Cato are MRIJ [Meuse-Rhine-Ysel 'Maas-Rijn-IJssel']
Piet shows a lighter vertical stripe on his back [Aalslag]

Family lines:
Mothers,
adoption mother,
adopted intersex,
daughters,
sisters,
half-sisters,
step siblings,
bonus calf
bonus mother

Generations Whole families Broken families

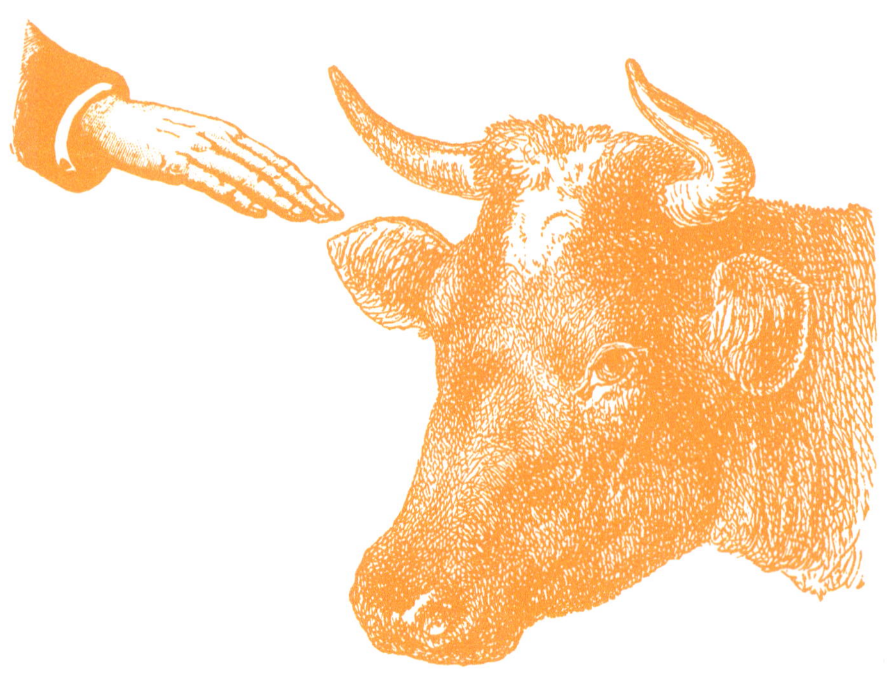

To touch lightly in passing

piet

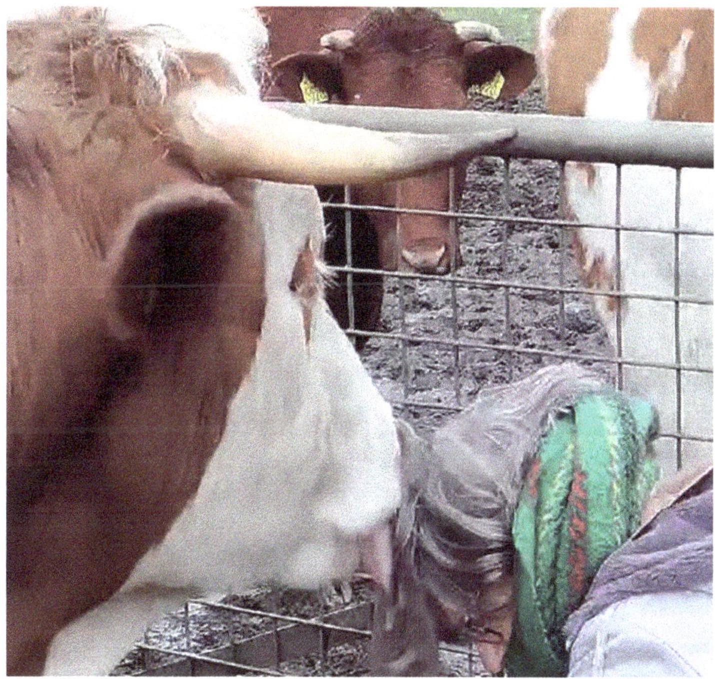

The bull
– in fact the intersex cow Piet –
is sniffing, licking and sucking at my hair
just like they were a small calf in their tiny wooden box
(fieldwork 12 March 2023).

Fieldwork over the past two years taught me
how Piet wishes to take the initiative
to approach and touch me:

I have to sit down,
bow down my head,
no eye-gaze
no moving,
no reaching hands towards Piet to touch him.

Noor behind the fence is watching us.

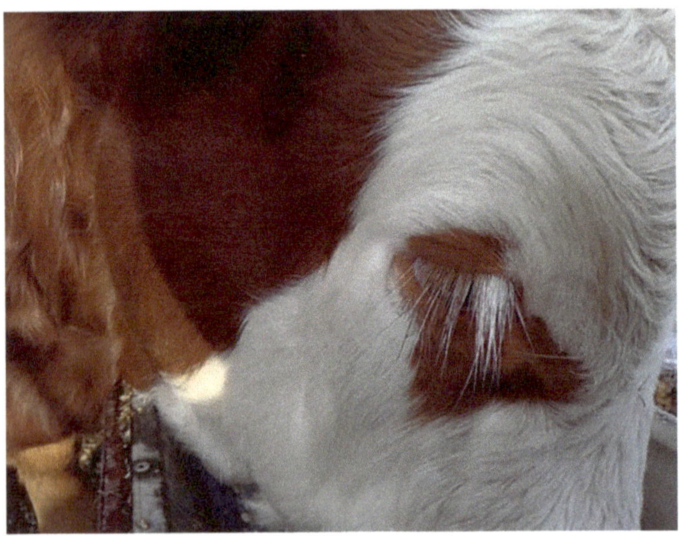

The white eye-lashes of Piet
Long eye-lashes
Big eye on the side of the head with a sight of 330 degrees
Piet's eye still sees me when standing right next to them, both faces nosing forward

To touch lightly in passing

Piet does not look at the feed
where wind can slip between bodies
someone touches my hand
a small child makes a noise
the bull's horns are warm to the touch

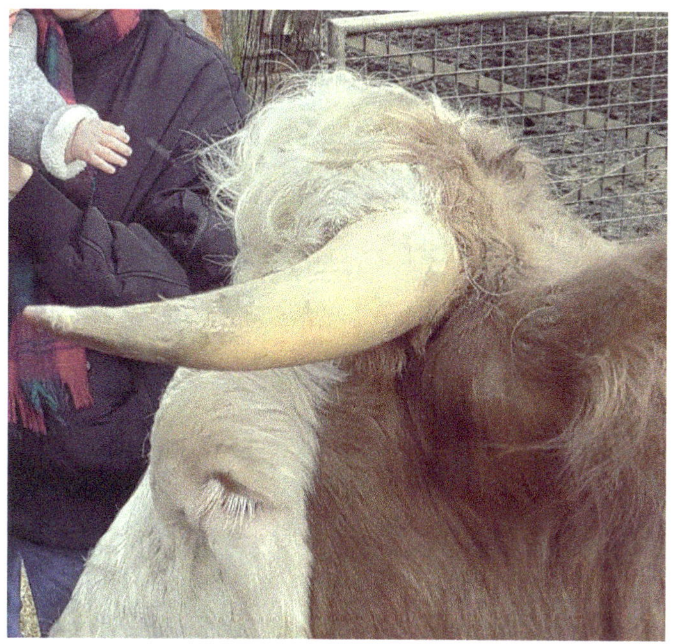

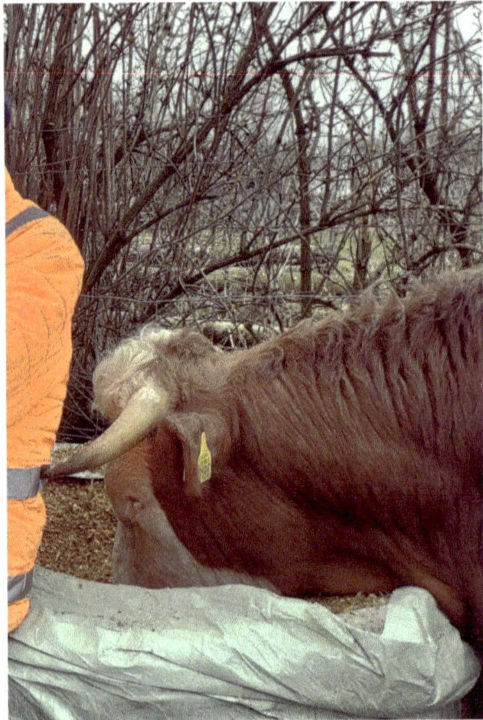

a bull is more body than we think
I'm right next to him

no one loses his body
and the pasture is the same body
and the pasture is a herd
and slowly we walk through the mud
to the feed

I look at the ground, the feed, the bull
I am only small while the bull is big
a bull is more body than we think

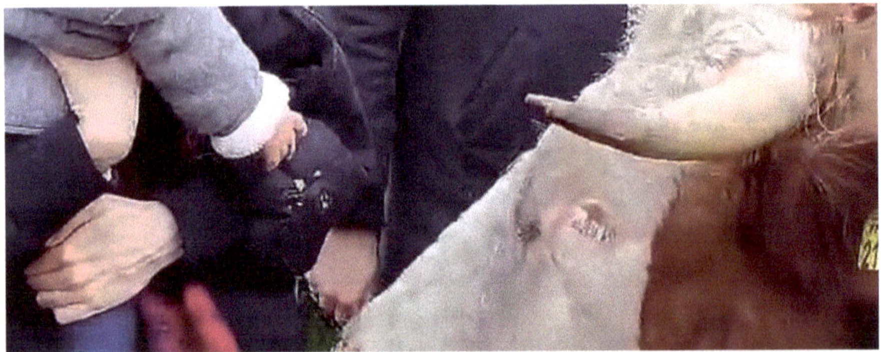

One horn and four hands, relaxed positions, mindful, holding. Four individuals reaching out to each other, interspecies-reaching-out-while-relating through smelling, sensing seeing, touching, belly-feelings.

To touch lightly in passing

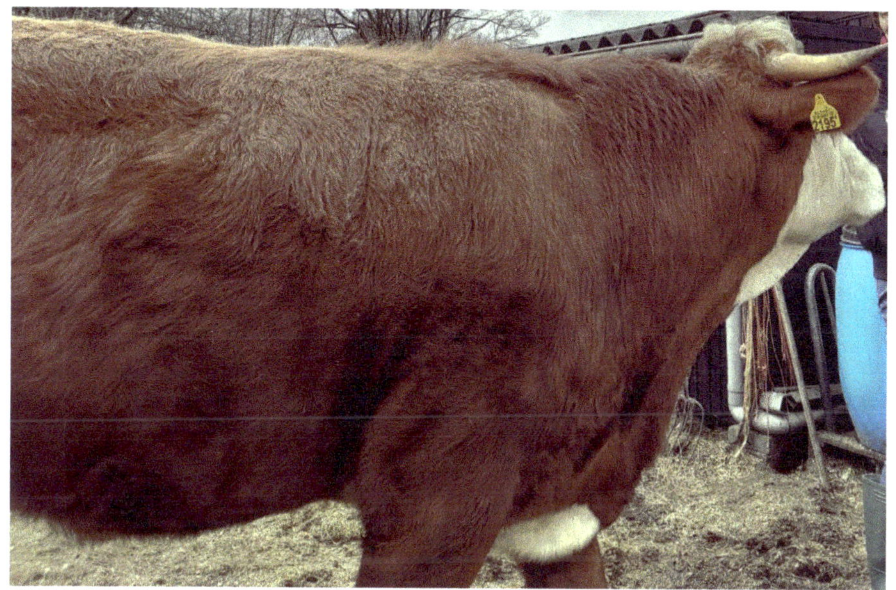

we move slowly to the next position
and stay there.

a small child makes a noise
the bull's tongue licks a baby sock.

with baby hands the beast is touched.
it is the biggest beast that takes the lead.

piet blows out.
what do leonie and nina and merlijn grasp?

the herd

to graze

transitive verb

[...]

1. to feed on growing herbage
2. to touch lightly in passing

ARTNOGRAPHIC STATEMENT

In order to listen to a cow like Piet and their herd, a decentring of humans in (socio)linguistic research is needed. Such a decentring presents theoretical and methodological challenges to understandings, conceptualisations and theorising of the animal Other. The main challenge becomes that of rethinking intraspecies and interspecies interactions as embodied, multimodal and sensory phenomena whose bodily mediation draws on material objects and environments (Cornips, 2024). Instead of academic writing, poetry ideally gives the opportunity to hide and/or approach something that is unsayable or untouchable in images. For example, the tension between a bull cow and a human baby hiding in a cow lick or a baby sock, is not present in biology or related academic fields but does exist 'in the poetry' of or between 'things'. That unsayable is then not necessarily in the written text but may (hopefully) subsequently arise in the minds of readers. That is another thing than capturing emotions or expressing them in academic language reserved in linguistics. Because tangible or measurable reality is bounded but our imagination is not, we need poetry to allow the world to shine through in us more completely.

Therefore, this project is a collaboration between Leonie Cornips (linguist and ethnographer), Merlijn Huntjens (poet) and Nina Willems (theatre/performance art). Nina and Merlijn have collaborated since 2015 in their art collective PANDA (see https://www.pandacollectief.nl/over-panda/). In 2024, we started developing the artistic research project called 'KOE' (cow), in collaboration with cow Piet and their herd, with whom Leonie has been working in the past few years. In 2023 we conducted preliminary field research with Leonie taking fieldwork photos, of which this small publication is the result.

Why did we choose to engage in this collaboration? The artistic methods, poetry in particular, allow humans to reflect and write about bodily and audible sharing activity with cows, hence synchronising together which is described by Argent (2012: 119) as part of 'kinetic, haptic, and proxemic communication modes to create meanings' and by de Waal (2012: 123) as 'identification' with the other, a process of 'bodily mapping the self onto the other (or the other onto the self)' which forms 'a precondition for imitation and empathy'. By using ethnography and artistic methods the authors became increasingly sensitive to and affected by Piet's expressive actions and movements from within our relationship through time (Servais 2018: 5) because we learned very soon to acknowledge Piet's personhood emerging out of what we both did and do (and didn't) in our relation (Servais, 2018: 6). Crucially, we learned almost from the beginning to consider and experience Piet not as a 'passive object waiting to be acted upon by a desiring human subject' (van den Hengel, 2021: 45) but that both Piet and we are 'part of an independent web of existence where the material, social, political and spiritual dynamics of living and loving meet in co-shaping motion and being' (Van den Hengel, 2021: 40). The strong point is that our relation is dynamic: Piet and we are being transformed by the other, articulated by what Piet makes us/our bodies do and perceive – or not – and what we make Piet/their body do and perceive – or not (Despret, 2004).

The more we collaborated the less our different roles (poet, linguist, ethnographer, performance artist, mother) became applicable; we became artistic researchers who, using all our qualities, discovered and described the world of cow Piet and their herd. Nina and Merlijn engaged in field research using Leonie's methods, Leonie started documenting through poetry, supported by Merlijn.

Nina also took her son Olivier with her as part of the field research, as a form of 'performance in everyday life' (Schechner, 2006). Olivier (now fifteen months old) is fully discovering the rules of behaviour and language in the human world. What happens when we confront him with the behavioural rules and language of Piet and their herd? How does his performance affect that of Piet and the herd, and ours as human researchers? An example: in their first encounter, during the preliminary research phase, Piet bowed their head to Olivier and approached him at a slower pace than the other humans. Finally, Piet started licking Olivier's sock. When Piet stood directly opposite Olivier, the child started to cry, and stopped when his mother placed her body between his and Piet. This affected the way Nina could perform in relation to Piet as well, because she had to turn her back to Piet, holding Olivier in her arms. Nina also noticed herself becoming very calm and slow in her movements, while she continued to try to move Olivier and Piet closer together.

The next step will be for us to design a new fieldwork method, based on our experiences so far, at the intersection of our disciplines, and to document through poetry. Poetry has our main focus for documenting, because it enables us to focus on the tactile, emotional side of communication between us and the herd we observe and interact with. We find that there are subtleties in this communication that need a different type of language from academic language. We also want to keep experimenting with hybrid presentation forms for our research.

For example, we presented a performative audio-walk as part of our project during Festival Cultura Nova 2024 in Heerlen, in collaboration with farmer Guus Huynen and the herd that lives on his farm. In the audio-walk, the audience could hear Leonie share her research, and recordings of the poetry that Nina and Merlijn created based on that research and their encounters with the cows on the farm of Guus Huynen. During the preparations, an article was published in the Dutch newspaper *De Volkskrant* (Embrechts, 2024) about their research. Positive reviews about the project also appeared in *De Volkskrant* and *De Theaterkrant*

REFERENCES

Argent, Gala. 2012. 'Toward a privileging of the nonverbal: Communication, corporeal synchrony, and transcendence in humans and horses'. In Julie A. Smith and Robert W. Mitchell (eds). *Experiencing Animal Minds: An Anthology of Animal-Human Encounters* (pp. 111–28). New York: Columbia University Press.

Cornips, Leonie. 2024. 'The semiotic repertoire of the dairy cow(s)'. *Language in Society*. Online first: 1–25. https://doi.org/10.1017/S0047404524000460

de Waal, Frans B.M. 2012. 'A bottom-up view of empathy'. In Frans de Waal and Pier Francesco Ferrari (eds). *The Primate Mind: Built to Connect with Other Minds*, pp. 121–38. Cambridge/London: Harvard University Press.

Despret, V. 2004. 'The body we care for: figures of anthropo-zoo-genesis'. *Body and Society* 10: 111–34.

Schechner, R. 2006. *Performance Studies: An Introduction*. London: Routledge.

Servais, V., 2018. 'Anthropomorphism in human-animal interactions: a pragmatist view'. *Frontiers in Psychology* 9: 2590. https://doi.org/10.3389/fpsyg.2018.02590

Van den Hengel, L. 2021. 'For love of the world: Material entanglements in ecosexual performance'. In D.C. Byrne and M. Schleicher (eds). *Entanglements and Weavings: Diffractive Approaches to Gender and Love*, pp. 34–53. Leiden: Brill.

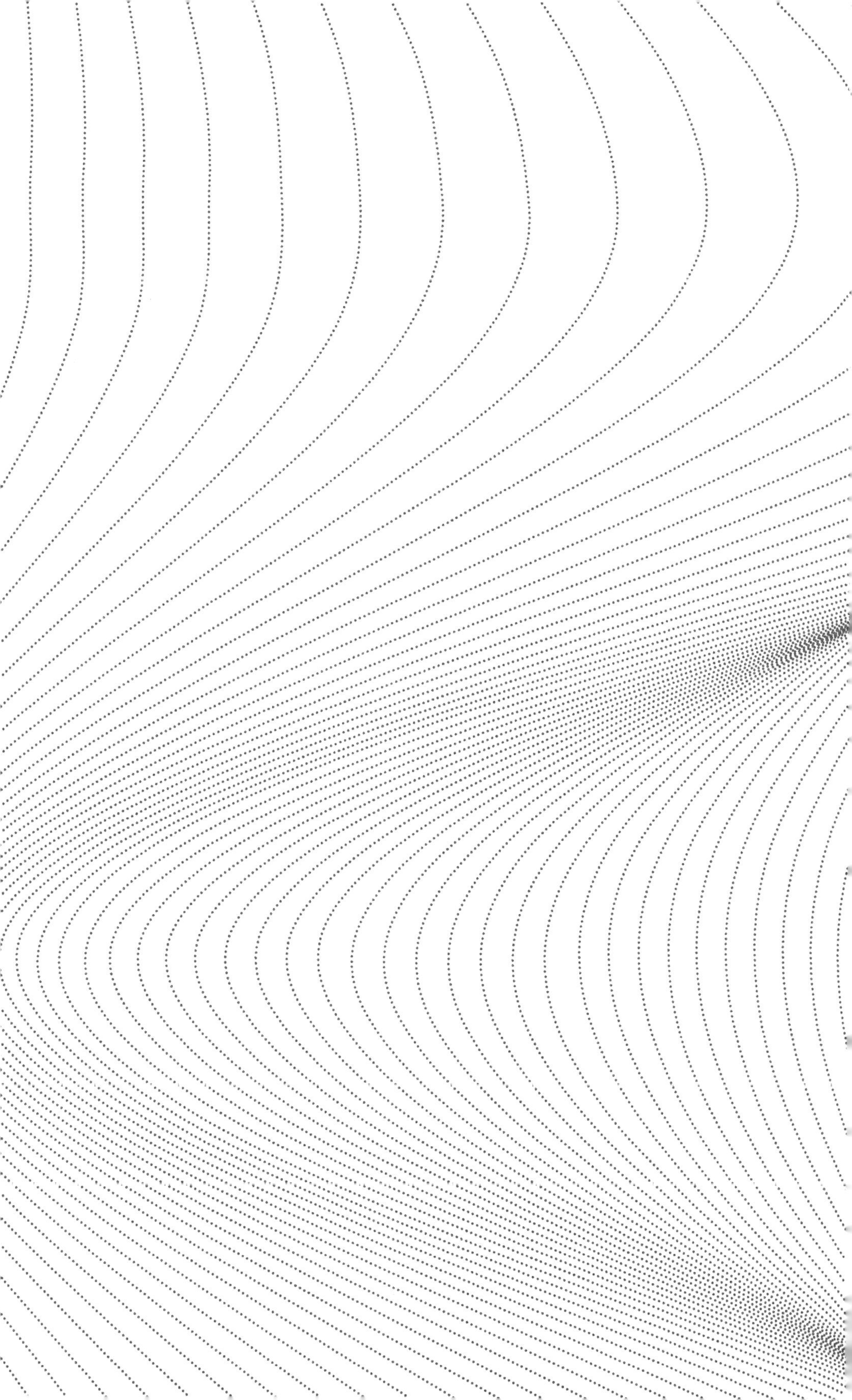

9. FREAKS OF NATURE: USING DEEP REFLEXIVITY TO UNDERSTAND TRANSGENICS

Lisa Jean Moore

Sociologist, Mother, Human, Writer

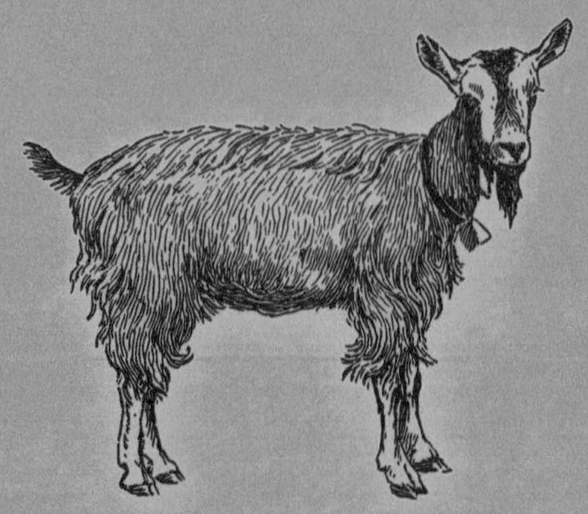

DOI: 10.63308/63878687083054.ch09

The kids are screaming their heads off as Amber holds the silver milk bucket above the pen. She's angling the bucket attempting to pour milk into the red plastic container but the kids are jostling around in a frenzy to be first in line. Some spills on their heads or mixes into the wood chips on the concrete flooring. What a waste.

I don't know if these baby goats have been typed yet to see if they are transgenic but they are definitely hungry. They've been watching the does on the milking stands for 10 minutes building anticipation, the Pavlovian response is probably triggered by the sound of the pump compressor. Maybe the kids are more attached to the compressor than to the adult goats. I wonder if there is any recognition between the goats being milked and these kids drinking the milk. Can the mom goat tell which one is their baby? Can the babies smell their mom? Are the screams pitched correctly to call to a specific mom? When I was nursing, I'd hear some random baby cry and experience let down. I always felt like I was cheating on my own baby as my milk soaked through my bra. Maybe it doesn't matter who cries out, female animals just produce milk for their kin.

(Fieldnotes 22 July 2019 South Farm, Logan, Utah)

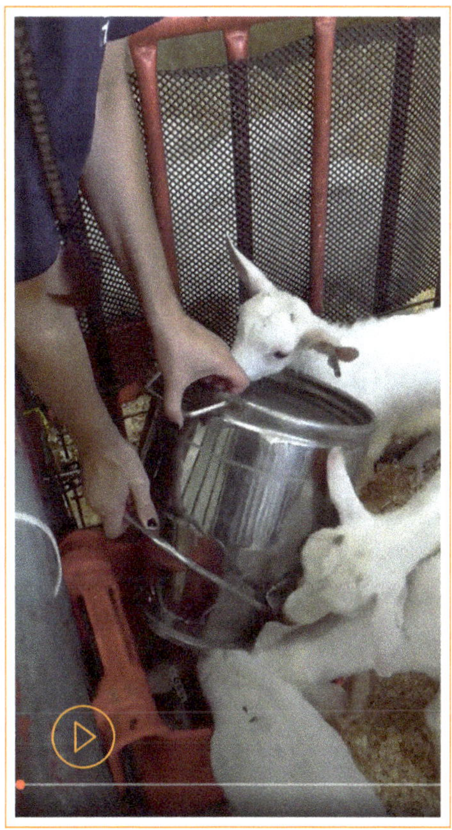

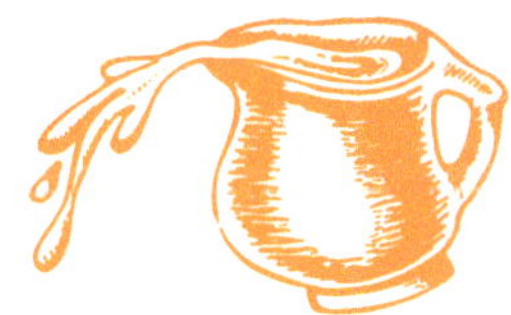

LINK TO VIDEO OF KIDS BEING FED NONTRANSGENIC MILK FROM GOATS AT SOUTH FARM UTAH:

https://youtu.be/0H0a0u2GrFM

These transcribed field notes and the accompanying video are from research I conducted during a project about transgenic goats in Utah from 2018–2021. As part of this work, I visited the Utah State University's farm and lab; interviewed several scientists, herdsmen and lab technicians; and observed the goats' everyday lives. By academic training, I'm a medical sociologist who uses feminist qualitative methods to explore the entanglements of humans and non-human animals in a variety of ecological settings. I've chronicled the interspecies relationships of goats, spiders and humans in the development and standardisation of spider silk production in my book, *Our Transgenic Future* (Moore, 2022). That book concludes by contemplating the possible end of the spider goats as their ability to make spider silk protein was starting to fail at the same time that the expense of maintaining the herd was rising. In several animal studies projects, I've used auto-ethnographic methods combined with multispecies ethnography to write deeply reflexive analysis. I'm becoming increasingly comfortable experimenting with artistic methods, more specifically creative writing techniques, as I grow my skills as an analyst.

My methodological tools are, however, not pursued without anxiety. In order to produce valid and reliable results, a hallmark of social scientific research, scholars are trained to mitigate subjective 'bias' in their analysis of data. Typically this training steers us away from the use of the first person in our writing. Feminist qualitative methods challenge these standards of methodological objectivity and push toward an approach of acknowledging the situated knowledges. From this feminist perspective, knowledge emerges from a context and is embedded in the historical and cultural context of the knower. Writing reflexively and drawing on the sensibilities of creative writing – plot, character development, imaginative narration – has enhanced my practices as a feminist social scientist. I blend these methods of qualitative inquiry (participant observation, meticulous fieldnotes, maintaining rapport) and creative nonfiction (imagery, vivid description, figurative language) to enhance my production of 'results'.

In this methods and creative writing piece, I explore my affinity to non-human animals by blending both my real lived experiences with my imaginative speculation about possible areas of mammalian and invertebrate connection. I have found using creative writing techniques to be valuable in my methodological rigour. In what follows, I explain my use of these creative qualitative and writing techniques in my multispecies ethnographies with bees, horseshoe crabs and goats (Kirksey and Helmreich, 2010). I conclude with some creative writing generated from my multispecies ethnographic fieldwork and data analysis.

AUTOETHNOGRAPHY, CREATIVE WRITING, AND MULTISPECIES ETHNOGRAPHIES

While autoethnography can be productive, it can also make me cringe (Ellis, 2004). I feel honest when I am deeply reflexive about my own lived experience and social position as I investigate different life worlds. But I also acknowledge how truly self-involved it feels. It's a delicate balancing act of sharing intimate details of my process and subjectivity, while also maintaining the critical sociological stance of my training. It feels risky, the potential perils of resisting the presumptive safety of an omniscient narrator. Accusations of bias abound, igniting me to swiftly assert that reflexivity is actually a way to engage with bias in an honest and open fashion. Trained in the traditions of feminist standpoint epistemologies (Smith, 1987; Harding, 1991), I maintain a stance of critical circumspection as I interrogate the dizzying flows of power between and among myself and the objects and subjects of my study. Entering the field sites of multispecies auto-ethnographic projects – urban honey beekeeping, horseshoe crab citizen science, and transgenic goat husbandry (Moore, 2022, 2017; Moore and Kosut 2013) – I have taken my whole self with me into the field: my body, my statuses and my memories. I have been variously accompanied by my partners, my children and my dog.

My formal methodological training began as a graduate student in a programme developed by Anselm Strauss, an originator of Grounded Theory. According to Strauss, it is through one's immersion in the data that these comparisons become the 'stepping stones' for formal theories of patterns of action and interaction between and among various types of data. By triangulating data sources from wide ranging data sites, analysts are able to establish various points of comparison to explore the range of dimensions of concepts. Working with analytic memos, researchers can establish interrelationships between concepts. 'Theory evolves during actual research, and it does this through continuous interplay between analysis and data collection.' (Strauss and Corbin, 1990: 273)

I have used Grounded Theory in many of my research projects because it is a flexible method that can be adapted to suit the needs of the research project. The approach is not prescriptive, and researchers are encouraged to be creative in their methods. Also, Grounded Theory is particularly useful when the research aims to understand the context in which a phenomenon occurs. The method emphasises the importance of understanding the social, cultural and historical context in which data is collected. Furthermore, Grounded Theory lends itself well to creative and artistic methods because it is an inductive theory; it starts with empirical observations and then develops theories or explanations based on those observations. Inductive reasoning involves moving from specific observations to broader generalisations and theories. In grounded theory, this involves analysing data in an iterative process, searching for patterns and themes, and gradually developing categories and concepts that explain the data.

One place I can generate a lot of ideas for my grounded theory on any topic is through the work of other creative artists, particularly the authors and illustrators of children's books. As a former child and now mom of three daughters, I have spent a lot of time reading children's books. Whenever I am beginning a new research project, I go to the Brooklyn Public Library and take out all the children's books available on the topic. When my daughters were younger, I enjoyed reading these books to them. I'd often ask the girls what they thought of the text or the illustrations. Part interview, part maternal nudging; for example, I'd ask them whether or not the Billy Goats Gruff were smarter than the troll and how they knew. Reading Eric Carle's pop-up book *The Honeybee and the Robber* (Carle, 1994) was an opportunity to think about how honeybees have to work together to protect the hive from honey thieves. From these conversations and my own reading and re-reading of the books, I developed research questions or themes that I was interested in exploring in my ethnographic work. Seeing first-hand how the anthropomorphism in children's books encouraged my daughters to establish empathy for non-human animals, I could see that the personification of bees, goats and horseshoe crabs (among other animals) offered humans some angle of connection.

Being able to represent the ethnographic field can be a challenge for social scientists. The writing techniques of using metaphors, similes and imagery can generate linguistic capacities. For example, channelling sensory perceptions of a place – the smells, sights, taste, sounds and textures – provides material to sketch out all the ways in which a place is sensed. In this vein, creative writing exercises often involve generating a vivid setting similar to the concept of thick description in the tradition of Clifford Geertz. Geertz's concept of 'thick description' is a method of interpreting and explaining cultural phenomena by providing detailed, contextualised descriptions of cultural practices, symbols and meanings (Geertz, 1973). I use voice memos to quickly describe my feelings when I come into a new field site. Taking many photographs of the physical site as well as recording some of the ambient sounds helps me to later free-write about my sensorial impressions. Transcribing my voice memos while flipping through my photographs often looks like stanzas of poems, which can generate new insights (Richardson, 1993).

Another technique I use to creatively generate ways of seeing and interpreting data from a multispecies field is stimulating my capacities for empathy. 'Verstehen' is a German term that means 'understanding' or 'comprehension' in English. It was introduced by the German sociologist Max Weber, who used it to refer to a method of understanding social behaviour and action from the perspective of the individual involved (Weber, 2011). In sociology, 'Verstehen' refers to the process of empathetic understanding the subjective meaning and motivations behind a person's behaviour, rather than just analysing it objectively based on external factors. This approach allows sociologists to gain a deeper understanding of social phenomena by considering the unique perspectives and experiences of the individuals involved. Conducting a multispecies ethnography typically means researchers must establish empathy for non-human animals. Taking on the perspective of the other is enhanced through creative writing skills, especially the reading of fiction, including fables and myths. For example, Perumal Murugan's *The Story of the Goat* (Murugan and Raman 2019) reminds me of the power of fables and allegories. This book taught me about our human capacities for cross-species compassion and love. The simple writing style and pacing of the story can sneak up on you as you develop sincere feelings for the main character, a small black goat.

Using these techniques – reading children's books, vivid setting exercises and sensory free writing, empathetic understanding and flirting with fiction – in what follows, I share an example of my creative writing about spider goats. By means of framing this creative writing, I share that I have used scientific innovations (however low tech, like at home insemination with a syringe) in order to reproduce my own children. In my previous work, *Sperm Counts* published in 2007, I 'came out' about this practice (Moore, 2007). I am a queer, menopausal mother of three daughters (ages 27, 24 and 16) conceived through donor insemination using both known fresh semen and unknown banked technosemen modified by scientific manipulation, stored in liquid nitrogen, and shipped across the country. While things have shifted in the sixteen years since *Sperm Counts* was published and queer reproduction has become more prevalent, contestations over the creation and existence of queer families persist – my daughters are 'freaks of nature'. Because of my personal life juggling the 'relatedness' of my kids, the 'naturalness' of our family, the incubation of biological experiments inside my body, and the cultural surveillance of my family, I feel an affinity toward spider goats. These goats are genetically modified through the addition of spider DNA in order to lactate spider silk for military and medical innovation. For three years, I spent time with these spider goats in Utah and found our ontological strangeness to enhance my epistemological interpretation of goats. I draw on my lived experiences to subvert the notion of the natural and the constructed. In many ways, my life reconstructs *the natural* and at the same time foregrounds the constructed nature of everything we call natural. Sometimes I do experience 'Nature' as oppressive, and believe it can be reconstructed to better serve those whom it oppresses.

AMONG THE FREAKS

I felt very activated during the weeks I was in Logan, Utah with spider goats. Even before leaving, I was primed by lots of opinions about my trip. In casual conversations with friends and family, I got an earful. One friend half-joked that I should be careful entering the lab as I could be abducted for 'some freaky experiments of splicing your genes' with a different animal. Most people referenced Frankenstein in some form or another. I was repeatedly warned about some nefarious and looming horror I'd soon encounter. 'Be careful', my mother texted as I boarded the plane.

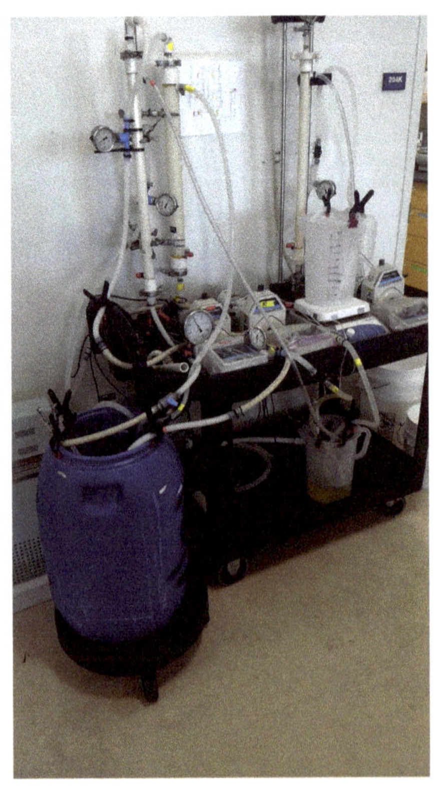

IMAGE 1.

Filtration system for running the purification of transgenic goat's milk to extract the spider silk protein

But the animals, the farm and the lab didn't appear out of the ordinary – even though something rather extraordinary was going on. These transgenically modified Saanen goats lactate spider silk protein and the entire operation – the laboratory, the offices, the farm, the fields – are designed to extract as much protein from the goats' milk as possible. They are literally and figuratively being wrung out for every last drop. Their breeding, feeding, veterinary care, surveillance, milking technologies all coalesce to create favourable circumstances for transgenic milk production. The lab with purification contraptions, centrifuges, filters, pipettes and beakers is designed to extract as much protein as possible. Imagine this gigantic udder just being twisted with as much force as possible to drain it empty.

I've also kind of wrung them out – I've taken hundreds of photographs and videos, produced pages and pages of field notes. Whereas the scientists, engineers and herdsmen want to get material and tangible products from the goats, I want to get something more ethereal. I am 'milking' the goats for meaning and metaphor. My extraction process also stimulates intrusive memories of my own reproductive experiences, breastfeeding and mothering. It's as if I can leverage my experience of motherhood, all the beauty and the horror, to see, hear, touch and know the goats. I jotted down these memories alongside my fieldnotes as a means to capture this generative opportunity. I also did a lot of free writing on what it is to be a freak and how freakish my experience of queer reproduction and parenting has been.

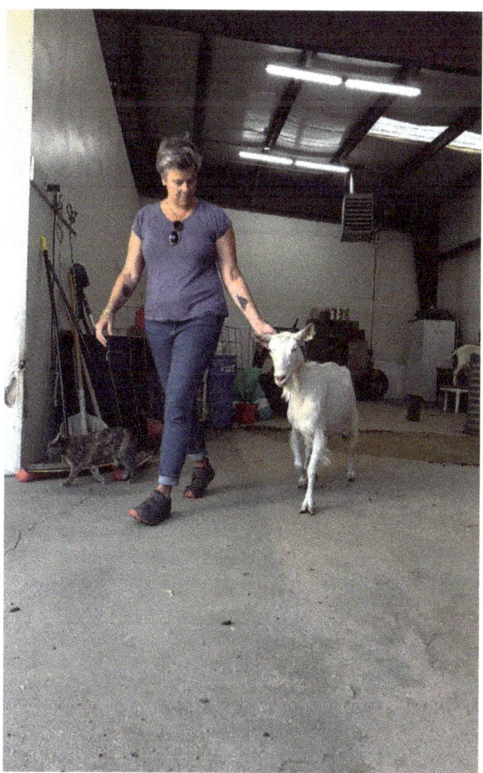

IMAGE 2.

Author walking Spider Goat back to pen after milking at South Farm at the Utah State University Barn.

What is a 'freak of nature'? A person, animal or plant that has unusual or abnormal physical characteristics that are not commonly seen in their species. In order to reproduce these particular offspring, the goats have been modified. Diverted from their reproductive standard operating procedures and reproduced through in vitro rather than in vivo methods. Spider goats were made through splicing and genetic manipulation outside of their bodies. Their offspring are queer, extra, new, special.

When the goat puts her chin into the palm of my hand, I feel the warmth and weight of her head. She pushes down into my hand and nuzzles, a gentle rub back and forth. I flex my forearm muscles as I take her weight. When she removes her head, a scent of goat lingers on my fingers and I smell it over and over again as I wander through the barn. This sense of wholesomeness reverberates through me while in the barn; all industry is stripped away. I'm fully present here with the goats at this precise moment, making physical contact. An affinity. One mammal to another. But all around us, reminders of the modifications and domestications, the artifice that scaffolds this entire operation. I want to trick myself into some sense that there is something natural, true, pure and real going on here. I don't want to admit to my complicity – I can lean heavy into being a mom as a way to purify myself. Is my motherhood a form of solidarity that cancels out my sociological grift?

Wanting to help and make myself useful to Amber, the herdsman, I walk the goats back to their stable pen after they are milked. It isn't totally necessary for me to hold the collar as the goat is leading me. On our walk, I briefly fantasise about us making a break for it. I loosen my grip to the collar but the goat doesn't seize the opportunity and quickens her pace to make it back to the stable. But we could just go over to that open field over there – I try to transmit this idea to the goat. I want her to taste the grass over in the field, wander aimlessly on the small hill next to the stable, experience a different view, or get energised by newness. We could be rebels and resist the milking routine but she seems almost relieved to get back to the confines of the pen. Domestication has produced a tameness that I both personally recognise and resent; I am after all a good girl despite my supposed rejection of heteronormativity. As I consider my fleeting fantasy about running in a field with a frolicking renegade goat, I realise how speciesist my ideas of liberation truly are.

We are strange sisters, me and the goats. Mothers that came to it through a combination of technical and folksy wisdom. I took a vial of semen from the liquid nitrogen tank and rolled it between my fingers. Then, to warm it up, I placed the vial under my armpit for a few seconds, melting the pellet of semen into a liquid. A syringe, a speculum and a pile of pillows all arranged to do the insemination on the couch. For some reason this procedure is freakish but a penis entering a vagina and ejaculating is not.

Because of the ways we reproduced, our kids are freaks. But when I look at these kids and my own kids, there is nothing different about them. They look ordinary. No one would know their origin story unless told. And then again, they are also exceptional, made differently, raised differently. There is some novelty in our offspring. But I have access to my kids, and theirs are taken from them at birth. They have to be milked to extract the spider silk protein, the remaining milk is thrown away since it isn't worth anything to humans.

I sit in the barn and take in all the low-tech interventions. The milking stands face a wall of the barn with square jaggedly cut wooden panelling over the wall. These two stands are constructed with a metal lever used to immobilise their heads. It looks like a sideways guillotine. Goats are voracious and indiscriminate eaters. While being milked, the goats took to eating the insulation of the unfinished barn walls, so the herdsmen had to block their access with a wood cut out. Before the suction cups are connected, the herdsman wipes down their teats with an antibacterial wipe. The feed is poured into containers in front of the goat's faces, the compressor is turned on. The noise of the machines is loud and grinding but the goats just eat their feed, seemingly unfazed, while the milk flows through the plastic tubing.

I'm reminded of the hours of pumping my own milk in faculty offices, counting the ceiling tiles above my desk while my undergraduate students waited outside. For the goats, after the milk stops flowing, about ten minutes, they are disconnected and their teats are sprayed with Fight Bac (a disinfectant to prevent mastitis in dairy animals). I sympathise with this as my breasts needed special care too. I recall applying lanolin, a wool wax from sheep, to my sore and cracked nipples after nursing and pumping to comfort and protect them. Our kinship is reflected in the routine of mammalian service, the repetition of providing precious liquid for others, the rituals of domestication. It feels as if our tameness is a commonality, our doing what comes naturally for someone else under unnatural circumstances with assistance of *man*-made machines.

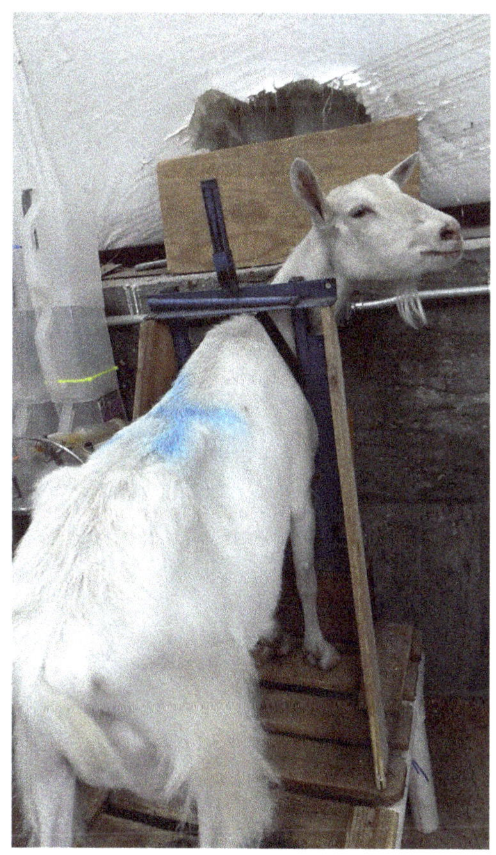

IMAGE 3.
Locked in to start being milked

I have brought my body, my history, my stories with me to the field. I cannot see the goats and

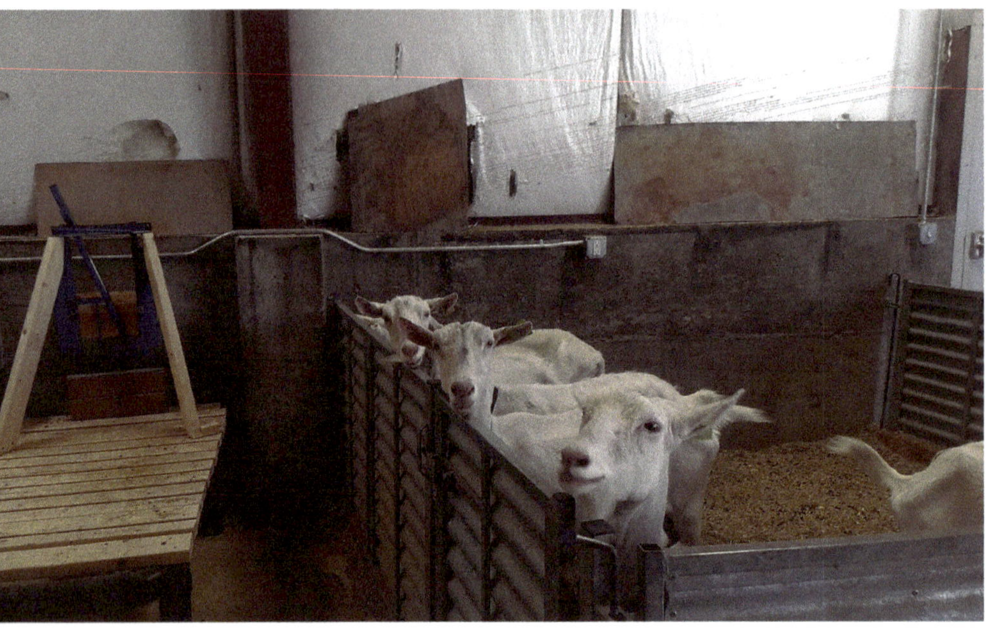

IMAGE 4.

Spider goats eagerly waiting to be milked at South Farm, Utah State University.

their kids without seeing myself and my kids. We are strange sisters, me and the goats. The yearning in me to be seen but not made exceptional, to resist what has been expected of me as a woman through my queerness, to raise my family in a hetronormative world where our relatedness is questioned all bubbles to the surface when I am with the goats. I want to help them break free but I can't, or I don't, and they do not seem to want it. For me, motherhood has been a taming force. Pregnancy, being milked, pregnancy, being milked, pregnancy being milked. Rinse, repeat. I think of how domestic my own life is, of food shopping and housekeeping, drop-offs and pick-ups, always returning to the house, not escaping. The goats return happily to their pen, submit willingly to their pumping, and eat intently while extraction hums along.

ARTNOGRAPHIC STATEMENT

In order to produce valid and reliable results, a hallmark of social scientific research, scholars are trained to mitigate subjective 'bias' in their analysis of data. Typically this training steers us away from the use of the first person in our writing. Feminist qualitative methods challenge these standards of methodological rigour and push toward situated knowledges. From this feminist perspective, knowledge is not a pure object or demonstrable fact but it instead emerges from a context and is embedded in the historical and cultural context of the knower. Writing reflexively and drawing on the sensibilities of creative writing – plot, character development, imaginative narration – has enhanced my practices as a feminist social scientist. I blend these methods of qualitative inquiry (participant observation, meticulous fieldnotes, maintaining rapport) and creative nonfiction (imagery, vivid description, figurative language) to enhance my production of 'results'.

In this creative writing piece, I explore my affinity to spider goats by blending both my real lived experiences with my imaginative speculation about possible areas of mammalian connection. I have used scientific innovations (however low tech, like at home insemination with a syringe) in order to reproduce my children. In my previous work, *Sperm Counts* published in 2007, I 'came out' about this practice. I am a queer mother of three daughters conceived through donor insemination using both known fresh semen and unknown banked technosemen modified by scientific manipulation, stored in liquid nitrogen, and shipped across the country. While things have shifted in the fourteen years since *Sperm Counts* was published and queer reproduction has become more prevalent, contestations over the creation and existence of queer families persist – my daughters are 'freaks of nature'. Because of my personal life juggling the 'relatedness' of my kids, the 'naturalness' of our family, the incubation of biological experiments inside my body, and the cultural surveillance of my family, I feel an affinity toward spider goats. These goats are genetically modified through the addition of spider DNA in order to lactate spider silk for military and medical innovation. For three years, I spent time with these spider goats in Utah and found our ontological strangeness to enhance my epistemological interpretation of goats. I draw on my lived experiences to subvert the notion of the natural and the constructed. In many ways, my life reconstructs *the natural* and at the same time foregrounds the constructed nature of everything we call natural. Sometimes I do experience 'Nature' as oppressive, and believe it can be reconstructed to better serve those whom it oppresses.

ACKNOWLEDGEMENTS

I'd like to thank the editors, the anonymous reviewers and my friend Megan Davidson for their help on this essay.

REFERENCES

Carle, E. 1994. *The Honeybee and the Robber: A Moving/Picture Book*. New York: Scholastic.

Ellis, C. 2004. *The Ethnographic I: A Methodological Novel about Autoethnography*, Ethnographic Alternatives Book Series, v. 13. Walnut Creek, CA: AltaMira Press.

Geertz, C. 1973. *Thick Description: Toward an Interpretive Theory of Culture*. New York: Basic Books.

Harding, S. 1991. *Whose Science/Whose Knowledge? Thinking From Women's Lives*. Ithaca: Cornell University Press.

Kirksey, E. and S. Helmreich. 2010. 'The emergence of multispecies ethnography'. *Cultural Anthropology* **25** (4): 545–76.

Moore, L.J. 2022. *Our Transgenic Future: Genetic Modification, Animals and the Will to Change Nature*. New York: New York University Press.

Moore, L.J. 2017. *Catch and Release: The Enduring yet Vulnerable Horseshoe Crab*. New York: New York University Press.

Moore, L.J. 2007. *Sperm Counts: Overcome by Man's Most Precious Fluid*. New York: New York University Press.

Moore, L.J. and M. Kosut. 2013. *Buzz: Urban Beekeeping and the Power of the Bee*. New York: New York University Press.

Murugan, P. and N. Kalyan Raman. 2019. *The Story of a Goat*, First Grove Atlantic paperback edition. New York: Black Cat.

Smith, D. 1987. *The Everyday World as Problematic: A Feminist Sociology*. Boston: Northeastern University Press.

Strauss, A. and J. Corbin. 1990. *Basics of Qualitative Research*. Newbury Park: Sage.

Richardson, L. 1993. 'Poetics, dramatics, and transgressive validity: The case of the skipped line'. *The Sociological Quarterly* **34** (4): 695–710. https://doi.org/10.1111/j.1533-8525.1993.tb00113.x

Weber, M. 2011. *Methodology of Social Sciences*. New Brunswick, NJ: Transaction Publishers.

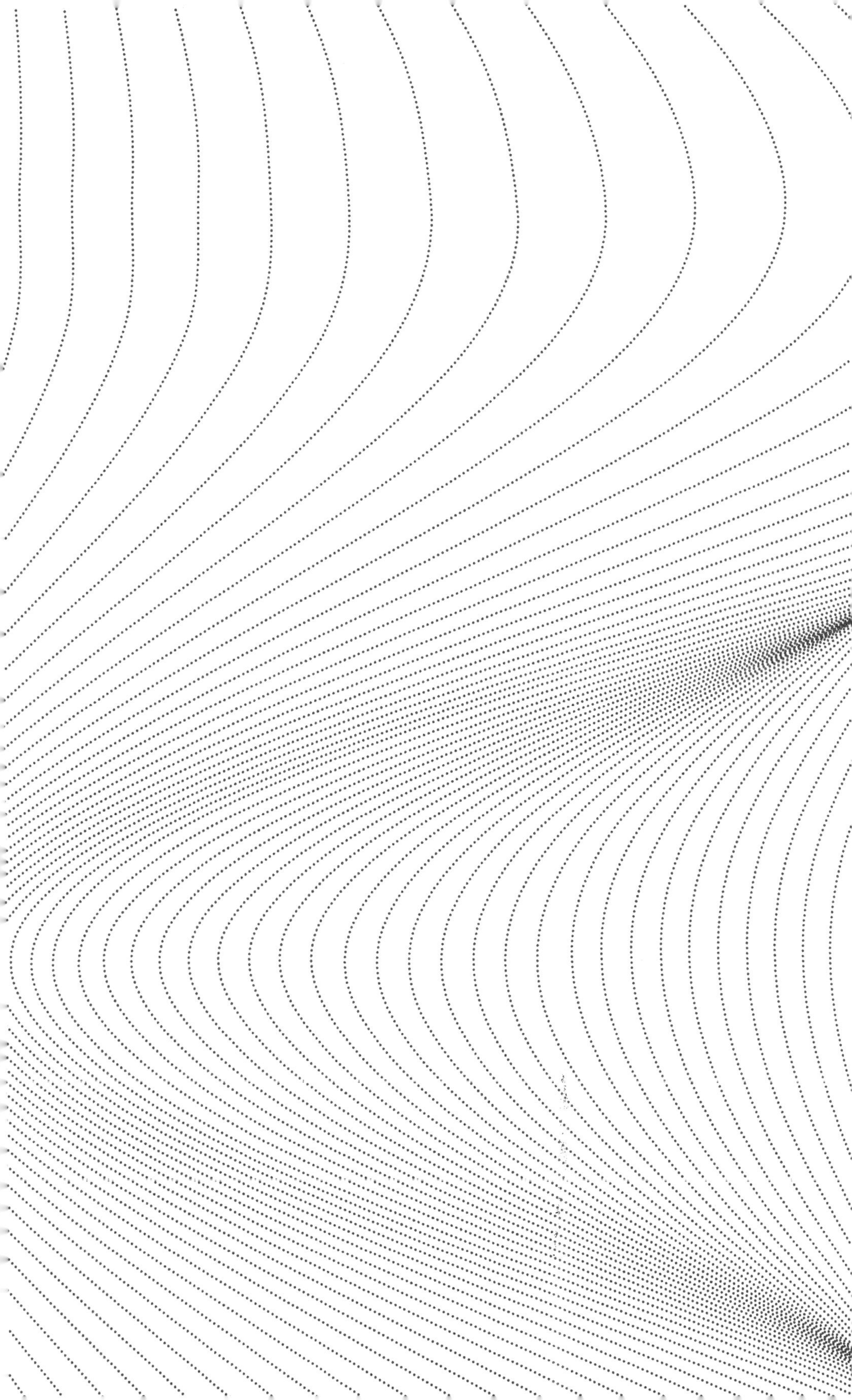

10. ETHNOGRAPHY OF WORKING COWHORSES: RHYMING SENSORY METHODS

Andrea Petitt

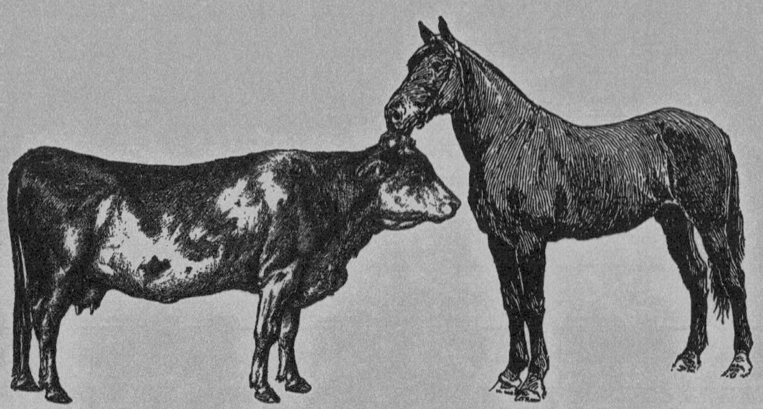

DOI: 10.63308/63878687083054.ch10

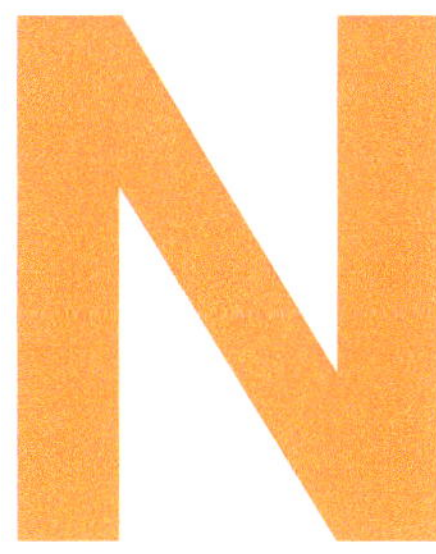o human has spoken for an hour or two
But the air is dense enough to cut through
The horse below speaks with movement of ear
And the message to cattle in front is quite clear

With loose reins and no pressure from spur
I can feel how my strawberry roan starts to stir
He motions to cow with his energy stance
In this power relation she does not stand a chance

He pushes her energy bubble through space
Expands his own bubble with grace
Without touching the pressure is on
Cow quickens her pace and the pressure is gone

Surely, it cannot be denied
That I'm dominating the horses I ride
But horses and cows under human dominion
Have, if we listen, their own opinion

They sure do more than just resist
They take initiative and insist
They have their own valued projects indeed
That go beyond sleep, reproduction and feed

With sensory methods of ethnographic collection
We can widen the scope of material selection
Tactile talk and sensing of pressure
Energy bubbles might be our treasure

These exchanges don't always fit into
An ordinary academic sentence or two
Conventional analysis and dissemination
Might struggle to explain and show sensation

Tapping into poetic methods traditions
We can challenge the norming academic conditions
Looking at structures that we want to transform
While letting local animal agency inform

Leaping beyond grammatic control
Poetry and rhymes can play a role
Rhyming can structure analytical thought
Poetic inquiry distils the data we brought[1]

1 For energy bubbles see Petitt (forthcoming); for valued projects see Ortner (2001, 2006); for sensory methods see Fijn and Kavesh (2021); for poetic methods traditions see Zani (2019); Petitt (forthcoming); for challenging norming academic traditons see Ohito and

ARTNOGRAPHIC STATEMENT

Drawing on a year of ethnographic fieldwork on working cattle ranches in the Rocky Mountains of Colorado, this ethnographic poem – an analytical 'rapstract' (Petitt, 2018) – speaks to the multisensory and multispecies methods necessary to understand the power relations infused in the multispecies triad of human, horse and cow in a ranching setting (also see Petitt, 2023a). Arguing for pushing the frontier of sensory ethnography to include what I am framing as 'energy bubbles', this piece strives to bring heightened attention to the dynamic nuances of multispecies and particularly non-human power performances. The rapstract typically breaks the 'fourth wall' in directly spelling out the analytical moves by its author, in addition to the elements of field poetry (Zani, 2019) or poetic inquiry (Fernández-Giménez, 2018), portraying the ethnographic setting and analysis. Moreover, this rhyme refers explicitly to method whilst simultaneously showcasing the artful research method of rhyming/ethnographic poetry itself.

The practice of poetry differs greatly between practitioners and poets, as does probably the motivation for and aim of writing poetry at all. Poetic attention, and rhyming in particular, are increasingly crucial for my understanding of the world around me, especially in research settings. In my research, which mainly takes a multispecies ethnographic approach and almost exclusively deals with gender and intersectionality questions in cross-species relations in agriculture across different continents, I use rhyming poetry in three overarching and entangled ways: in data collection, for analysis and to disseminate research results.[2]

When I first started conducting data analysis through rhyming, I didn't know there was a whole field called 'ethnographic poetry' (Maynard and Cahnmann-Taylor, 2010). Because the first pieces I wrote and performed at conferences struck me as some sort of rhyming abstracts, and because I read them to some kind of beat, I called them 'rapstracts', although they do not stem from a rap tradition. After I was asked to publish some of these texts in a Swedish journal for gender research (Petitt, 2018), the word 'rapstract' stuck.

What I had discovered and somewhat formalised was that writing analytically through rhyming helped me to focus on the core of what I wanted to say – there is not space for fluff and over-explanation in a rhyming poem – and the

Nyachae (2019) and Petitt (2023b); for rhyming structuring academic thought see Petitt 2018; 2023a; 2023b; 2024; for poetic inquiry see Fernández-Giménez 2018; Faulkner, 2020.

2 Together with Véronique Servais, I write about this at length elsewhere (Petitt and Servais 2024; Petitt forthcoming), as well as how I also use drawing as a method in these three entangled research activities.

process helped me to discover unspoken premises and potential logical stumbles that I needed to work through. The rhyming itself allowed me, forced me, to come up with different ways to say the same thing – find different words that rhymed – and still convey the essence of what I was trying to say. This practice sharpens my analysis in that it helps me feel what part of the sentence – and thus the idea itself – is crucial to my conceptualisation, in my analysis and that absolutely has to make it into the next version of the phrase or stanza. It is a little bit like moving between different languages, making sure that the right nuance of a word is translated when I choose between potential synonyms in other languages. Building text one verse at the time, it becomes easy to see if one line actually follows logically from the verse before, and if any verse or stanza is unnecessary. In the analytical phase, the poem thus works as my 'bullshit detector'.

As a method to collect data, the ethnographic poem in my rhyming version has been crucial at times during my field work. Inspired by Leah Zani's (2019) *field poems*, I write about *field rhymes*, as a particular kind of field poems. During my yearlong *horseback ethnography* on two working cattle ranches in the Rocky Mountains of Colorado, where I conducted multispecies ethnography focusing on the multispecies triad of the humans, horses and cattle living, working and moving together, these rhymes helped me distil the essence of an experience, meeting, happening, a day or relation or even everyday practices over a longer period. The word 'distil' pops up continuously when I read about the experience of writing poetry or songs, such as in Mary Gauthier's (2021) thoughtful book *Saved by a Song*. While catching every single detail of a day or event might seem ideal in the field, often it is simply not possible. We always make editorial and subjective choices.

At my 'home ranch', where I lived during my fieldwork, I spent my days together with the mother and daughter who were the only other humans living and working there, and I took part in whatever they did. Not only did they do the horseback cattle work, but they also tended to fences, hay, equipment as well as taking up all the managing work of an owner, manager, cowboss and so on. At the neighbouring ranch, where I spent roughly two days a week during fall, late spring and summer, in order to get a different perspective, the days in the saddle were longer as they had more cattle, vast grazing lands and a hired (all male) cowboying crew. Sometimes, after ten hours in the saddle I would come home to my house at my home ranch absolutely exhausted. Mustering the energy to eat, shower and prepare for the next day, the writing of field notes could feel like an insurmountable wall. I would do what I could during the day, scribbling down words and sentences, mumble into my voice recorder and use my cell phone and the mounted camera strapped to my chest to capture events, thoughts and feelings. But most of the time I needed all parts of my body, brain, energy and focus to 'read' the cows in front of me and around me, communicate with the horse beneath me and to pay close attention to how my fellow humans were moving and potentially signalling what I needed to do next. Many days I simply did not manage to write much on the fly.

Sitting down at night and letting the feelings, images and thoughts run through me, paying poetic attention to it all, in addition to ethnographic attention, the rhymes would roll into my head and body and I would write them down. Rather than struggling to try to capture as much detail as possible about everything from morning to evening, I would lean in to the pleasure of poetic pondering and the sharpness it could bring to a heightened sense of perception. I could capture that which struck me as most remarkable about the day, a particular event or social relations. I could capture thoughts that were hard to express in ordinary language. I could get something down on paper where I would otherwise write nothing. Over time, these field rhymes collected into a rich and varied multispecies ethnographic portrayal. Most days I also wrote some additional field notes, but as I went through my material, I often found the rhymes became particularly useful in the analytical process – together with field drawings.[3]

Both field rhymes and analytical rhymes have made their way into my research dissemination. When teaching or presenting at conferences I often, almost always, use a rhyme to either portray an ethnographic piece or make an analytical point. Sometimes I make a rapstract for the particular presentation to sum up the main take away points, including as a part of the second MEAM conference that links with this volume. People have come up to me afterwards expressing that it was when they heard the rhyme that they really understood the theoretical framework I had been explaining during a presentation, or that they really could imagine the field setting and the context. These poems also reach a wider academic audience beyond academia. My choice to use the cowboy poetry format has meant that I can share my work with my cowboying interlocuters in the field, giving them an idea of what I have been up to and conveyed in a way that they find more accessible. Cowboy poetry is a tradition amongst working cowboys and performed at rodeos and cowboy gatherings of different sort. It tends to rhyme, use a ballad structure and heed no particular verse measure; and it typically tells of cowboying life with a funny twist or tone.

3 I write about my use of field drawings elsewhere, in Petitt and Servais, 2024; Petitt forthcoming.

The poetry at the beginning of this piece, a rhyming ethnographic poem, came about a couple of years after the fieldwork took place. I had been kneading the material I collected and had come quite far in analysing my ethnographic data into explicit theoretical development and methodological advancement and the rhyme sprung from a need to clarify the use of these artful methods. The rhyming poem is thus based on my original field work, and draws – as most analytical work – on other scholars' theorisation and methodological contributions as well as my own conceptualisation of the 'energy bubble'. The concept of the energy bubble is an emic formulation and more-than-human concept whereby power is felt in space. I build here on the idea of 'feel', which horse writers have conceptualised as that elusive and embodied feeling of interconnection between horse and rider (Brandt, 2004; 2006; Zetterquist Blokhuis, 2019; Blokhuis and Lundgren, 2017; Dashper, 2016; Fijn, 2021). Horse riders strive for this connection and in my field setting of working cattle ranches, not only the human and horse are taken into account when striving for smooth connection, but also their triadic interaction with cattle. Moving cattle smoothly and calmly, which is the stated goal at these cattle ranches, human and horse need to gauge their own energy bubble towards that of the cow or cattle that they are trying to move. The bubble is not referred to as a physical entity but as a socially felt pressure in space. Learning from humans, horses and cattle alike to perceive these bubbles through various senses, I started to understand them as the very core of the local and situated multispecies power relations of the multispecies triad of the American West.

The main point of the rhyme, however, is the usefulness of artful methods and poetic ones in particular. Such analytical poetry has served to 'w/rap up' some of my talks at conferences and teaching spaces and is thus meant for dissemination, as a way to think through a particular theory or understand and portray a particular piece or angle of field-based material. Yet most of what I rhyme never meets the eyes or ears of others – the rhymes are ways for myself to think through, or feel through, my data collection and analysis. Moreover, as they follow the ballad structure of cowboy poetry, rather than any particular verse measure, they are rhythmic in my head and when I read them out loud myself, but they might stumble and seem rhythmically erratic when others read them. In this way, engaging poetry can be relational. A bit like riding a galloping horse – you need to synchronise with the horse's movements in order to find the 'feel' and to not bump about on their back. Try it, read it again, and see if you can get the poetic 'feel'.

REFERENCES

Blokhuis, M.Z. and C. Lundgren. 2017. 'Riders' perceptions of equestrian communication in sports dressage'. *Society & Animals* **25** (6): 573–91.

Brandt, K. 2004. 'A language of their own: An interactionist approach to human-horse communication'. *Society & Animals* **12** (4): 299–316.

Brandt, K. 2006. 'Intelligent bodies: Embodied subjectivity human-horse communication'. In *Body/embodiment: Symbolic Interaction and the Sociology of the Body*, pp. 141–52.

Dashper, K. 2016. 'Learning to communicate: The triad of (mis)communication in horse riding'. In Donna Lee Davis and Anita Maurstad (eds). *The Meaning of Horses: Biosocial Encounters*, pp. 87–101. New York: Routledge.

Faulkner, S.L. 2020. *Poetic Inquiry: Craft, Method and Practice*. Second edition. New York and London: Routledge.

Fernández-Giménez, M.E. 2015. '"A shepherd has to invent": Poetic analysis of socialecological change in the cultural landscape of the central Spanish Pyrenees'. *Ecology and Society* **20** (4):29. https://doi.org/10.5751/ES-08054-200429

Fernández-Giménez, M.E., L.B. Jennings and H. Wilmer. 2018. 'Poetic inquiry as a research and engagement method in natural resource'. *Science, Society & Natural Resources*. https://doi.org/10.1080/08941920.2018.1486493

Fijn, Natasha. 2021. 'Human-horse sensory engagement through horse archery'. *Australian Journal of Anthropology* **32**: 58–79.

Fijn, N. and M.A. Kavesh. 2023. 'Towards a multisensorial engagement with animals'. In Phillip Vannini (ed.) *The Routledge International Handbook of Sensory Ethnography*. London: Routledge.

Gauthier, Mary. (2021). *Saved by a Song: The Art and Healing Power of Songwriting*. New York: St Martin's Essentials.

Maynard, K. and M. Cahnmann-Taylor. 2010. 'Anthropology at the edge of words: Where poetry and ethnography meet'. *Anthropology and Humanism* **35** (1): 2–19.

Ortner, S.B. 2001. 'Specifying agency: The Comaroffs and their critics'. *Interventions* **3** (1): 76–84.

Ortner, S.B. 2006. *Anthropology and Social Theory: Culture, Power, and the Acting Subject*. Durham, NC: Duke University Press.

Ohito, E.O. and T.M. Nyachae. 2019. 'Poetically poking at language and power: Using Black feminist poetry to conduct rigorous feminist critical discourse analysis'. *Qualitative Inquiry* **25** (9–19): 839–50.

Petitt, A. (forthcoming). *The Multispecies Triad of Cattle Ranching: A Horseback Ethnography in the Rocky Mountains of Colorado*. Multispecies Anthropology: New Ethnographies series. Abingdon and New York: Routledge.

Petitt, Andrea. 2024. 'Gender and intersectionality in agriculture on three continents: A rapstract compilation'. In S. Swart (ed.) *Gender and Animals in History: Yearbook of Women's History 42*, pp. 307–12. Amsterdam: Amsterdam University Press.

Petitt, Andrea. 2023a. 'Conceptualizing the multispecies triad: Towards a multispecies intersectionality'. *Feminist Anthropology* **4** :23–37. https://doi.org/10.1002/fea2.12099

Petitt, Andrea. 2023b. 'At arm's length. Open forum'. *European Journal of Women's Studies* **30** (1): 103–05.

Petitt, Andrea. 2021. 'Cow paths and horse trails: in academia and around the world'. In L. Birke and Harry Wels (eds). *Dreaming of Pegasus: Equine Imaginings*, pp. 99–115. Uttoxeter: Victorina Press Ltd.

Petitt, Andrea. 2018. 'Rapstract: genus i jordbruk på tre kontinenter'. Frispel. *Tidskrift för Genusvetenskap* **39** (4): 97–102.

Petitt, A and V. Servais. 2024. 'Artful multispecies ethnography: reflections from ongoing practices'. *Anthrovisions*.

Zani, L. 2019. 'A fieldpoem for World Poetry Day'. *Anthropology News website*, March.

Zetterqvist Blockhuis, M. 2019. 'Interaction between rider, horse and equestrian trainer: a challenging Puzzle'. *Södertörn Doctoral Dissertations*: Stockholm.

AFTER WORDS: TOWARD A NEW KIND OF FIELD GUIDE

Karin Bolender

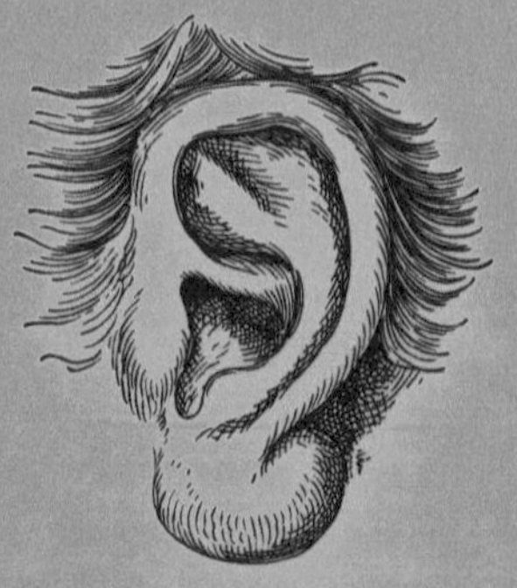

DOI: 10.63308/63878687083054.after

Because printed words on a page are not enough.

Because prescribed patterns of prose constrain, even as they create vital channels for meaning and memory to flow.

Because worms seek warm places, whether we pay attention or not.

Because trees, snow, and herbivores speak for themselves – even if their stories are illegible.

Because bubbles' edges shimmer, expand and contract, holding kaleidoscopic refractions of shared lives inside of them.

Because eyelashes. Ear flicks. Whiskers fit exactly to a tunnel's dark width.

Because *a bull licking a baby's sock.*

If you've ventured deep into this collection, or even given it a cursory glance, you already know it offers new openings for researchers seeking to expand encounters in more-than-human worlds. This volume is not the sort of standard manual that provides easy directions for how to get from one popular site to another, or a checklist of the names of species to watch out for. Here, the paths are not paved or well-trodden – nor do they aim for or arrive at places one might expect to come across. Really what this volume does is guide one into wandering beyond marked and bounded fields, so we might learn better how to get lost and thus discover different ways to navigate through always-elusive, richly inhabited places. The terrain is varied here, unpredictable. The signs guiding us appear at times in unexpected forms: a scribbled line in the dirt, a murmured sound from underground or above in the trees, or a scent faintly streaming from within a shrub, or floating free on the breeze.

What we find here is like a series of curious landmarks, presented in a kind of field guide for intrepid researchers into more-than-human worlds. By necessity these are unmapped territories. By necessity, the marks we follow to find our ways are subtle, fluid as wind and water, and do not always adhere to recognised forms of authority – they overflow them.

But isn't this one of the main reasons we are drawn into more-than-human worlds as researchers, hoping to step lightly rather than bulldoze in search of insightful meetings with dynamic others in earthly places? Not to stake claims, or kick ass and take names, or even to extract valuable resources for the market or discursive exchange: we come into unknown worlds with wonder and curiosity – to practise becoming more humbly attentive, more alert to possibly significant scents, sounds and faint tracks on the ground that deepen our senses of who lives here and how.

In all these ways, this volume presents an array of openings into rich layers of fields, forests, pastures, shorelines, undergrounds, barnyards and open ranges where we go in the hope of learning from, with better respect towards, those we meet in these places. The collection ventures beyond the usual form of staid academic publication, a predictable sequence of prose chapters in which individual authors or teams report their fieldwork and shape their findings around an armature of disciplinary theories and standardised forms of delivery. Instead, the brave editors of this collection bring together generous intermedial spaces for both contributors and fellow researchers to explore. These projects offer unique sets of tools, methods and media to trace their own meanderings, which in turn lead to unforeseen encounters and insights.

Each project invites its own modes of encounter: various speeds, sensory apprehensions, ways of reading text/ures and the spaces between words or hearing words spoken. In her photo essay on ancient gum trees surviving amid suburban sprawl outside Canberra, Natasha Fijn reflects that the spatial arrays of images and text invite visitors to choose among various ways to engage with the media presented and at what pace (Fijn, this volume). This is true across the variety of forms presented throughout the collection – including still and moving images, sound, drawings, prints, handwriting, documents of time-based performance, alongside different kinds of text that range from densely poetic to expository. The unique marks of the human hand are present, as are voices (human and others) that come from singular bodies and merge with others present in places: birds, wind, insects, hums and grinds of machinery. The weave of media and distinct methods they each invite are not ornamental; this diversity is fundamental to the aims of each piece and the MEAM project as a whole. Each piece invites us to remember that meeting the mystery of others humbly and openly is a task that requires bottomless curiosity and openness.

Because there is no expert way to do what has never been done before. No authority who can affirm from outside whether or not we have met another being as respectfully as we might.

When I, an artist, tumbled down the rabbithole (or better yet a mole tunnel, following Hermione Spriggs) of multispecies ethnography over a decade ago, anthropology as a discipline was new to me. A burgeoning enthusiasm to include interdisciplinary perspectives made it possible for me to connect my artwork's core questions and desires with ideas and research across an emerging field. Yet a big conundrum remained; it bothered me profoundly that in most academic fields, the Book (or the Paper) stands as the ultimate end and mark of achievement. Because, frankly, I have never been satisfied that written publications on their own can be adequate as the primary product of encounters with more-than-humans worlds. The prospect of limiting reflections to standardised forms of expository prose to trace the joys and vicissitudes of making worlds with others (for whom language is not primary) has always seemed to me at best an absurdity and, at worst, something more treacherous.

With this in mind, I was both relieved and apprehensive to read this collection and its ambitions to integrate ethnographic research with artistic methods and media. Relieved: because the aims of the project foregrounded the limitations of traditional academic disciplines and outputs to respect the autonomy and agency of those who inhabit their worlds in other ways. But, as an artist, I was a little worried, too. Often the experience of artists engaged in academic-scientific realms involves compromising core principles and practices in uncomfortable ways. Such discomforts arise in what Andrew Yang calls the 'drunken conversation between two cultures', art and science (Yang, 2015). Sometimes in academic venues, this exchange can tend to feel, well, a bit uneven.

When Science sidles up to Art at the university bar, it's usually the one buying the drinks and determining the parameters of what gets talked about. Looming and leaning, and however fast and loose it plays, the Discipline decides what will be taken seriously or dismissed as silly, insensible, irrelevant, or passe. In such situations, art is allowed to speak its own language so long as it respects the terms and conditions of its admission to the conversation. It must be responsible to the common goals of rational, progressive knowledge-making discourse, even if it doesn't exactly share them … even if its aims are otherwise, impossible to articulate by means of expository prose and (politics of) citation. Even if it believes, alongside Hugo Ball, that its own goals as art are to 'speak a secret language and leave behind documents not of edification but of paradox' (Ball, 1974). Art might feel especially inclined to believe this when it proposes to speak with (if not for) other beings whose languages it must fail to fully grasp.

This failure to grasp the fullness of more-than-human worlds is in fact at the heart of the MEAM project's success. Rather than asserting authority through deployment of traditional disciplinary forms, the projects assembled here embrace a more experimental ethos in the making of hybrid forms for sharing their research. Of course, the creation of unrecognisable forms carries inherent risks of misapprehension. But a great success of this collection is that it is willing to take such risks, with an eye to the possible rewards that might be found on the other side.

One consistent way this project reaps the benefits of such risks is through its embrace of poetics through and across the different projects. Poetics serve many different roles across the chapters, but first and foremost is the overt recognition, as Merlijn Huntjens, Nina Willems and Leonie Cornips have it, that: '… there are subtleties in this communication that need *a different type of language* than the academic language' (this volume). It is worth noting how this might be particularly salient for academics, because there is real danger in the threat that one's thesis might not come across clearly. As linguistic communication, poetry grapples with and revels in this risk – and collects its rewards – in ways that traditional forms of expository prose do not.

The precarities I evoke here are generally integral to artistic practices, to poetic and nonlinguistic, visual, forms of communication. The artist usually holds that the danger of venturing into uncertainty is worth the novel encounters it leads to. While such wanderings afield may lead to dead ends at times, they are also a means to forge new crossings to uncharted, undisciplined spaces where we can meet others on more open grounds. For instance, Andrea Pettit describes how wrangling with the lyric traditions of cowboy poetry is not so much about the production of poems as it is a means to deepen her ethnographic practice, encouraging different rhythms and unexpected insights to emerge within her thinking on the range, moving between the differential force fields of cows, horses and the unruly sounds and meanings of words (Pettit, this volume). Bartram+Deigaard make the value of creative risk-taking explicit in documents of their artistic practices, which open and frame radical spaces of agency for dogs, horses, and others they invite into their investigations: 'We embrace classical views of failure as successful outcomes through our commitment to reciprocal and non-hierarchical values' (Bartam+Deigaard, this volume).

Yes, there is always a danger that when I make an unexplained intuitive leap from one thing to another, you the reader will not make that leap with me, and whatever meaning we might have exchanged flutters down into the abyss between us. But when you do leap with me, here we are: suddenly together in new territory, full of unforeseen possibilities.

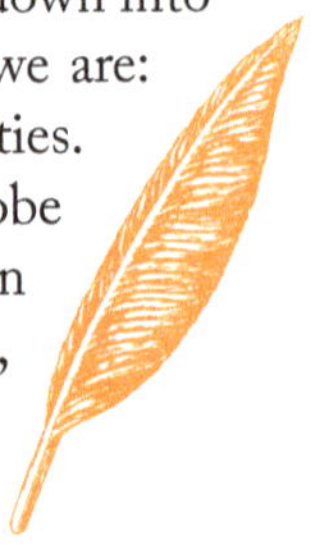

When faced with the prospect of a book that proposes to probe multispecies encounters, it always comes back to the question of whether and how words – whether poem or prose, written, spoken or sung – can speak to or for others belonging to worlds where human languages do not hold sway. Angela Bartram wryly reflects this ongoing conundrum in the images that document the performance, 'Reading Theory to Animals – Horse'. The horses are politely attentive and apparently interested in the artist's presence, but it's hard to say to what extent they are edified by the nuances of argument in the text she presents to them. Ironies aside, we must believe to some degree that our communicative labours in whatever media can change things in some ways for the better. If not on our words, what other forms can we rely on to navigate and affect lives we want to better understand and honour? This is a question that any quest to respectfully inhabit more-than-human worlds must live with.

The outstanding value of this project is not only in what it presents in the way of images, or texts, or discursive interventions. Rather its most vital gift is the encouragement of experimental ways of approaching more-than-human worlds, which invites researchers to depart from standardised modes of authority and move more softly, with humility, into gentler modes of listening and gathering. Most radically, these hybrid modes of attunement demonstrate that research does not have to be extractive or even productive of particular forms of output in ways that tend to dominate and prescribe what can be sensed and shared. Research's traces might be otherwise: continuous, radical acts of respect for what flows through, and just beyond, our efforts to represent meetings with each and every other, who is not circumscribed by any form of knowledge and so 'remains mysterious' (Dorn, this volume). Or as Merlijn Huntjens, Nina Willems and Leonie Cornips (this volume) offer via pictures, prose and fragments of poetic observation, such differently sensitised research modes might work more like gestures that both give and take in unexpected ways – new kinds of exchanges across the charged and porous edges of fields and bodies where tongues and skins, whiskers and welts might 'touch lightly in passing'.

REFERENCES

Ball H. 1974 [1915]. *Flight out of Time: A Dada Diary*. New York: The Viking Press.

Yang, A. 2015. 'That drunken conversation between two cultures: Art, science and the possibility of meaningful uncertainty'. *Leonardo* **48** (3): 318–21.

www.ingramcontent.com/pod-product-compliance
Lightning Source LLC
LaVergne TN
LVHW052353100826
845147LV00013B/824

* 9 7 8 1 9 1 2 1 8 6 9 3 8 *